Oliver Messel

CHARLES CASTLE

Oliver Messel

A BIOGRAPHY

FOREWORD BY SIR JOHN GIELGUD

THAMES AND HUDSON

For Anne, Oliver's devoted sister

Frontispiece A portrait of Oliver
Messel by Angus McBean

© 1986 Charles Castle

First published in the United States in 1986 by
Thames and Hudson Inc., 500 Fifth Avenue,
New York, New York 10110

Library of Congress Catalog Card Number 85-52297

Printed and bound in Great Britain

Contents

*I attempted to use every device to make
as much magic as possible.*

OLIVER MESSEL

*Oliver was many things to many people, but in my
memory it is always the child that I see — Oliver
bubbling with laughter, with delight, with
excitement, with astonishment, with inventiveness,
tender, caressing, dreamy and wicked, as only a child
can be wicked — and also old and wise, as only a
child can be old and wise. . . .*

PETER BROOK, 1984

Foreword

OLIVER MESSEL AND I were exactly the same age and I knew him from my boyhood. His father was my own father's senior partner, whom I met a few times but found rather alarming. Mrs Messel, on the other hand, was extremely gentle and kind, though I thought that I detected a somewhat steely character, which occasionally emerged from beneath her gracious exterior. I used to be taken to dinner parties at their great house in Lancaster Gate, which impressed me very much, though I never went to their country house, Nymans, with its famous garden.

Both Oliver and his sister Anne were ingenious and talented craftsmen. Anne was a skilled needlewoman and she helped Oliver with his early experiments in mask-making, which first brought him success in the Cochran revues of the 1920s.

Years later, in 1940, when I worked with him for the first time in a hastily — and cheaply — contrived production of *The Tempest* at the Old Vic, I well remember sitting behind him in the stalls during a later rehearsal and discovering that his hands were busy in his lap fashioning an Elizabethan ruff out of pipe cleaners. As one could see in the recent exhibition of his work at the Victoria and Albert Museum, he was something of a genius at handling unlikely materials: models of his scenes and properties made of paper, cardboard and scraps of tin or anything else that came to hand, and sketches for head-dresses and jewellery for Hugh Skillen to realize for practical stage use — and all light and elegant to wear.

Oliver had enormous personal charm, allied to a very firm conviction of what he wanted and a way of getting it done by the scene painters, wardrobe mistresses and wigmakers with whom he worked so successfully. He was also very funny and in great demand for his sketches and imitations at parties.

I once heard him give a hilarious version of a conversation between Mrs Somerset Maugham and Lady Colefax, two rival hostesses whose accents he caught to perfection, and also, at one of his own parties in the big studio which he lived in at Yeoman's Row, he regaled us with a succession of imitations, first of his own Nanny, with much grunting and belching, then of some grand lady in an opera box, wielding a formidable lorgnette and fan. Finally he mimicked a tart plying her trade in some imaginary oriental dive. He played this sketch by leaving the room and from behind a door gave vent to shrieks and giggles with money being thrown about at intervals. It was wildly comic but went on rather too long, so that when he finally emerged after about ten minutes he found that a number of his guests had become exhausted and slipped away — a calamity which, I must say, he took in excellent part.

After the war when he had moved to Pelham Place — just opposite his equally sharp but more spiky rival Cecil Beaton — he invited me to a party at which I was the first to arrive. The dining room was a dream of beauty, as well as *gourmandise*. Marble tables without cloths, cabinets and shelves were spread or filled with wonderful dishes, sent from Denmark, such as one had not seen for many years. Shrimps, lobsters, vegetables and salads, all displayed and set out with the most exquisite elegance and graded colour schemes. How charmed I was and how lucky to see it in such pristine splendour, before the other guests arrived to make speedy havoc of its delights, and how I should have loved to have had a photograph to remind me of its beauty.

The Lady's Not for Burning was one of Oliver's most perfect achievements in decor, matched only by his equally striking set and costumes for *Ring Round the Moon* and *Helen!* — while Fry's other play, *The Dark Is Light Enough*, gave him another fine opportunity, which he enjoyed to the full, especially in the costumes he designed for Edith Evans, which she wore as superbly as she had previously in the film of *The Queen of Spades* and in the Old Vic production of *The Country Wife*. The only crisis I encountered with Oliver (similar to the one I was to encounter with Cecil Beaton some years later over some costumes and scenic disputes in his otherwise brilliant decor for *Lady Windermere's Fan*) was an *impasse* with Pamela Brown, whose refusal to wear a costume which Oliver had designed for her in the cast of *The Lady's Not for Burning* brought about endless quarrels which lasted all through the weeks of the provincial tryout before we opened in London. Pamela Brown was crippled with arthritis. She never referred to this, but many weeks later I noticed that her wrists and one hip were both badly affected, and she alone knew exactly what she could wear and carry off effectively in order to conceal her defects. After a number of violent letters and recriminations, she and Oliver were finally reconciled at a tea party, to which I was not invited, and he contrived another dress for her to wear during the last week of the tour. It was the only occasion when I saw the steel emerge from behind the charm and brilliance, and glimpsing his mother one evening at Glyndebourne when she greeted me from her car, shortly before her death, I could not help wondering whether he had learned from her how to manipulate charm with unexpected firmness. His talent was also, of course, inherited from his grandfather Linley Sambourne, a brilliant *Punch* cartoonist who was contemporary with Tenniel. Nevertheless, Oliver's work was enchantingly original and he was certainly a master of design, sharing with his friend, Rex Whistler — whose death in the war was such a calamity for all who knew him — the distinction which he contrived to give to all the great variety of productions which he adorned with so much wit and consummate taste.

JOHN GIELGUD

Preface

MEETING THE SMALL, mercurial, comfortable and immaculately dressed man that was Oliver Messel, one would never have suspected that he was the most famous theatrical designer and decorator Great Britain had produced. He was rare among the practitioners of his art in being a painter first and then a scene designer, having acquired his craft through making theatrical masks and painting portraits.

In the fleeting moments which made up his infinitesimal allowance of spare time, he devoted himself to portraiture of great charm and sensitivity, and cultivated his instinct for Negro art. But it was in the spangled world of theatre that he pursued his vocation with energy and earnestness, and it is there that one searches for the qualities which made him unique.

His originality did not depend so much on his being a specially incisive draughtsman or a resolute architect of shape and form, but rather on a knowledge of art and culture inherited from his forbears. Gothic, Renaissance, baroque, rococo and the eighteenth-century style were his particular penchants. His sense of fun, his fantasy and humour gave his contribution to the theatre the extra dimension which set him above so many other theatrical designers.

When the curtain rose revealing his set, the audience became immediately involved in the play even before the actors made their entrances. The onlooker quickly settled into a sense of confidence and anticipated delight at what was to follow.

The variety of scenes, the diversity of the palaces and pump-rooms, parks and parlours were typical of Oliver's style. The Messel magic was as unmistakable in a Crusoe-mocking desert island scene for a French farce like *The Little Hut* (where the breadfruit ripened in the noonday sun and monstrous flowers burgeoned like gramophone horns), as in the grandiose arrangement of pillars, arches, foliage and festoons for his *Sleeping Beauty*, the one ballet for which he became famous above all the others he designed — palaces which evoked something of the stately pomp and grandeur of a seventeenth-century court masque. His style was equally evident when making its effect with the minimum of means — as in the flimsy, spun-sugar lightness of the conservatory in *Ring Round the Moon*, floating, as it were, on the fantastic airs of the comedy itself — and no less obvious when it was tethered closer to reality, like his vision of the stables of an Austrian castle for *The Dark Is Light Enough*. The qualities which were to be found in each were constant — a warm romanticism salted with wit; a relish for luxury always controlled by an exacting finesse.

'He plucked his talent off the tree as nonchalantly as a faun picks a pomegranate,' recalls John Barber in *The Daily Telegraph*.

But what of his origins?

Elizabeth and Thomas Linley Jr when they were respectively fourteen and twelve years old. A study by Gainsborough, *c.* 1768

Oliver Hilary Sambourne Messel, the youngest of the three children of Maud and Lieutenant Colonel Leonard Messel, was brought up in a twenty-room house in London staffed by ten servants. The Sambourne and Messel grandparents owned another two houses: one in Stafford Terrace, now in the care of the Victorian Society and kept as it was in its fully Victorian glory; and the other, a magnificent country home, Nymans, in Staplefield — 'the best-kept village in Sussex' — now bequeathed to The National Trust and open to the public. His forbears on his father's side were bankers of Darmstadt, Germany, and financial advisers to the Grand Dukes of Hesse, and of Jewish lineage. The distinguished stockbroking firm L. Messel & Co. was founded by his grandfather in London during the 1870s.

Oliver's sister Anne, now Anne, Countess of Rosse, was three years older than he and a noted beauty of the day. She married Ronald Armstrong-Jones, a K.C. They had two children, Susan — and Tony, who married Princess Margaret and is now the Earl of Snowdon. The third of the Messel children, Linley, was three years older than Anne. He became a stockbroker with L. Messel & Co. and a Colonel in the Territorial Army.

Edward Linley Sambourne (1844–1910), Oliver's maternal grandfather, was a well-known artist and illustrator who took over from the famous Sir John Tenniel as the political cartoonist of *Punch*, but is best remembered for his illustrations to Charles Kingsley's *The Water Babies*. His mother, Frances Linley, was the daughter of one of twelve talented musical children who lived at Linley House, No. 1 Pierrepont Street, Bath. The father of this brood, Thomas Linley, a prominent composer, was Director of Music at Bath and taught music privately as well.

Elizabeth Ann, one of Frances's aunts, was a brilliant singer and celebrated beauty, who became a national idol worshipped by an enthusiastic musical public. Her main claim to fame, however, was to have eloped to Calais with the playwright Richard Brinsley Sheridan in 1773, when she was eighteen. Gainsborough, living in Bath at this period, painted her portrait several times, as well as those of her father, her brother Samuel, and her together with her sister Mary. They were hung in the Dulwich College Picture Gallery in 1955.

For a while, the nursemaid to the Linley family was Emma Hart, who later married Sir William Hamilton and was the mistress of Nelson. In 1775 the family left Bath and went to London, where Mr Linley was musical director of the

Oliver Messel's family tree

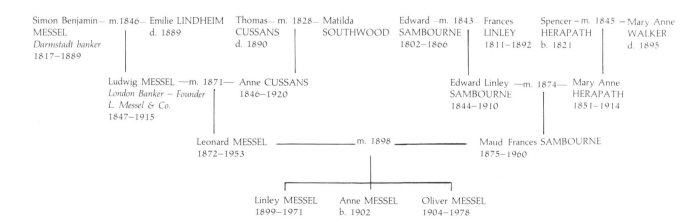

The Messel family and friends. At the top, from left to right: Ludwig Messel (Oliver's grandfather); Mrs Linley Sambourne (Mary Anne Herapath); Linley Sambourne. Centre row: Maud Sambourne; Oliver's grandmother (Anne Cussans); Mr and Mrs Frank Gielgud. Bottom row: Roy Sambourne, Muriel Messel ('the Kid') and 'Lennie' Messel (Oliver's father)

Theatre Royal, Drury Lane, until 1781. Sheridan's first comedy, *The Rivals*, was performed at Covent Garden in the same year the family settled in London; two years later, in 1777, *The School for Scandal* was performed at Drury Lane after Sheridan had acquired the theatre in partnership with Thomas Linley.

Linley Sambourne's only daughter, Maud, inherited his talent and also became an illustrator (at the age of fifteen), contributing a good deal to *Punch*. Her drawings were a mixture of Kate Greenaway and Edwin Abbey: beautiful drawings with fine detail. Her uncle Mervyn Herapath was a well-known sculptor and her first cousin Hylda painted in oils; all three — Sambourne and the two Herapaths — had exhibits in the Royal Academy in 1908.

Maud's mother, Mary Anne Herapath, was the granddaughter of the scientist John Herapath who had been one of the pioneers in the invention and design of the steam engine. His son, Spencer, became a director of the railway companies and a Fellow of the Royal Society. He bought 18 Stafford Terrace for Mary Anne when she married Linley Sambourne.

Oliver's paternal grandfather Ludwig Messel — the first of the German family to settle in London and founder of L. Messel & Co. — married Anne Cussans, daughter of a family of plantation owners of Amity Hall, Jamaica, who had made their fortune in the eighteenth century. Ludwig changed his Jewish faith to Church of England when they married.

Oliver's great-uncle was Alfred Messel, a famous German architect of the nineteenth century, who was known as the Kaiser's architect. A book by Walter Curt Behrendt was published in Berlin in 1911 in appreciation of Alfred's contribution to German architecture. Possessed of an inventive and artistic mind, he designed baroque banks and opulent residential palaces, and was the first architect to use steel and glass through several floors. Alfred's brother Rudolph became a noted scientist. It is clear that all the Messels more than satisfied their ambitions.

Ludwig's son Leonard married Maud Sambourne, and their three children were Linley, Anne and Oliver Messel. Linley died in 1971, leaving a son Thomas and daughter Polly by his second marriage, and two daughters, Elizabeth and

Victoria by his first. Anne, Countess of Rosse, spends her time at Nymans but much prefers the Rosse family seat at the forbidding but unquestionably romantic Birr Castle, County Offaly, and her late husband's Yorkshire estate, Womersley Park.

It was my good fortune to secure invaluable sources of recollection for this tribute to Oliver Messel from his family. Firstly, his sister has contributed from her wide knowledge about the early days; the Earl of Snowdon, the nephew who inherited Oliver's estate, has allowed me access to the archives of letters, reviews, art-work and photographs. Spencer Herapath, Oliver's second cousin, helped to authenticate the family tree. Princess Margaret, who had a high regard for Oliver, her uncle-in-law, has offered her own thoughts and permitted the reproduction of the photographs of her house in Mustique, designed by Oliver.

After Oliver's death on 13 July 1978 Snowdon had his art-work and memorabilia shipped back to England where, together with the designs, costumes, masks and maquettes stored at Kensington Palace, they found an appropriate home at the Victoria and Albert Museum, where they rightly belong to posterity, given on permanent loan by Lord Snowdon.

On 20 June 1983 Princess Margaret opened an exhibition of Oliver's work at the Theatre Museum at the Victoria and Albert where the public were at last able to examine Oliver's genius at close quarters. Her speech offered Oliver a high accolade, presenting him posthumously with the final seal of Royal approval for the unending delight he had given audiences for over half a century.

Princess Margaret signing the visitor's book at the Georgian Ball at the Mansion House on 1 July 1964. The costume and hair ornaments were designed by Messel (the latter made by Hugh Skillen) and the wig by Stanley Hall. Photograph courtesy Central Press.

Princess Margaret: Although I only had the pleasure of knowing Oliver well for the last fifteen years of his life, I had admired his creative genius as long as I can remember going to the theatre. For genius he was, along with a number of other things — magic-maker, mimic, raconteur, entertainer, designer and painter.

The combination of his immense talent and creativity, his care for detail, endless research and true love of the theatre, with his passion for work, made him one of the greatest designers this country has produced, although I think he himself would admit that on occasions he wasn't always the easiest person to work with because his demands for perfection came before anything else.

C. B. Cochran was, of course, his first and perhaps greatest patron. For Cochran he designed the now legendary sets for *Helen!* in 1932, which set the vogue for the 'white on white' style of interior decoration of the thirties.

He contributed more than anyone else to the glorification of Covent Garden after the drabness of the war years, even when materials were still scarce. Headdresses that looked beautiful from the auditorium were simply made by him out of wire, sticky paper and pipe cleaners. He was a craftsman as well as artist, as you can see from the details of the models. The sets and costumes for Glyndebourne in the fifties were stunning make-believe romanticism, and, in contrast, his inventiveness for sets like *Ring Round the Moon*, *The House of Flowers*, *The Little Hut*, to mention only a few, was unrivalled.

It was terribly sad for the theatre (and for his many friends) when he decided to go to live and work in Barbados, but it gave him a new lease of life to create things more permanent than those in the theatre. In the West Indies he turned his talents to architecture; it was out there that I came to know him well, as I think he took me round every inch of every house he had designed. He was immensely

Part of the Victoria and Albert Museum's exhibition of Oliver Messel's work (1983): in the centre is the tunic worn by the ballerina Moira Shearer when she appeared in The Royal Ballet's production of *The Sleeping Beauty* with Messel designs and costumes.

practical and understood about the climate and the workability of the house, as well as its beauty; he had perfect colour sense.

Before he left England, I found him tearing up drawings in his studio, so I asked him if I could store all his models, otherwise they would have to be destroyed, or sold; we were delighted to find the space at Kensington Palace.

When he died and left Lord Snowdon all his models and sketches, it was felt that these would best be preserved for the students of theatre design and the public in general if they were kept at the Theatre Museum.

I would like to congratulate the Victoria and Albert Museum for creating this beautiful tent room and Carl Toms for designing it in the mood of Oliver. Before becoming one of the best theatre designers of today he was, of course, Oliver's assistant in the fifties, and I know would be the first person to credit Oliver for his training.

I hope this exhibition will be an enormous success and remind us all what a truly outstanding creative artist Oliver was, and I have great pleasure in opening it.

Scheduled to run for five months, the exhibition was so successful that it was extended for two months and closed on 13 January 1984 — Oliver's eightieth birthday.

In searching through Oliver's files and papers, I discovered the notes he had prepared for his own autobiography; with the family's permission, I reproduce excerpts from them here for the first time, together with private letters and other correspondence.

1

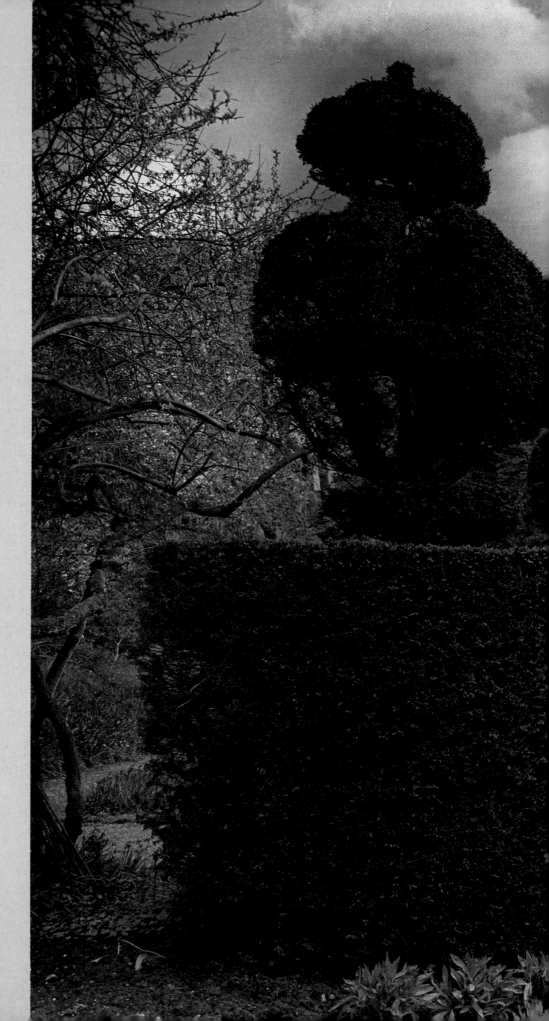

The gardens at Nymans,
Sussex, which was the Messel
family home from 1890, were
created by Oliver Messel's
grandfather and continued by
three succeeding generations.
They are now owned by the
National Trust.

Right, the Wall Garden with
the Italian fountain and clipped
yews.

1 * Family feeling

IN 1932 the white-on-white set for C. B. Cochran's *Helen!* received an ovation every night — it was the work of Oliver Messel, unquestionably the most outstanding theatre designer of his day. The sets for practically every other production he designed were also well received — from ballets at Covent Garden and the Met to musicals on Broadway, from operas at Glyndebourne to plays in the West End. He developed his own style of romantic baroque with a flair for creating magic, which was what everybody longed for after the austerity of the 1914–18 war. He was a master of illusion and make-believe, a craftsman who taught those with whom he worked the art of creativity. He would make a chandelier himself with sticky paper and fuse-wire, or construct a dancer's head-dress out of pipe cleaners. His nephew, Lord Snowdon, remembers as a child finding a bird's nest in his London garden — on inspection, he discovered that it had been made by Oliver and that the eggs were china and hand-painted.

He had the respect of everyone in the theatre because he knew which way the fabric should be cut and how every stage property could be made. He was a perfectionist — often to the great cost of those with whom he worked or who had to foot the bill, for he might have an item remade three times until he was satisfied with the result. He had the good looks of a film star and an abundance of charm, a wry wit and a tremendous sense of humour. He worked with every major leading artist and theatre director; he achieved the distinction of a CBE, an Oscar nomination for his work on *Suddenly Last Summer*, an Antoinette Perry Award for *House of Flowers* on Broadway; and although he was the highest paid theatre designer, rivalling his friend Cecil Beaton, he died in debt in Barbados in 1978, after spending the last fifteen years of his life carving out a new career as architect and interior designer of over a dozen houses on that island and twice as many in Mustique.

We turn to his early days to discover how he set upon his path to success.

Oliver himself says, 'It was in the early hours of 13 January 1904 that I am given to understand I first made an appearance in my parents' London house.'

He was born with a silver spoon in his mouth, in circumstances as comfortable as he would doubtless have chosen for himself. The house was 27 Gloucester Terrace, but soon after Oliver's birth the Messel family moved to 104 Lancaster Gate.

Oliver always felt a certain restlessness in the quiet of the country, whereas he felt more at home in a big city like London. Even when working and leading a hermit's life, he found the necessary solitude more congenial if encircled by the hum of the city.

Maud Messel, Oliver's mother

Oliver: All my childhood sentimental attachments, and my awareness of what was going on around me harked back to Balcombe House in Sussex where I was very happy as a child. It was a beautiful mid-eighteenth-century Georgian house with little Trafalgar balconies added. That was what first planted in my mind my consistent hankering towards an eighteenth-century influence in my work.

The gallery was covered with jasmine, honeysuckle and roses, giving almost the effect of a welcoming bird's nest. From a wide hall where the Georgian panelling was painted white, doors opened — left into his father's study and right into the morning room. The latter was a room of great atmosphere filled with favourite objects his mother had collected.

High-backed William and Mary chairs stood beside the fireplace, which sparkled with an array of polished brass: rare fire-dogs, pierced brass fire curb, and all the ornamental paraphernalia that make a fireplace look complete and inviting. Some finely carved bellows hung on ribbons beside the chair rail. A set of Neapolitan costume pictures of about 1790 always intrigued Oliver; perfect designs for *Così Fan Tutte*, he felt. These had been brought back from one of his father's many visits to Italy and Sicily. There were needlework pictures, silhouettes, embroidered firescreens, and everything arranged with the instinctive artistry of his mother's creative taste.

The dining room was further down the hall beyond the study on the left. A congenial room with three long windows opening on to the trellised gallery and the vines which made an arboured foreground as a frame to the view over the garden. On the right, opposite the door to the dining room, was a sturdy carved Georgian staircase, where the three Messels used to sit as children in dressing gowns to overhear what seemed an overwhelming noise of chatter and laughter, rather like a parrot house, from the dinner parties. They would snatch some of the goodies before they disappeared.

Oliver said that 'Mrs Parsons, the crotchety old housekeeper, was ogress in chief, and darling Addy, my mother's dear personal maid was guardian angel in whom all secrets could be confided without fear of betrayal. She remained our dearest friend.'

Beyond the dining room, sometime at the end of the eighteenth century, there had been built on a large drawing room, forty feet long with a simple Strawberry Hill gothic window at the end, which led out onto a balcony of its own and down into the rose garden. It was a casual living-drawing room, but filled with treasures collected and brought back from the Messels' travels. In one corner stood a fine ornate sedan chair lined with Genoese cut velvet. As the door was opened there was a delicious aromatic smell. Possibly ingredients and oils for pot-pourri kept in one corner enhanced this magic atmosphere. Very special toys were kept here, only to be peeped at as a great treat. There were wonderfully painted Hungarian peasant dolls with many petticoats in layers and English Queen Anne wooden dolls with naïvely painted faces. Their dresses were made of brocade and lined with paper. Possibly the children's favourite excitements were the imaginative toys which their parents had brought back from one of their expeditions through Germany. A whole world in miniature: villages of houses, farms, trees, streams with bridges, complete with peasants, their cows, sheep, animals and birds and market produce, all ingeniously carved in wood and exquisitely painted: a toy Brueghel setting to be put together and arranged however they might choose. These gave Oliver infinite delight and influenced his interest in making detailed models. His father had also given him one of the Pollock's of Hoxton Penny Plain and Twopence Coloured toy theatres, with a great variety of scenes and figures to cut out. This he adored, and he soon began innovating miniature stage settings himself, with tiny figures which he jointed and weighted so that they could move on strings like marionettes.

Oliver's father was a sensitive man, capable of great kindness and affection, and Oliver loved him above all for his touching devotion to his mother. At Oxford, Leonard Messel's friendships had been with Max Beerbohm and others of an intellectual rather than a sporting group, although any mention of Oscar Wilde always caused a hushed silence which roused the children's curiosity. Over the years Oliver's father developed into a passionate collector of furniture, *objets d'art*, fans, china and glass. Apart from his dedication to gardening, Messel collected one of the finest private libraries of botanical books, which were unfortunately destroyed in a fire at Nymans.

Brought up in this ambience of beauty and art, Oliver encountered no serious opposition from his father when he decided to become an artist. In fact he had made this decision as early as six or seven years old and never wavered from it.

Oliver: The first thing I ever remember was when I was about four years old at Balcombe. I was dressed up as a little French soldier, in a fancy dress that belonged to my father. I thought how terribly grown up I was, and decided to get out into the world and away from my pampered life. I decided to explore the world for myself, and when nobody was around, I slipped off into the village. There was a great outcry at home, and hours later somebody found me wandering down by the cricket field. I couldn't imagine what all the fuss was about. All I wanted to do was explore and be alone. That is the way I felt the rest of my life. I've always liked being alone.

Oliver as Cupid, at the age of nine

At Balcombe, the three children were continually being dressed up. One of their mother's great friends, Gladys Beattie Crozier, wrote books for children; and so, to illustrate innumerable games and caprices for children, they were dolled up for dear 'Aunt' Gladys (as she became known to the children) to photograph. Anne was decked out in simple tucked muslin dresses that looked like pictures by Renoir, and Oliver as Cupid with crepe-paper wings or as a jester. Linley, being the eldest, was let off the lightest by being allowed to appear in more conventional variations of Eton jackets. Gladys Crozier's books were very popular at the time.

Linley was the first to be placed into the hands of male tuition and sent off to school. Oliver and Anne remained together at home and became inseparable.

Oliver: Our devoted nanny, Maimie, who made life at Balcombe so blissful for us, had to be superseded by governesses of varying nationalities because she was thought to be far too easy with us, and so arrived in rapid succession a unique array of grotesque old hags with scarcely an exception. To keep our spirits up we would work out imitations of them in secret; many of our parents' guests were also prey to our merciless mimicry. As screams of laughter resounded from the schoolroom, could they have suspected that it was they themselves who were being parodied?

My darling mother, always having an eye for the picturesque rather than the practical, used to dress Anne and me in twin matching coats and crocheted hats, almost until time came for school, unaware of the shame and embarrassment I often felt at being mistaken for a girl.

Anne: Oliver's upbringing with me was a very different one from many others. My parents were enormously cultured and knowledgeable people. I think that Oliver inherited their craving for culture and knowledge, which, once acquired, he later projected into his work. This beautiful mother of ours was the most romantic person in the world. She was really Oliver's inspiration.

I am afraid that Oliver and I practically never went to school. We were both too delicate, I suppose. We adored each other and did everything together, rather like inseparable twins although I was three years older than he.

Life at Balcombe was built on a fairyland of imagination, no doubt because their mother often read fairy stories to them. Films and television assume that role nowadays. It seems that Oliver's great knowledge and his feeling for romanticism came from this sort of fantasy existence in his childhood.

Anne: There were months when we had to be in bed. We both had a bit of tuberculosis. At least we thought we had, and that was really when we made so much with our hands. We'd sit up in bed making things; little *maquettes*, perhaps a chapel, little candlesticks, altars and a tiny bishop, all dressed up, because we both adored sewing.

That's where perfection came in. Oliver was a great perfectionist. We loved that thing of being ill in bed. *Pretending* to be ill in bed. Wallowing in it.

We lived in a world of imagination and making things from our earliest childhood. If we had a mouse that died we'd have a lovely funeral and make wreaths for it and Oliver would make a glorious coffin out of a soap box. But beautiful, absurd childish things.

When Oliver was at Eton he would go to school for perhaps a fortnight and then get ill so my mother, who loved him so much, would have him brought home. And when it was time for him to go back, he would say, 'Darling, I'll tell you what you must do. Now I've got this beastly cough. Promise me that every ten minutes you'll come in and keep me awake coughing.' So there was vehement coughing. He'd cough all night and I'd run in saying, 'Go on, keep coughing,' so that he wouldn't be forced to go back to school.

Oliver's mother forbade his father to bring his City colleagues home to dinner. Theirs was a private world to be shared only with friends who enjoyed similar domestic tastes.

An absorbing picture of the Messel family and their 'upstairs-downstairs' pattern of life emerges through Addy, the lady's maid to Oliver's mother. Addy became a much respected, life-long friend of the family and continued to live with them. Shortly before her death, Lord Snowdon asked her about his family's background, and she recalled that 'The old housekeeper Mrs Parsons wrote to me and said that if I called at Balcombe House on Saturday afternoon I might hear of a situation that would suit me. This was in 1913, when I was twenty-one. I went along and Mrs Messel said after a while, "Oh, yes. Your hair is neat", and that I should have to wear a black coat and skirt, a white blouse and a toque and a veil to travel in. I could choose either grey or black gloves. I would be paid £24 a year. My daily duties used to be to call Colonel Messel at eight o'clock; the breakfast was brought up. They always had their breakfast in bed. The Colonel had a boiled egg every morning and then he used to dress and come down and go straight out to the City. I had to see to Mrs Messel's clothes, of course, but I didn't do any housework or anything like that.

'Mrs Sambourne [Oliver's grandmother] died in 1914, just before war broke out. Mr Messel, the Colonel's father, died in 1915 and we moved to Nymans in 1916. They started rebuilding it after the First World War and it took seven years because the architects kept breaking the contracts.'

It was in 1890 that Ludwig Messel, Oliver's grandfather, bought Nymans, beautifully situated in a part of Sussex which was particularly suited to experimental gardening. Messel took a great interest in creating a distinctive garden and introduced many exotic plants from all parts of the world into the site. After his death, his son Leonard continued to enlarge the scope of the garden, and made a significant contribution of his own. This work was carried on into the third generation by the Earl and Countess of Rosse.

The house itself, described by Lady Rosse as having a 'Regency flavour', and evidently nineteenth-century in origin, was not architecturally distinguished nor of any great size, but additions were made to it in various stages, and it was a comfortable family home.

In *Country Life* in 1932, the late Christopher Hussey described it: 'So clever a reproduction is it of a building begun in the fourteenth century and added to intermittently till Tudor times, that some future antiquary may well be deceived by it . . . Nymans is not a copy of any existing building. Rather is it an exquisite example of pastiche – a form of invention that in literature holds an honourable place and is capable of producing works of art in their own right. . . .

'During the transformation of the apparently nineteenth-century house into its present state, the entire walls, with several door-heads of a late fifteenth- or early sixteenth-century building, were revealed, almost complete to first floor level. These evidences of an earlier building, which, in a sense, confirm the type of the new, were not discovered, however, till the design had been decided upon.'

Addy: At Nymans we always had three housemaids and a housekeeper, three kitchen maids and four in the pantry; the butler, two footmen and an old man, and me. I never had to do any cooking. There were about fourteen gardeners in those days. There was a chauffeur, and there was Beech with the horses and there was a groom. The horses were for the carriages. They had an open landau, and a closed carriage that was used for going across London. At weekends I used to go down to Nymans in the car with Mrs Messel, but the staff went by train. A big brake would meet them because we used to take the silver chests down for the weekend. They always left two housemaids up at the house in Lancaster Gate. And then I used to travel abroad a great deal with the Colonel and Mrs Messel, to places like Bruges and Brussels. They never took a manservant with them because the hotels always had a valet, but the Colonel didn't like them to look after him, so I used to do so.

We used to go for six weeks at a time. We went the second week in March and came home before the first of May, because when we went to Menton, for

Nymans. Above, the house in
the early years of this century,
showing the extensive
alterations by Sir Ernest George
and Leonard Stokes to the
original

Right, design by Oliver Messel
for a new wing after the fire of
1947; opposite, the gazebo and
part of the new house designed
in a Cotswold style by Sir
Walter Tapper

instance, the Colonel wouldn't travel through France on the first of May because of it being a national holiday with all those people about. When we got back to Nymans we'd spend the summer there, or they used to go down to Bath and very often to Scotland.

In Italy, if they went out for the day, sometimes they would take me because the Colonel used to hunt for these wild orchids and I would help him. On another day they would go out to buy Italian cloths, tablecloths in Florence. They used to buy them in the market.

The Colonel was a very strict man. He didn't have the patience of Mrs Messel, who was wonderful. He could be very frightening and Mr Linley never got on with him. But the Colonel did get on with Mr Oliver, because he was always very funny when he was a little boy. He wouldn't be perturbed about

Oliver's father, Lt Col Leonard Messel

anything or anybody, Mr Oliver. Also, he was always delicate; he had impetigo. Miss Anne and Mr Oliver always got on very well together. I used to take them to see Granny Messel before they went back to school. Sometimes they got half a crown and sometimes they might just get a few sweets. And I used to have to take them to old Dr Rudolph in Victoria Street because he used to give them a pound always when they were going back to school. We always went by bus. Mr Oliver was so polite that I had a job to get him on the bus because he wanted everybody else to get on before him. You used to have to push him on, to get him there, otherwise the bus would be off and he would still be standing on the pavement.

But Miss Anne and Mr Oliver were always very bright and cheerful and they were kept very strict by Miss Blain, their governess, who went there about the same time as me. But Mr Oliver would defy anybody. He was nine at the time and he'd only just left off the irons; he'd had a caliper on his legs because he had weak legs. Of course, that meant he couldn't go out and play like the other little boys and so he used to be seated on the balcony in London a great deal, and there he used to knit and crochet. He used to crochet hats for his sister. Very nice hats, they were.

Anne: In our childhood days 'American Tournaments' of tennis were the vogue. They lasted all the long afternoons with the players consisting of fat middle-aged men in white flannels and ladies in circular skirts and hats. To our agonizing boredom Oliver and I were called upon to collect the balls at each end for them to serve. The game on one occasion was wrecked by Oliver in his little smock; having collected the lot, he sat on them insisting that if he remained there for an hour they'd hatch out — as he believed he had the same qualities as a hen. He had that gift as a child of getting away with fobbing off grown-ups. But then we both hated games, especially the Teenage Tournament which we managed to ruin by turning it into a ballet. They all thought it very rotten of us and we were never asked again, thank God.

Having been spoilt to distraction as a child, Oliver's father appeared to him as something of a pocket Napoleon in those days. Leonard Messel's old nanny had never allowed him to be crossed, which left uncurbed a peppery temper that exploded on the slightest provocations. This was frequently vented on Oliver's Uncle Roy, his mother's brother, of whom Messel disapproved because of his compulsive interest in cricket. The two men had few interests in common.

It was still the era when children were meant to be seen and not heard; and to Oliver his father's severity, even if only put on for effect, represented something of the King Rat figure to the child. Linley was frightened of his father and never managed to overcome that fear. Even Anne, until she reached years of independent security, was apprehensive of brewing tempests.

On a few occasions Oliver managed to stand up to him and, as they were fond of each other *au fond*, it worked. There were great scenes of reconciliation. At the same time Oliver observed his mother's flawless tactics, her quiet methods of achieving her own way over everything — methods he employed in later life.

Oliver: Having myself by nature what could have been described as an uncontrollable temper, the supreme self-control of my mother was an example I

Sketches by Maud Messel of her three children: Linley, Oliver and Anne

tried to follow. I never cease to wonder or to realize fully how amazing this rare inspiration has been for the three of us children: a faultless being as a mother. Her presence had, as it were, an instant effect upon everyone who came within its orbit. Frailty which was by no means weak. She set a standard for us which we always tried to keep.

My parents were so much taken up with each other that we children were more like toys to be brought out on occasions.

It was really in the later years that we were perhaps more fully able to appreciate each other, when the generation barrier had dissolved.

Anne: My mother was enormously clever and refined but very vague. She was on to every trick in the book, though. For instance, when she visited the opera at Glyndebourne she was rather wry. She managed to get her car parked on the lawn — which was out of bounds to everyone — and then all the singers would come round to see her and enjoy the champagne and smoked salmon she'd had prepared for the long intermission. She'd have her wary little eye on everything that was going on and notice who was with whom. There was absolutely nothing she wasn't very clever about.

Unfortunately Maude Messel was arthritic — a family ailment that both Oliver and Anne inherited — but she made good use of it. She moved slowly and graciously down the stairs and all would rise from their seats as she made her studied entrance into a room. She was also slightly deaf, which gave her a rather distant air; she managed all the same to hear exactly what she wanted to hear.

Anne: Father was very dark in complexion. All the Messels were dark, including Oliver. Although he loved us dearly, he was immensely intolerant. He never talked about the City although when Frank Gielgud became a senior partner in his company, L. Messel & Co., all the Gielgud children — John, Eleanor and Val — were constantly quoted to us as being brilliant, which put us three Messels to shame. All his conversation was about art. The people who came to Balcombe and Lancaster Gate were collectors, by and large; museum people. And therefore museums came into our lives very early on. Oliver and I started being taken to the V & A as small children — which was my only real schooling.

I looked upon our father as this great collector and when we took an interest in the things he loved, like the Japanese allegorical stories on the fans, for instance, he warmed to us tremendously. I've got his two famous collections: his great Japanese collection which is really entirely original drawings, and the European collection. He would tell us all the stories about them. He was most knowledgeable about Spanish and Italian art.

Apropos money, I remember something that our grandmother said one day when we were children. A Lady Alexander called and I overheard my grandmother say to her: 'Oh, that's dreadful. You should never make your daughter marry for money. Mind you, I don't think you should ever let her meet anyone who hasn't got any!'

This portrait of Anne and Oliver Messel, painted by Glyn Philpot in 1913, was destroyed in the fire at Nymans.

Oliver was first introduced to the applied arts through an artist, Glyn Philpot, who was a friend of his parents and a regular visitor to Balcombe House. He had painted a portrait of Mrs Messel's uncle, the sculptor Mervyn Herapath. Herapath was a charming and sensitive artist from whom Oliver later learned to model in fine wax. At this time Glyn Philpot was in his mid-twenties and came to paint all the Messel family. His portrait of Oliver and Anne was painted in his studio in Tite Street when the children were seven and ten respectively.

Philpot was to be the first and possibly the most influential person in Oliver's creative life. Born in 1884, he became one of the most adventurous Royal Academicians of the first half of this century. His style changed constantly and, although it was always typical of the best aspirations of his time, it remained throughout very personal. His versatility of manner was equal to his diversity of style, for he produced memorable work as an engraver, a book illustrator, a theatre designer and a sculptor, apart from his main preoccupation as a painter. His paintings, too, were extraordinarily various; there was an extremely accomplished series of portraits, ending in the studies of Negroes which so much interested him towards the end of his life and which impressed and encouraged Oliver. His works were shown in the National Portrait Gallery in 1985.

Anne: Glyn taught us how to make beautiful butterflies out of paper (but Oliver used to be very naughty and blow them down my neck.). Oliver was fascinated by Glyn's abilities and through him learnt to draw hands and other fine detail. If one were to compare Glyn's Negro paintings which hang in the Brighton Museum with those of Oliver's, one would hardly be able to tell them apart.

Oliver: The pictures Glyn painted of us were beautiful. Anne sitting in one of her white muslin dresses with a wide yellow sash [Oliver was to emulate the design of this outfit many years later for Evelyn Laye in the Cochran production of *Helen!*], and I standing beside her in a black velvet suit and Peter Pan collar. He did a charming portrait of my mother in a black dress, and also painted Linley in a white shirt, but these too were destroyed in the fire.

Oliver saw his new-found friend and mentor as one of the great masters of the Renaissance. Observing him in his studio, the youngster always felt an exhilaration at first and afterwards — as if he had been in the presence of Raphael or Leonardo. Philpot played with Oliver and Anne as children and as Oliver grew up he encouraged and guided his work. It was with him that the aspiring young artist was to have the thrilling experience of seeing Italy for the first time.

Oliver: Grandpapa Sambourne, alas, died before I was really able to know him well and only his illustrations for Hans Andersen's fairy tales and *The Water Babies* made an impression on me. As Anne and I used to read a great deal to each other, it was always the saddest stories with which we became involved and we would sob so uncontrollably that we became really ill.

Grandma Sambourne, who had been severe in bringing up my mother, was, to us children, the essence of leniency and understanding. Every Saturday afternoon when we were in London we would walk to 18 Stafford Terrace, her home, with its wonderful atmosphere of William Morris and Burne-Jones which, thanks to my mother and Anne, remains intact to this day.

Glyn Philpot (*c.* 1934) played a strong role in Oliver's artistic awakening.

The house, a perfect example of Victoriana in the middle of Kensington, has been described by Sir John Betjeman:

Sir John: I doubt if there is anything like it in the country. First, the hall has racks with thirty-nine walking sticks of variously elaborate design. The hall is dark, as all Victorian halls were, with looped curtains, a barometer, and feather pictures on the wall. On the right is the dining-room with ferns, a fringed chimney-piece with bobbles; Morris wallpapers almost obscured by brown photographs, in frames, of pictures that stunned the Royal Academy in the late eighteen-nineties; no inch of undecorated space: plates, polished brass, lampshades of pleated silk, and fine furniture scarcely discernible in the half-light.

I walked through the looped plush curtains to the morning room, which has stained glass of a vaguely medieval character to shut out any impression of

London and to transport us into a separate kingdom of artistic social life in the days of hansom cabs and Sherlock Holmes. Here in the morning room there are oil paintings and Japanese prints and a Morris paper on the ceiling.

On the first floor is the *pièce de resistance*, the drawing room, a vast L-shaped room, dimly lit by stained glass in daylight and by gas fittings, adapted in King Edward's reign to the glorious invention of electricity, by night. The room is so crowded with furniture, satinwood, mahogany, marqueterie, Japanese pots, plates along a shelf under the frieze drawings by Charles Keene, Phil May, and other cartoonists on the walls – the floors are so studded with sofas and chairs and tables of all shapes and sizes – that the richness is overwhelming and the ghosts of full Victorian diners are sitting everywhere ready for conversation and song after dinner.

Linley Sambourne, a cartoon by Spy, 1887

Opposite, the drawing room of the Sambournes' house in Stafford Terrace. The young Oliver did not find this type of decoration to his taste.

Anne: Our mother's parents continued living at Stafford Terrace while we lived in Lancaster Gate. In fact, we ourselves never lived at Stafford Terrace. Oliver never liked it. Far too fussy and Victorian for him. We thought it was like a sort of lodging house, but on the other hand we didn't much care for Lancaster Gate either, which was a collector's house very much in the mould of the great collector and adviser to collectors, Hugh Lane. It was (and still is) full of wonderful oriental art and marvellous Spanish and Italian furniture. I did, however, pity the staff because there was no lift and thirty-seven buckets of coal had to be brought up every day. My mother simply ignored that sort of problem. She didn't think, 'Poor man . . .' – if she did, she'd still allow him to take it up.

Oliver: In a special corner by the fernery in the morning room in Stafford Terrace there was a stained glass decoration.

Lily Elsie would visit regularly and I thought her a raving beauty when I saw her. By this time she was quite plump but had compelling charm. Edna May was another frequent visitor.

My Uncle Roy had been so in love with Edna May that he went three hundred times to see her in *The Belle of New York*. His room and bedroom are still lined with her pictures and those of Gertie Miller, Gabrielle Ray, Lily Elsie and all the other famous beauties of 1910. We gazed at those photographs with wide open eyes and were subsequently thrilled to meet the beauties in person.

Grandma Sambourne would take infinite trouble to show us how to make things. Anne developed an amazing artistry in needlework and Grandma's tuition in handicraft was something that I loved and always remember. Among the many treasures at Stafford Terrace are some of the delicate drawings and illustrations by my mother who, as a young girl, did some work of great distinction.

At Nymans, my father's parents were benign but more remote figures than my mother's parents. Granny was always ailing, and moved slowly supported by elderly crones. She presided at a tea table of splendour (with additional tiered stands) laden with almond macaroons, a vast array of sandwiches, rich cakes and innumerable goodies for innumerable grandchildren dressed in those frightful hats like tea cosies of *broderie anglaise*, with dresses to match. All the nannies, uncles, aunts and cousins galore made it quite a *do*.

Grandad had fine features and a beard like an El Greco portrait, and his brother, Uncle Rudolph, was a brilliant scientist of whom I was very fond. As small boys they had set out together from Darmstadt with gold coins in their shirts, leaving behind their brother Alfred, who was to become one of Berlin's leading architects. Although I never saw him, I admired examples of his neo-classical architecture years later.

Grandad, a generous Father Christmas figure, gathered all his brood on every occasion for blessings. I am told that he was a martinet in his office and that he had a brilliant business brain. None of that, unfortunately, have I inherited.

Nymans was an exceptionally hideous house with a really monstrous conservatory. Its only redeeming feature was the garden. When the time came for us to leave our beloved Balcombe, my mother was as reluctant as I.

'Aunt' Gladys [Beattie Crozier] remained a constant visitor to Balcombe as well as to Nymans. She was basically a rather pre-Raphaelite beauty; the end of her nose quivered like a rabbit's as she shook with suppressed laughter while telling stories that were audible only in fragments. She was a dear person, with great enthusiasm to be helpful. I remember her excitement over a young artist who had been slaving away in a garret, making exquisite designs for the *couture* house Lucille. He turned out to be Norman Hartnell!

As I grew to a receptive age, 'Aunt' Gladys took me to see her uncle Percy Anderson, who designed many settings for the theatre. He showed me little models for *Chu Chin Chow*, *The Mikado* and a number of other productions. This lasting impression was to inspire me to make my own models in the years to come. I was thrilled. He also arranged for me to go to the Harkers Scenic Studio where the small models were being enlarged to giant canvases hung on pulleys. The skeleton structures of platforms in the immense studio buildings, like compositions by Piranesi, and the smell of the size, with all the tins and pots of colour dribbling everywhere, made a great impression on me, as did the kindness of the Harker brothers.

Later, a dear man nicknamed Numph, who had helped with the decorating of Lancaster Gate and of Nymans, took me on fascinating expeditions through a range of Dickensian side streets of London, to see fabulous materials being woven in Hogarthian surroundings, secret havens for fringes and tassels of all kinds. Another winding alley would lead us to masters of woodcarving and the gilders with their miraculous, deft handling of precious gold leaf and skilful burnishing of it with polished agate stones. On another visit I was shown the cutting and engraving of glass, and glass being blown into fantastic shapes. All this was a revelation from which I gleaned more useful education than I did from school.

Schooldays were unadulterated hell to me, banished as far as possible for ever out of my mind. The abject misery of being plunged from the pampered life at home into a private school of Dickensian horror was a total ordeal. I realize now that such unhappiness at an impressionable age, however painful, may have had some advantage. For instance, life ever afterwards has seemed one glorious holiday by comparison. Also, loathing every moment of the day as I did, at night I could shut myself up alone and create in my mind an imaginary life, seeing vividly in dreams or pictures, as I closed my eyes, scenes and people or costumes that obliterated and compensated for all that I dreaded during the day.

Oversensitive and vulnerable, too young at that age to put up a defensive armour or to see the funny side of things, Oliver was overtaken by a religious mania. Through prayer and concentrated effort, he found that these pictures of an imaginary world could form themselves as clearly as reality. He was convinced that, because of these childish problems, he had been stimulated in developing a special vision, which became a help to him in designing for the theatre and films.

Oliver: I was what might be termed a seedy child, always a bit ailing, which of course I played up to the hilt, in order to avoid being sent back to the dreaded school.

To make things even more tense for the fledgling pushed out of the home nest, it was war time. Everything German was taboo. Dachshunds were put down and faithful old German governesses stoned and interned. Plates and many other German products were smashed in the hysteria. My name, of course, was German. Fiendish little schoolboys quickly caught on to that, and their taunts and torments knew no bounds.

The headmaster was an ogre with an insatiable passion for beating little boy's bare bottoms; he inaugurated a special ritual and had birch rods soaked in brine for the occasion.

Craving a glimpse of spring, I remember one day climbing over a garden wall just to look at an apple tree in blossom. It reminded me of home, seeing its branches from outside. This transgression of the rules was deemed an unpardonable sin. I was sent for. 'Not allowed to be beaten, eh?' shouted the old brute at me, as he grasped me between his obese thighs. A quaking little figure peered up at the fearsome bloodshot eyes which were popping out of his head. 'I'll get permission to beat you and I'll thrash you within an inch of your life!' 'Yes, sir. No, sir.' I was not called Oliver for nothing! But during the following holidays at home, I learned that the headmaster had died. I could hardly shed a tear for the old tartar, nor did I ever return to that hell-hole.

Thereafter, I was sent to Eton. There were a thousand individuals there, rather than the handful of little fiends at the other school. At least Eton might be far more congenial. Among the much wider range, there were bound to be at least a few friends of less conventional outlook than the relentless tiny minds of a private school.

'What the f... you think you are doing, you ruddy little c..t?' were the first words of greeting shouted down the corridor. A little bewildering on arrival, as I remember! Four-letter words were the only vocabulary used on the new boys as they rushed helter-skelter to answer the calls of 'boy!' The latest arrival was committed to any task of servitude required by the privileged mature members of the fraternity.

My brother Linley was still at Robeson's, the house at Eton, for a half term when I arrived. It seemed a point of some embarrassment to him, for I was given strict instructions never to greet him in the street, but to pass him by on the opposite side.

At one stage I was appointed fag to Ian Campbell-Grey, who later became a distinguished artist. We subsequently became great friends and were together for a short while in the army. I learned to appreciate his caustic humour and remarkable mind in later years.

In my early days at Eton, however, unaware of the facts of human eccentricities, I found the duties of fagging sometimes alarming, and extremely painful. Whatever task was attempted was met with disapproval and resulted in a flying leap with a switchy cane. Only later did it become possible for me to endure the sting and treat it as a a joke. Campbell-Grey died tragically of leukaemia during the Second World War.

I was soon joined at Eton by my cousin Rudolph [who at 42 married Judith, daughter of Field Marshal Lord Birdwood of Anzac and Totnes]. All through childhood we had been more like brothers, so at Eton we were constant companions. He developed a passion for Wagner and sat closeted for hours hypnotized by the emotion of the music. He was extremely handsome and looked remarkably like pictures I had seen of Ludwig II of Bavaria. He died early, at 53.

At Robeson's life was fairly lax — sometimes a bit more than anyone might have asked or bargained for. Mrs Fagan, the Dame, was a kindly soul and encouraged any artistic efforts, as her daughter was an artist. Among my close friends at Robeson's were Billy Clonmore [later the Earl of Wicklow], Irish and delightfully eccentric with an irrepressible sense of humour, and Robert Byron, who would warrant an entire book to do him justice. He could draw pictures with Hogarthian savagery, could write and felt violently about everything. Later he was one of the original founders, with Michael Parsons and others, of the Georgian Society.

At Eton, Harold Acton, whose mind and diction even then seemed to me as individually brilliant as they have remained, became a close friend whose companionship I have valued over the years. Brian Howard, whose friendship and feuds with Harold were superbly imitated at Oxford by John Sutro, also entered our little circle.

Young Acton, who was to become Sir Harold Acton, CBE, author and poet, later wrote *Memoirs of an Aesthete* as well as many other notable works. He was born in Florence, where he continues to live when not travelling the world. John Sutro became a film producer and writer, and died in 1985. His father, a banker, helped finance Alexander Korda's London Film Productions, of which John was to become a director.

John Sutro and Harold Acton had many tastes in common; Sutro was a privileged court-jester and an extraordinarily accomplished mimic; Acton was the 'aesthete' *par excellence*, poet, raconteur and man of discrimination. When he first reached Oxford, the Christ Church 'hearties' regarded him as a highly suspect figure and he was obliged to barricade his door against assailants. Later, however, he achieved the status of a distinguished local institution, and even the Bullingdon Club were proud to entertain so witty and so blithe a guest. He had a romantic, yet fatherly attachment to Evelyn Waugh, and Waugh enjoyed the splendid luncheons served in Acton's rooms in the Victorian annexe of Christ Church Meadows, which had a balcony where, after consuming draughts of steaming mulled claret, Acton would declaim his own verses through a megaphone to the crocodiles of school-children who passed beneath.

Brian Howard, the third of Oliver's triumvirate of long-lasting friends, was perhaps the most colourful and controversial of the group. Howard played Beau Brummell to the good-natured grandees whom he thought it worth his while to educate, instructing them in the secrets of modern art, lecturing them about the clothes they wore, or urging that, like himself, they should have their racing colours designed by the Paris firm, Charvet. 'Mad, bad and dangerous to know' is how Evelyn Waugh described him in a phrase borrowed from Caroline Lamb who had written it in her diary in her description of Byron. But Howard was more complicated than that. Incontestably the wittiest man of his generation, he could be cruel and compassionate by turn. He bulged with talent, but achieved very little. Waugh, who detested him, took some hints from his character when he created 'Anthony Blanche' in *Brideshead Revisited*. He could not deny, however, that this blend of Brummel and Disraeli — Howard was of Jewish-American descent — exercised a curious fascination: 'he had dash and insolence . . . a kind of ferocity of elegance that belonged to the romantic era of a century before our own'.

Sir Harold: At Eton I learned nothing scholastically. Entirely my own fault, of course. The only education that I absorbed was on holidays, or when semi-ill, from Jimmy Marshall, a charming tutor we called Jemima. In London he would take me to see places of interest. We would explore, and he would explain details of history which linked up with what he had discovered. It was far more vivid than learning dates at school. What I learnt at Eton, from almost the first moment of shock and discomfort of it all, was to be able not to take life so seriously, to laugh instead of cry — and that was possibly the most helpful and valuable of lessons.

Oliver and I were born in the same year, 1904, and started at Eton in the same year. I left Eton a bit earlier than he did, not because I was sent away but because I hated the house so much and I passed my entry for Oxford. I implored my parents to let me go, otherwise I'd just have stayed another summer half, as the term was called, and go to camp because one was obliged to join the O.T.C. Besides, the camps were, well, filthy. That must have been 1921 because my first volume of poems was published in 1922.

Before going to Oxford I went to Strasbourg to polish up my German, but I can't say that I did very much work there: and then from Strasbourg I went to Oxford to Christ Church. But Oliver was never an undergraduate, although he might just as well have been because he was always the guest of undergraduates. He would come over because there was a club there, a very Bohemian club called the Hypocrites, which was extremely lively. Even dances took place, and not always with women although sometimes women were smuggled in. Oliver designed the walls. He painted amusing pictures of Queen Victoria and Prince Albert on the walls of the Hypocrites Club for these dances and parties. He was a brilliant comedian and mimic.

Oliver: Many of my friends from Eton had gone on to Oxford and it was there that I managed to spend many hilarious weekends. My cousin Rudolph, Harold Acton and his brother William, Michael Parsons and Robert Byron, and a host of old and new friends who formed a galaxy of individual and eccentric personalities, rather than jolly college youths, made Oxford at that time a very lively centre.

Emlyn Williams — not part of this set but studying at Christ Church as well — became a close friend of Oliver's.

Emlyn Williams: The first time I heard the name 'Oliver Messel' was about 1925, when I was an undergraduate at Christ Church, Oxford. It was at a charity concert in the Town Hall. This very dark boy came on — I thought he was Italian

79113

August, 1997

Emlyn Williams aged 18

— with a charming diffident smile, did some very funny sketches and imitations: I was pretty naïve, but was delighted to catch on to some pretty sophisticated stuff, involving personalities like Tallulah Bankhead, Noël Coward, Gladys Cooper, Gwen Farrar . . .

I inquired eagerly about him. No, he was not an actor, a painter or something, very much in the top-flight Oxford set: Harold Acton, Evelyn Waugh, Michael Parsons, Brian Howard, Bryan Guinness [later Lord Moyne]. I did not meet Oliver at the time as I don't think he frequented the O.U.D.S. [Oxford University Dramatic Society], which was my spiritual home. I only got to know him, and then intimately, just after the war, in 1945.

However, he saw Oliver again later in 1925 — in Venice. Oliver was holidaying there and Emlyn Williams had gone on a three-months tour of Italy before the Autumn term. His trip ended in Venice where he took a tiny house in the Campo San Geremia. From there he walked and absorbed the culture while he polished his Italian. In the first volume of his autobiography, *George*, he describes his daily routine, visiting the Lido as a break from studying: 'Once, looking down from the steamer at the quayside crowd, I noticed among a cluster of golden boys and girls one striking bare-breasted Venetian, a youth even more bronzed and white of teeth than his companions, all carrying bathing shorts and waving addios to friends next to me: remembering him in the distance in Tom Quad [Oxford] I saw it was Oliver Messel and nearly waved back.'

The two young men returned to Oxford; Emlyn Williams to sit a paper — Oliver to rejoin his social circle.

Oliver: The feuds between Brian Howard and Harold Acton continued unabated in dialogue that might have come from *The Importance of Being Earnest*, and relayed to our constant delight in mimicry by John Sutro, who was the life and soul of many parties.

Sir Harold: Brian Howard was a contemporary of ours. His life and times were recorded in a book called *Portrait of a Failure*, written by Marie-Jacqueline Lancaster. She had married a man called Lancaster — her maiden name was Nicholson — and lived in Tite Street, Chelsea. She was in love with Brian Howard, but it was to no avail because he was not a person for the ladies. This did not prevent women from falling in love with him, though — even Nancy Cunard had feelings for him — and he probably occasionally went to bed with them, but he was the most impossible character. His life ended rather tragically. He committed suicide.

Brian Howard had taken to drugs and picked up somebody at the BBC who finally inherited some money and pictures, one of which hangs in the National Gallery: a Titian which had belonged to his father. I never wished to see Brian because whenever we met we had terrible rows and he was offensive. They were very bogus Howards. I believe their name was really Gassaway, but they adopted the name of Howard. His father, Francis Howard, married Laura Chess. She was the daughter of William Chess from Louisville, Kentucky, a captain of artillery on the Northern side during the Civil War — his wife was a well-known journalist called T. P. O'Connor who edited a weekly magazine. Laura Chess was from the American south, 'Southern, you know', terribly pretentious, who ruined

Brian's career because she never left him alone. She was always telling him what to do, and of course, 'You must do the right thing. You must get into the Bullingdon, and hunt and ride.'

Brian was rather delicate, slender with huge eyes, rather good-looking when young. And there he was galloping and riding and trying to be with the hunting set at Christ Church when he went to Oxford. This rather hard set regarded him as *outré* and strange, but they liked him all the same. He was entertaining and he amused them, but he wasted those years running about with the Bullingdon and athletes.

He fought with me because I was just myself and he disapproved of what I wrote. Originally at Eton we edited together a magazine called the *Eton Candle*, known as the *Eton Scandal*, but it was very handsome. In later years it could be bought in second-hand bookshops for £150. It was a bound publication which was most unusual for a schoolboy magazine. It was bound in boards, a brilliant sort of puce colour, and inside we had an Old Etonian supplement, with contributions from the Sitwells and Aldous Huxley, for example. Among the contemporaries was Brian, myself and Anthony Powell, who is now such a very popular novelist. But he didn't write for it; he did the drawings. My brother, who was then alive, was a painter. It was a very curious and interesting thing. Brian was very precious and brilliant and witty — but wicked.

Oliver: There were continuous gatherings and parties, and I would work out preposterous invitations to amuse increasing groups of friends. I concocted absurd mimes to music for which I would make a large variety of elaborate masks. I remember once making a full-sized figure of a terrible bedraggled tango dancer in a Spanish shawl, and a rose in her dark tangled hair. The feet were weighted so that I could manoeuvre the puppet to follow the steps and appear to be a live dancing partner, as I led it through the routine of a ridiculous tango. The crudely painted face clearly said, 'No Lady!' — and she was walked or carried round the streets of Oxford or for rides in taxis, and under cover of night taken into one of the colleges. The proctors pounced on the sinister, lurching figure and arrested her escorts for keeping bad company.

Sir Harold: Oliver had certain set pieces, such as a woman who had diarrhoea in a train, or he would mimic various figures from his youth. He would also imitate Mrs Gibson, an American who was his cousin Rudolph's grandmother. Rudolph Messel was at Eton at the same time; according to some people he was very beautiful. Lots of people fell in love with him, but he was very precocious and over-sexed and had a tremendous number of affairs even at Eton. And then he rather burned himself up. He too, like so many others there, became a terrific socialist. I think he stood as a socialist though he never got into Parliament. But he was very, very rich. All the Messels were.

By the time he was twenty-one, Oliver had cemented his friendship with Glyn Philpot, who was proving to have a strong influence on him. Philpot was tall and elegant and wore an eyeglass. His attire was more that of a City stockbroker than an artist and he was known to have charm. The companionship they found in one another deepened, and the forty year-old artist and his pupil would regularly holiday together.

Oliver's painting of the Virgin and Child, now in St Mark's Church at Staplefield

Oliver: As a human being, the standard Glyn set for me persisted even after his death. I felt as if he had been borrowed from another age. How lucky for me to have had the privilege of working with him during that time. An imaginative sense of the absurd would make every moment hilarious and dispel the seriousness or awe of the Master. His sense of values was the truest I have ever known, spurning worldly successes.

Under Philpot's tutelage Oliver had painted an oil of the Virgin and Child; it was left unfinished and hung in the nursery at Nymans where his niece Susan (who became Lady Vesci) and his nephew Tony spent much of their childhood. It escaped the fire which devastated the house in 1947. Oliver subsequently completed the painting and gave it to his mother, who bequeathed it to St Mark's Church in her local village, Staplefield, where it now hangs on the right of the chancel arch.

By the mid-twenties, Oliver was enjoying the journeys he took with Glyn Philpot to the Continent, but Venice had a particular charm for him and continued to beckon him for many years to come.

Oliver: On my first visit to Venice, Cole Porter and his beautiful wife had taken a famous palazzo. It was there that I first met Elsa Maxwell, who was embarking on her singular career of giving parties and squeezing crowned heads together. Venice was a whirl, evoking every dramatic form of entertaining.

The ball the Cole Porters gave in this superb setting was the first of its kind I had ever seen. The guests were all dressed in red and white. Musicians played guitars as one arrived by gondola, and this created a magical atmosphere as one admired the set of rooms with ceilings painted by Tiepolo. As the night drew on, surprises were presented in rapid succession. Acrobats dressed in white performed their masterful acts; clowns danced on tightropes against the skyline while guests, bewitched by the unforgettable sights, gazed from the windows of the courtyard. Six in the morning came all too soon.

There were no unfortunate mischiefs comparable to the one that had taken place at a great ball given earlier by the Marchesa Casati. Apparently she stood on the steps of her palazzo, a romantic unfinished ruin, with a leopard on each side of her in the mood of Bakst's *Schéhérazade*. The wild beasts took a good nip at the guests as they arrived, and two attendants dressed as Nubian slaves, dipped in gold, barely survived the exotic reception.

Despite the pleasures he derived from his annual trips abroad – financed by his rich parents – Oliver worked diligently on his returns to London and was commissioned to paint Nancy Cunard for whom, at that time, he had prepared some drawings.

Oliver: I first met Nancy in the mid-twenties, in Venice where I visited often and for as long as I could spare the time in the summer of those days. Her cousin, Victor, owned a beautiful palazzo. It was rather a long walk from the piazza, long past the Accademia, over innumerable bridges and a maze of little streets and piazzettas.

I remember one evening when there was one of the usual dramas with her mother Emerald who had, I gather, criticized certain of Nancy's friends.

Lady Cunard's Christian name was Maud, but she disliked it and was always known as Emerald. She was American, but soon became an important figure in London society and together with her rich husband, Bache Cunard, cultivated celebrities. She was intelligent, amusing, and elegant, as well as being forthright and eagerly inquisitive. She delighted in flinging challenging remarks at her guests on every kind of topic as she sat at the head of her table in her large house in Grosvenor Square. She had spent considerable sums of money as a patroness of opera and ballet seasons at Covent Garden and Drury Lane before the First War and her parties were always peopled by musicians and dancers, as well as writers and politicians.

Oliver: On one occasion there had been a public demonstration in Paris by some *avant garde* artists, and Nancy had been at the hub of it. At that time, there was a young American John 'Jack' McGowan, a playwright, director and actor who formed part of Nancy's entourage, and against whom Emerald was venting her scorn. The rebellion against her mother seemed one of Nancy's main preoccupations. In later years I got to know Emerald and appreciated her special qualities immensely. Her unpredictable remarks would shoot out at random, sounding spontaneous and clownish, but in fact they were cleverly staged. She had a flow of the wittiest repartee and would strike a match to the general conversation among her distinguished guests, who, aside from Sir Thomas Beecham and George Moore, included Lord Berners, the Sitwells and Harold Acton.

After a summer in Venice I remember going with Nancy and Jack McGowan on a pilgrimage to Florence to worship at the shrine of the writer Norman Douglas, who wasn't very well. He was in a rather grumpy mood, possibly aggravated by a bit of a rumpus caused by the parents of one of his protégés who was demanding more money. It was in the early days of October and we felt that the first nip of autumn in the air as we sat in a café sipping Pernod.

Harold Acton, a friend from my Eton days, appeared together with Peggy Turner, a notable figure in Florence, distinguished for having been an intimate friend of Oscar Wilde, and incidentally, of my father's at Oxford. Harold has one of the most beautiful villas in Florence and I remember him giving me a beautiful book, the earliest on costumes, by a nephew of Titian.

Nancy and I became friends at our first meeting and saw a lot of each other. Then there would be long intervals of separation, yet when we met again it was as if time had stood still and the threads were soon gathered up again. We would see each other in London and in her flat on the Ile St-Louis in Paris, but for longer periods each year in Venice.

When the Venice summer season ended in late September Oliver enjoyed rambling with Nancy Cunard, exploring the network of little streets and small piazzettas off the beaten track of tourists, making quick sketches at small cafés of passersby – of interesting types, or of 'wandering troubadours'. Sometimes they went for walks along the far shore of the Lido. One of those late summer evenings they discovered at the Luna a black American orchestra whose playing they enjoyed immensely. They soon became friendly with them and Nancy and Oliver ended up sitting around with them as they sang and improvised.

Oliver: At that time, Nancy Cunard had a flat on the Zattori and one evening she gave a party which scandalized some of the rather conventional snobbish Venetian set because she had invited the black orchestra as her guests — and not merely as entertainers. This was the beginning of an era for Nancy, as the pianist in this orchestra became her great friend. He was neither a sensational pianist, nor an astounding specimen of black manhood, but more a cosy black daddy-figure, rather podgy with a slight hint of halitosis.

But the friendship served to scandalize Emerald, which was precisely what her daughter had set out to do.

Nancy Cunard, the Marchesa Casati (of the bright red hair and white-wash face) before her, and Isak Dinesen all created a striking effect by the forceful accent of black kohl around the eyes, inspired no doubt by the work of Bakst for the Ballets Russes.

Isak Dinesen was born in 1885. She grew up in her native Denmark but left to study English at Oxford University and painting in Paris and Rome. In 1914 she married her cousin, Baron Blixen, and went with him to run a coffee plantation in British East Africa. When they were divorced in 1921, she took over the management of the farm herself and 'began to write . . . to amuse myself in the rainy season'.

She left East Africa and returned to Europe in 1931 and three years later published her first book *Seven Gothic Tales* under the name of Isak Dinesen; *Out of Africa*, her next book, was published shortly before the war. Back in Denmark, Baroness Blixen continued to write profusely, in Danish and in English, and was visited by many younger writers and praised by many older ones. She became a friend of Oliver, whose companion in later years, Vagn Riis-Hansen, was also Danish.

Oliver: Nancy turned out to be one of the pioneer devotees of African culture and to this end wore a collection of massive bracelets carved from ivory tusks. At times she would set about her causes far too violently in order to achieve the success she craved. However, that individual, unconventional spirit, without compromise, is something that I love, and I treasure the time I spent in her company.

There had been another rumpus shortly before my next return to Venice. The atmosphere of Venice, with its compelling, legendary magic setting for romance, always had the disturbing tension of a sirocco preparing itself to spark off another incident. Princesse de Polignac [*née* Winaretta Singer of the sewing machine empire, for whom Stravinsky composed *Renard*] held court in one of the splendid palazzi on the Grand Canal. She was a commanding woman in appearance, not unlike pictures I had seen of Catherine the Great. Her musical salon was not to be taken lightly. Members of the Paris musical world were carefully selected (among whom was Misia Sert, the discoverer of Chanel and Diaghilev's closest friend), and the concerts were usually heavy going, apart from the joy of hearing masterly piano playing by Arthur Rubinstein on occasion.

That year, Princesse de Polignac had planned one of her largest *soirées*. An eccentric Englishman, Ralph Peto, the possessor of great charm but also of wild and unpredictable behaviour, had fallen into disfavour and had not been invited. He appeared, plastered, half an hour before the guests were due to arrive, and threw every morsel of the banquet into the canal. From a gondola, he sent up a message to the Princess: 'If you are the man you claim to be, come down and fight!'

Oliver's visits to Venice were rarely without incident. He once set off to return home by car — with his new-found friend Isadora Duncan at the wheel — and when they reached Avignon, according to gossip of the time, she tried to sell Oliver to a rich gentleman because they were short of money.

Apart from the great impact Glyn Philpot had on Oliver's life, there was another friend of the Messel family who was to influence the young artist's career.

Oliver: That man was Dr Archie Propert, a scholarly connoisseur in the field of art and the author of the first expert books on the Russian ballet [*The Russian Ballet in Western Europe* and *The Russian Balllet, 1921–1929*]. I am the lucky possessor of copies, left me by C. B. Cochran.

Archie Propert had a fine head, rather like Savonarola: perfect casting for Prospero! For me he was a very real magician. First, he persuaded my father to let me leave school early, and as he was an old friend of the eminent and austere Professor Tonks, he arranged for me to be admitted as a student at the Slade. That miracle performed, he was soon like a conjuror pulling more tricks out of the hat.

Professor Tonks, a gaunt figure and superb draughtsman, gave short shrift to the swarms of aspiring students. The arty girls in Augustus John-style dresses who were permanently draped around the entrance were greeted with an icy glare, and given no encouragement. To me he was very kind and Rex Whistler was the apple of his eye. Rex and I became instant friends.

It was entirely by chance that I ever arrived at designing for the theatre. Instead of always slaving away in the somewhat uninspiring atmosphere of life classes (always flabbily grotesque models) at the Slade, Rex Whistler and I were inclined to fritter away the time in each other's company, doodling and drawing fantasy palaces and imaginary people. During the weekends we started making masks of *papier mâché*. I was always fascinated by masks, and I continued until I had made quite a collection.

(From James Laver's Introduction to *Stage Designs and Costumes by Oliver Messel*, London, 1933, pp. 14–15)

The method Oliver adopted in making the masks was to model the head with the desired features in wax. Then small pieces of brown paper dipped in boiling water and saturated with flour paste were stuck all over the modelled face until the required thickness was reached. The surface was worked over while still wet, and the whole left to dry, when the mask could be separated from the wax and then painted.

Oliver was intrigued by masks with all their possibilities of dramatic expression and hieratic repose, and it was this craft that was to guide him into the theatre.

But a good deal of study — and play — was to take place before an eventful meeting with Diaghilev, which led to an introduction to the great impresario Charles B. Cochran.

Oliver Messel as a young man;
photograph by Elwin Neame

Oliver: The time at the Slade was one of awakening! Each day was filled with discovering friends anew and new experiences, finding for the first time how interesting life could really be. Apart from my friendship with Rex Whistler, I developed other close ties with Adrian Daintry, Robin Guthrie, Roger Furse, John Mansbridge and a number of other exceptional fellow students. Visits to the Slade by idols such as Augustus John or Stanley Spencer, whose strange primitive compositions I admired so much, were not unusual. Other celebrated artists would drop in to give words of advice.

However, I felt I might learn more somewhere less like a railway station, so I became apprenticed to John Wells, a portrait painter of distinction. He taught me to study the painting techniques of the Old Masters. Underpainting in *terre verte*. With him I could share models more inspiring than the freaks at the Slade. There were to have been a number of student apprentices but as it turned out I was the only one. This was all the better for me, to be the focus of attention, as John Wells had a cultured and sophisticated mind. His studio, No. 10 Abbey Road, St John's Wood, was an ideal studio building, set back from the road in a small garden. As well as being an ideal setting for painting, the rooms provided a congenial atmosphere for many uproariously wild parties.

Once, a little later, when Oliver had been lent the Abbey Road studios, he gave the first party to welcome the Blackbirds, members of the Harlem production that Cochran had presented at the London Pavilion in 1923 in *Dover Street to Dixie*. The black cast was headed by Florence Mills, 'the queen of coloured America', who received an ovation each time she came onto the stage — before she even sang. Edith Wilson, Johnny Huggins and the rest of the dynamic cast had taken London by storm. Beatrice Lillie, Alice Delysia and a number of other London star attractions turned out to meet them and combined to make an impromptu non-stop cabaret.

The occasion of the English set entertaining blacks in the early 'twenties caused a mild sensation, and needless to say Oliver's parents were none too pleased — even though it was through their close friend Glyn Philpot that he had been introduced to Negro art.

Oliver: In spite of the concern of many of our parents and irresponsible as some of the pranks may have appeared to the serious-minded, we were full of the exuberance of life and enjoyed every moment of it. The most complicated efforts would culminate in some absurd escapade, and so emerged what was known as The Bright Young Things. Parties of this kind were not extravagantly beautiful, nor were they competing with the more affluent but conservative social functions. They were organized with little money by the young generation themselves. It was the crazy resourcefulness of ideas, the oddness or incongruity of the setting which was aimed for.

We chose unusual, unexpectedly tatty settings like St. George's swimming baths, Victoria; some unknown pub on the way to the East End; or dinners arranged on a railway train on a journey to nowhere in particular. And so the Railway Club was started and stunt parties of endless variety took place. There were Baby Parties, Hollywood Roman Parties at which practical jokes, not in the best of taste, it must be admitted, but with imagination, were carried far too far.

The old Brasserie at the Café Royal was the haunt of artistic Bohemia.

Nothing of the kind, alas, has ever replaced it. Jacob Epstein, Augustus John, Ambrose MacEvoy, Sir William Orpen, and a host of exciting and sometimes sinister figures in a smoky hubbub were reflected in the mirrored walls among the gilded cherubs and red plush of the legendary atmospheric decorations. I would sit wide-eyed at the marble brasserie table as all the famous or notorious personalities were pointed out. Some indeed might join us for a drink, as John Wells had a wide circle of friends in the Bohemian world.

By now almost twenty, and living at home in Lancaster Gate, Oliver would have to creep up the stairs as noiselessly as possible in the early hours, past the parental landing, to reach the upper floor. Sometimes there would be an unexpected disaster: his father waiting, grim-faced, as City colleagues had reported back that his son had been seen with unwholesome or undesirable friends – and he would have to attempt to dispel such illusions.

Although his father was now happy for him to be a respectable portrait painter, the idea of his being mixed up with the theatre was another matter. To him, the very word 'actress' was akin to 'whore'; Oliver's parents assiduously avoided seeing his first efforts for Cochran – but in later years they were thrilled with each production.

Oliver: Archie Propert had just started the Claridge Gallery with Eva Mathias, one of the Wertheim sisters of the famous Sargent picture. The gallery was in Brook Street, and it was a venue especially launched to foster the work of young artists. They were to invite me to exhibit some of my masks at their gallery, but before that event, I received letters from both Eva and Archie asking me to do some work for Diaghilev!

> 15 Montagu Square
> London W1
> Sunday 2 November 1925

My dear Oliver

Diaghileff has just rung me up to ask if you would do some work for him for *Zephyr & Flora*, the new ballet – but he says he wants his own designs translated into *papier mâché*, or something, and thought you would do this so well. If you care to, go and see him at the Coliseum tomorrow morning between 11 and one, or ring him up at the Savoy. If you are not back until Tuesday, ring him up.

> Yours in haste
> Eva Mathias

> 100 Gloucester Place
> Portman Square, W1
> Saturday 1 November 1925

My dear Oliver

You may have heard from Mrs Mathias that Diaghileff wants a helmet and a lyre or some such things. Can you do them, or want to? They'd have to be hustled through, as the first performance of *Zephyr and Flora* is set for Tuesday week.

42

> Of course, you're quite aware of Diaghileff's odd ways and I'd think you're quite capable of taking care of yourself. . .
>
> love
> Archie

Masks by Oliver Messel shown in an exhibition at the Claridge Gallery, London (1925): left, 'Jehanne', and above, 'Hyacinthe'

Oliver went along to see Diaghilev, as arranged, and was duly commissioned to do the work. Their friendship developed, and when the Russian left London, he invited the young artist to visit him in Monte Carlo.

Oliver: Archie Propert was a close friend of Diaghilev and through him I had the opportunity while still a student to meet this dynamic personality and to be commissioned to take the first tentative step towards the theatre.

Diaghilev's supreme flair, taste and knowledge, his equal understanding of painting, music and choreography and also his absolute authority, which could weld all these elements into one complete working-out, made him an impresario apart, and a god to all those who were dedicated to creative work. I can never forget the compelling impact of his personality. He seemed able to mesmerize everybody around him.

The ballet *Zéphyre et Flore*, with decor by Georges Braque, was to be produced by Diaghilev at the Coliseum in 1925. It was being mounted as a vehicle for Lifar with music by Vladimir Dukelsky. Some masks were needed. A few large grotesques were to be propped about the stage, and the ballerinas at the opening were to have masks on top of their heads, creating a curious bat-like effect, as they were first seen with heads bowed down.

Boris Kochno took me under his wing, and insisted that I was to be given special credit in the programme for my work. That is something that I shall always remember! Also, a little later Kochno's impeccable taste and his kind advice concerning some designs I did for Cochran proved to be of immense help.

Diaghilev was most appreciative of Oliver's contribution to the ballet: 'Thank you very much, again, for your work for Zephyr,' he wrote. 'Should you be in Monte Carlo this winter don't forget to come and see me at the Hôtel de Paris, otherwise I hope to see you in Paris, London or Turin in the spring. I should be very happy to see your new productions and to greet you again.'

Archie Propert was sufficiently convinced of Oliver's talent to invite him to show some of his masks at the Claridge Gallery.

(From Laver's Introduction to *Stage Designs and Costumes*, pp. 15–16).

One of the most striking Oliver showed was 'Jehanne', the line of the austere profile continued by the butterfly head-dress. Another was 'Hyacinth', a Negro mask with a hat decked with ostrich plumes and trailing draperies looped round the face. Two 'Heraldic Masks for Decoration in a Room' set a fashion that was widely followed, although none of the imitations had the beauty or vigour of the originals.

There could be no doubt of the interest which the exhibition of Oliver's masks aroused. Among those who made purchases was the actor Ernest Thesiger, and it was at his house that C. B. Cochran first heard of Oliver's work and, having seen it, summoned the young artist to his office.

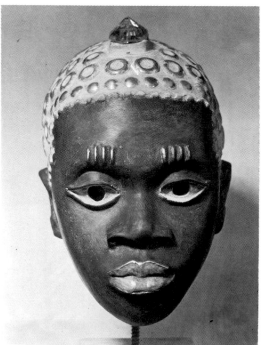

Three more of Messel's masks:
above, 'Icarus', below,
'Narcissus', opposite, 'Queen
Elizabeth'

44

2

The dancer Tilly Losch and
chorus in the 'Dance Little
Lady' number from Noël
Coward's 1928 revue for C. B.
Cochran, *This Year of Grace*

2 * The Cochran connection

OLIVER HAD JUST TURNED TWENTY-TWO when he received his first commission from C. B. Cochran and was launched into the world of theatre that he was to inhabit for the next fifty years.

Oliver: I first had a letter from him to ask if I would make a mask to the design of another artist for the next Cochran revue. This I had the nerve to refuse. Fortunately, only a short time later I was summoned to his office in Bond Street.

I had a slight lump in my throat as the dingy lift carried me up. The corridor and the walls were lined with fantastic sketches by Lautrec and Bonnard together with a rare collection of theatre playbills. I was soon in the presence of the great impresario.

There was no pompous nonsense aimed at impressing the visitor, such as Oliver encountered later in the film world. 'Cocky' had a commanding presence, immense charm and consideration coupled with authority, which enabled him to deal so well with temperamental stars.

He commissioned Oliver's first set of designs and gave them star promotion in his 1926 revue which opened at the London Pavilion on 23 April after a Manchester tryout. Entitled *Cochran's Revue* (1926) it was written by Ronald Jeans and featured Ernest Thesiger, Douglas Byng, Hermione Baddeley, Joan Clarkson, Mlle Spinelly, the popular French actress, and the incomparable Florence Desmond. Leonide Massine choreographed and appeared in two ballets.

For Oliver, it was the masks he created for one of the scenes of this revue that were of prime importance. 'One must not omit passing mention of a particularly striking (and all too brief) scene called "The Masks",' reported *The Daily Telegraph*, 'wherein a wondrous company of Chinese, Greeks, Russians, Hawaiians, Ethiopians, and so forth are seen wearing masks conveying in Oliver Messel's graphic designs an extraordinary wealth and range of suggestive physiognomy.'

Although he enjoyed mention of his work for the first time in the national press, Oliver was put out by a piece in the *Daily Sketch* after a dress parade at the Lyceum: 'I prophesy that these masks, which have been designed and executed by young Oliver Nessel, will make something of a sensation.'

Oliver took *The Sketch* to task over the spelling of his name, and the newspaper printed an apology:

Messel, Nellel, Missel, and Muscle. I have had an amusing letter from young Oliver Messel, who has designed the masks and dresses for Cochran's "Ballet of the Masks" in his new revue.

It seems that I inadvertently called him Nessel. "I am accustomed", he writes, "to being called Missel, Mossel, and even Muscle, but if ever you do me the honour of mentioning my

A youthful portrait of Oliver
Messel by Hoyningen-Huene

48

Oliver's Chinese costume and mask for Cochran's 1926 Revue

unworthy name again, will you be merciful and choose one that sounds less humiliatingly familiar than Nessel?''

I apologise, and I will be merciful.

Although Oliver contributed to Cochran's next revue at the Strand Theatre the following year, it wasn't until Noël Coward's *This Year of Grace* in 1928 that his name became known to the general public. He was given two scenes to design, 'Lorelei' and the 'Dance Little Lady!' sequence. Other designers for this spectacular revue included Ada Peacock, Doris Zinkeisen and Gladys Calthrop. In the 'Lorelei' sketch, Adrienne Brune and Sonnie Hale sang the number danced by Lauri Devine, who played Lorelei, with William Cavanagh as the sailor. Adrienne Brune and Sonnie Hale's clothes were designed by Kitty Shannon and Oliver designed the set as well as the costumes for Lauri Devine and William Cavanagh.

'Dance Little Lady' was sung by Sonnie Hale, and Lauri Devine, who was 'pale of face and ascetic', as recalled by C. B. Cochran in his memoirs, 'dancing with strange mechanical precision and followed by exotic masked figures. She mimed the role of a modern girl dancing in a lifeless, exhausted, unsmiling fashion evoking the young who were reared on food-tickets and bombed into neurosis during the First World War. The masks designed by Oliver faithfully reproduced the mirthless, vacuous expressions that could be seen any night in smart restaurants and clubs, where empty-looking youths danced with empty-looking girls in an empty shuffle. The scene was almost cruel in its veracity, but nonetheless a genuine satire of its period. The grotesque masks were brilliantly conceived by Oliver and won him tremendous praise.'

A chorus girl appearing in the routine was Marjorie Robertson, one of the first British actresses to win international stardom in a number of films – including *Victoria the Great*, *The Lady with a Lamp*, *Nell Gwynn*, *Odette* and *Spring in Park Lane* – after she had changed her name. But at that time she was one of the Cochran Young Ladies.

Dame Anna Neagle: There was a marvellous day when we were in this great bare rehearsal room in Poland Street, when the numbers were first being tried out, and Sonnie Hale was to sing 'Dance Little Lady'. Now 'Dance Little Lady' at that time was such a new rhythm altogether, and we didn't really know what to make of it. We were the girls and the boys dancing as robots in the background, wearing rather sinister masks, with Sonnie singing this number.

Sonnie was in despair at rehearsal, not knowing how to do the routine, and the rather young Noël Coward was sitting there watching him. One could see him getting agitated because it wasn't going the way he wanted it, and Sonnie said to him, 'I don't know what to do with the number.'

'Well, let me show you, dear boy, let me show you,' Noël replied, and got up and did it. Well, the vitality, the *magnetism* when he went into it – it was astonishing!

This Year of Grace was a triumph. Maisie Gay, Jessie Matthews and Tilly Losch scored their own successes in it, the show netted Noël Coward £1,000 a week in royalties, and Oliver's name became synonymous with masks of unique character.

But his talent was not limited to masks. When it was announced that Cochran had commissioned Gordon Craig to stage a play for him (it never materialized for various reasons), Arnold Bennett said to Cochran, 'Why bother about Craig when you have a real genius in Oliver Messel?' Cochran took Bennett's advice and continued to cultivate the young artist's talents.

Through his progressive successes, Oliver was beginning to acquire new and different friends, not only in the theatre, but in the aristocratic, social and literary sets as well. Another friend of his family was the British caricaturist and writer Max Beerbohm, whose economical and often caustic drawings stand as a sophisticated commentary on the social and literary life of his time. Before he left Oxford, where he had befriended Oliver's father, Beerbohm had made a reputation as an essayist of wit and polish; his reputation was maintained when he succeeded George Bernard Shaw as dramatic critic of the *Saturday Review* (he was always too much of a gentleman to attack his half-brother actor Sir Herbert Beerbohm-Tree in his official notices). His story, *The Happy Hypocrite* (written in 1897), was later dramatized by Clemence Dane as a vehicle for Ivor Novello in 1936 with Vivien Leigh as his leading lady. Beerbohm used the title of the story as a play on words in a letter he wrote to Oliver on 4 October 1928 from his home, Villino Chiaro in Rapallo.

Oliver was on his way to Venice to spend a holiday and Beerbohm had asked him to stay at Rapallo either on the way there or on his return to England. Their lines crossed in Italy.

> Dear Mr Oliver
>
> I seem to have no luck with the Messels! Two years or so ago my wife and I were going away just when your father and mother arrived here. And last Spring, when we went to Florence, the first thing that we heard from our friend Reginald Turner was that your father and mother had gone away that morning.
>
> I was determined to avoid another fiasco, when, last Sunday morning, your letter reached me at the Poste Restante in Vicenza. I wired to you at the Hotel Luna. And then I thought it would be well to telephone. I was told that you had just telephoned from the Hotel Terme at Salsomaggiore to say that you weren't arriving until the following Sunday. So I wired to the Hotel Terme — and later, I wired also to the address from which you had written.
>
> What more can a man do?
>
> But it is useless to struggle against fate, if fate is in a bad mood. Fate is determined to go on dividing Messels and Beerbohms. Fate had ordained that you shouldn't turn up here yesterday, as we'd hoped you would.
>
> Conceivably you will appear today or tomorrow, on your way *to* Venice. Fate *may* be less determined than she seems.
>
> But I send this letter, all the same, to you at the Luna. I daresay you won't be there — and if there you are, fate will steal the missive from the bureau! And so I won't express any view on *happy hypocrite* — cinema notion.
>
> > Yours very sincerely
> > Max Beerbohm

One of Cochran's greatest financial successes up to this time was *Wake up and Dream!*, which opened on 22 March 1929. With music and lyrics by Cole Porter, it featured two of his now popular songs: 'Let's Do It', performed by Jessie Matthews and Sonnie Hale, and 'What Is This Thing Called Love', sung by the then famous radio artist Elsie Carlisle to the accompaniment of Leslie Hutchison,

Top, Anne Neagle in *Wake Up and Dream*, Cochran's 1929 revue. Above, Tilly Losch as the Manchu Marchioness in the same show.

'Hutch', the black favourite of London society and Royalty alike. The book was written by John Hastings Turner and the show, under the direction of Cochran himself, was choreographed by Tilly Losch and Max Rivers. One of the principals, George Formby's leading lady in ensuing years, recalls her part in the show.

Polly Ward: I didn't sing or dance very well but I had a terrific amount of drive. Although I had my own part to perform in the various sequences, I was Jessie Matthews' understudy and went on for her several times — even though I couldn't dance as well as she could. But I often had the chance to sing 'Let's Do It', and enjoyed that tremendously.

I was cast as 'link man' under the heading 'Little Johnnie Energy' and Oliver made me some gorgeous skin-fitting costumes encrusted with jewels. When I came on stage it was like a flash of lightning. Oliver had a terrific personality, and as he was a genius as far as we were all concerned, his designs were naturally brilliant. He was way ahead of all the other designers, standing out on his own as a creative artist. I found him rather aloof, though — he was always on his own and never entered into the spirit of the company's general *bonhomie*.

The scenes, costumes and masks for the opening three scenes and three other sequences in the second act were designed by Oliver; all the clothes for them were made by his sister, whose credit in the programme reads: 'Costumes of Tilly Losch, Alanova and Edwin Lane executed by Mrs Armstrong Jones'. Some of the other scenes were designed by Rex Whistler, Oliver's friend from the days at the Slade.

(From Laver's Introduction to *Stage Designs and Costumes*, p. 18)

Weeks of experiment had taken place with Tilly Losch's dress as the Manchu Marchioness in the 'Girl in a Shawl' sequence, as Oliver wanted something that shone like porcelain yet fell in folds like heavy silk. The right material did not exist, so he discovered a medium which enabled him to paint on the finest rubber sheeting without stiffening it. The head-dress was also of rubber with little delicate scrolls in the likeness of a Ming figure. The dress of the singer William Stephens as the Chinese coolie was similarly contrived, and his masked figure seemed to be made entirely of porcelain. The set consisted of a frail vermilion bridge against a background of bluish-green gauze, in several layers, dense like a heavy mist, and this, with the lemon-yellow of the singer's robe, made up a stage picture of astonishing beauty.

Dame Anna Neagle: I was one of the eight ballet dancers in the show, and we did the opening routine 'on points'. The scene was so imaginative — it is what we used to call 'futuristic' in those days. The scene was a dream sequence and the whole thing was in shimmering white and silver. Our dresses that Oliver designed were also silver and white, mid-calf, and we wore head-dresses made by him in translucent celluloid with a white velvet band encrusted with large pearls.

We went to New York with the show, but it didn't do well. Nothing did. It was just after the Depression; we opened in December and closed in the following May. Even Jack Buchanan, who came over with the show, wasn't as

Costume parade for the Coppelia number in *Wake Up and Dream*. Cochran is seen examining Tilly Losch's costume; Oliver Messel is at the desk second from the right; Anna Neagle is third from the left behind.

well received as he was in the earlier Charlot revues on Broadway with Gertie Lawrence and Beatrice Lillie. I do remember the rivalry, though. Tilly Losch, who was known to be difficult, didn't know what Cochran was planning for the final curtain call at dress rehearsal. Jack was the star of the show and Tilly had scored a big hit in it in London, and I remember them eyeing each other when Cochran rehearsed the curtain calls. Jessie Matthews took her call with Sonnie Hale – and then Tilly came down, followed by Jack.

When the cast returned to London in May 1930, Jack Buchanan planned to produce *Stand Up and Sing*, of which he was part author with Douglas Furber. It was scheduled for an opening the following year at the London Hippodrome following an extensive tour which began at Southampton in December. He was casting the part of Mary Clyde-Burkin, and Marjorie Robertson, who had by now adopted her Irish mother's name, Neagle, had new photographs taken and handed them to a stage director friend who sent them along to Buchanan. She was asked to audition for the part. 'It's *you*,' Buchanan said. 'I *thought* I recognized that face, but I didn't recognize the name.' He gave her the part and she made a great success both on tour and in London. She never danced in the chorus again.

Oliver's next commission was Cochran's 1930 revue by Beverley Nichols, with songs by Vivian Ellis and Beverley Nichols, and ballets by Boris Kochno, with whom Oliver had first worked on Diaghilev's *Zéphyr et Flore*, and George Balanchine. It opened at the London Pavilion with a cast headed by Maisie Gay, and scored another success for Cochran. He had employed the most notable designers available: Christopher Wood, Christian Bérard, Rex Whistler, Ada Peacock, Doris Zinkeisen — and Oliver, who was entrusted with both scenery and costumes for the 'Piccadilly 1830' and 'Heaven' sequences which were elaborate and offered peculiar scope to his creativity.

The highest praise came from the distinguished critic of *The Sunday Times*, James Agate:

It is a pity that Mr Oliver Messel is an Englishman. If he had been a Roosian or a Proosian practising decor on the marges of some Czecho-Slovakian crocodile-infested swamp, we should have long ago hailed him as a great scenic-artist. As he is merely a Londoner, the play-going world is content to be completely ravished once a year at the London Pavilion and then forget all about this fine artist until Mr Cochran next reminds us. Mr Messel has two scenes plumb in the middle of this revue, and they are so lovely that we look before and after and pine that none other is by him. The first is 'Piccadilly, 1830' in the course of which a Highlander (M. Serge Lifar), appears wearing a head-dress which impinges on the mind almost as terrifyingly as Garrick's delivery of the dagger-speech from Macbeth. But then, Mr Lifar is actor enough to carry that gear. The rest of the scene is like walking through an old-print shop. This is succeeded by a view of heaven, and those who normally hold white to be an insipid colour suitable for blanc-manges, babies, snowdrops, Alps and almonds are recommended to note Mr Messel's way with blamelessness. Mr Messel is a *blanchisseur* of riot.

(From Laver's Introduction to *Stage Design and Costumes*, p. 20)

Ivor Brown in *The Observer* was almost as enthusiastic, and concluded his notice: 'Whoever makes Mr Cochran's next revue, we can do with more and more of Mr Oliver Messel.' The result of the two scenes Oliver designed was that his name became familiar to a large public and he was recognized not only as a stage decorator of infinite competence, but as an artist with a highly individual style of his own. The set he designed for the 'Heaven' sequence, in particular, was an important stage in his development when he used it as the basis for the design of *Helen!* later on.

The Daily Sketch reviewer said, 'I was interested to see that Oliver Messel had used Pollock's Hoxton prints, to which I was referring some months ago — and to which, actually, I introduced him — in his "Piccadilly 1830" scene.

'He sat in a box with the Baroness d'Erlanger, who might have seen her own Piccadilly house on the back-cloth.'

Oliver: Catherine d'Erlanger was the most inspiring personality. She had Venetian red hair, rather like a Veronese or Titian. Many pictures by Larby Lazlo and other artists are recorded of her beauty in books on costume, such as 'Modes and Manners'. She was basically French, but claimed to be descended from Bianca Cappello, the famous mistress of Francesco de' Medici. I wouldn't have liked to get on the wrong side of her. But to those she cared for, she was a fabulous friend, and was one of the first people to commission me to paint a portrait of her daughter, Baba. She was eccentric in an age that had been so conventional; she

The 'Piccadilly 1830' number designed by Oliver for Cochran's 1930 Revue

set out to help all artists and at one period she was devoted to Hugo Rumbold who did beautiful designs for *Figaro* at Covent Garden and had that flair for designs.

Hugo also enjoyed a double life *en travestie*, and for a while they lived happily together at Bath. He dressed up as a charming lady companion.

Archie Propert and Eva Mathias had opened the doors to the world of the Russian ballet. In the lovely house of Catherine d'Erlanger, in Piccadilly, which had belonged to Byron, parties were given in their honour and I became friends with Danilova, Tchernichova, Lifar, Massine and many of the ballet company.

(From James Laver's Introduction, pp. 21–22)

Cochran's 1931 revue disappointed most of the critics, chiefly because it relied more on boisterous humour and less on spectacular and beautiful settings than some of its predecessors. But all gave high praise to Oliver's only two contributions – 'Stealing Through' – and 'Scaramouche', which brought the first act to an end with an orgy of fantastic forms and vivid colour. *The Evening News* called particular attention to it:

> My own favourite item, and, I submit, by far the most distinguished and beautiful thing in this revue, was 'Scaramouche', a scene and ballet with music derived from Pergolesi and characters and costumes from the Commedia dell'Arte of Venice, in which Mr Oliver Messel's scenery and costumes were theatrical in the very highest sense of the word. It was comparatively simple yet superlatively brilliant.

The first complete production entrusted to Oliver was *Helen!*, a new version of Offenbach's opera bouffe *La Belle Hélène*, with a libretto by A. P. Herbert, destined for its British premiere at the Adelphi on 30 January 1932. It was produced by C. B. Cochran with choreography by Massine, and its cast, directed by Max Reinhardt, included Evelyn Laye, George Robey and W. H. Berry. The opportunity of designing scenery and costumes for such a production does not occur twice in a lifetime. Oliver seized it with both hands.

The production of *Helen!* was not a sudden whim, but a dream which had been maturing for years. And, granting everything that is due to Max Reinhardt, who conceived the idea of the production and first performed his original version of it in Germany, the English *Helen!* was the artistic creation of Cochran. He took Oliver and A. P. Herbert over to Berlin to discuss Reinhardt's production at the Schloss Leopoldskron. 'We sat in a circle of high leather chairs', Cochran reported in his memoirs, 'with long cigars, and Messel and myself, I think, in some alarm.' This was the great Reinhardt, quiet and courteous but tremendous in his own great castle; and this was the great Cochran — two kings and veterans of the European theatre.

'In *Helen!*,' Cochran continued, 'the supreme passage was the Bacchanale, superbly arranged by Massine. Oliver Messel who had designed the entire production — scenery, clothes, and accessories — reached a pinnacle of beauty with the white bedroom of Helen.'

Since there was no question of any need for archaeological correctness, Oliver decided to emphasize the Greek themes but modified them with the influence of the Baroque. For his colour scheme, inspired by the success of the 'Heaven' sequence in Cochran's 1930 revue, he chose with great boldness to let white dominate the stage for the greater part of the play. Other colours were not lacking, but most people, if they had been asked what colour they had seen in the performance and what stage picture had impressed them most vividly, would have replied, 'White', and 'The white bedroom'.

The stage was hung with white curtains, the low divan-bed rested on a dais of two steps flanked by white swans in honour of Leda, Helen's mother. Above it rose four slender pillars, topped with palm leaves and supporting a kind of half-dome. From this hung a baldacchino and, from the baldacchino, immense lengths of white muslin looped with great swirling curves to the flies. Other white curtains hung at the head of the bed, at the back of which could be seen a relief of a dancing figure.

Evelyn Laye as Helen was at the peak of her beauty, and had enjoyed a recent success on Broadway in Noël Coward's *Bitter Sweet*.

Evelyn Laye: I had never met Oliver before this, and when Cochran asked me to play Helen, I thought, 'How marvellous. How wonderful. I'm going to sing Offenbach.' I didn't think about Oliver at all. He was an also-ran as far as I was concerned. I was thinking about the score and was thrilled to think that I had been chosen by Charles, whom I had met many years before through my father, and who had given me a contract as my twenty-first birthday present! I was chosen to be the face that launched a thousand ships. But then Charles said to me, 'Oliver is going to do the decor and the costumes, and I am leaving you entirely in his hands.'

I felt a little apprehensive about this, because I was to be entrusted to someone I'd never met. I've always been punctilious about theatrical clothes and have never left anything to chance. I studied my body, what is good for my body, and what is bad for it; in fact, exactly what I can wear. I learned in America from Ziegfeld that I could not wear a lot of fussy things, that as a personality I must dominate my clothes. The clothes must not dominate me because they kill me. So in the theatre I always wear good clothes, made of good material of plain design, but I never explained any of this to Oliver.

I met Oliver and agreed with Cochran that I would not choose anything

Evelyn Laye at the height of her career, and (opposite) in the 'white on white' bedroom set for the Cochran/Max Reinhardt production of *Helen!* (1932), a successful frolic which established Messel's talent in his early career.

The costume designed by
Messel for the character Ajax in
Helen!

except one thing, which I eventually told Oliver about, but he wanted to have *carte blanche* in choosing the materials, the designs – and everything else. Why I agreed, I don't know, because it is very unlike me. I think it was Charles's persuasive manner that did it. He said, 'Put yourself in his hands. I assure you that if you do, he'll do it right.' So I did. I left everything to Oliver. All my materials came from Paris, but I said to Oliver, 'There is only one thing I do insist upon, that there is no hard line around me. I don't like a hard line. I like a soft line and plain clothes. Beautiful material, yes, but not a hard line on the dress!' And he agreed. We got to the first fitting, which was a beautiful black velvet dress, the first dress I wore in the play. There was a line around the bust, but I didn't say anything. I thought it best not to do so. So I shut up. Finally, much to my satisfaction, the dress was fitted perfectly – and it had a long white train which I liked. People always say that when I walk on the stage my train is still in the dressing room! Anyway, it wasn't quite as bad as that this time, but I waited and waited and finally Oliver went over and got a piece of white chiffon which he draped around my bust and said, 'I do hope the dear little darlings will be happy in that.'

He was a strange little creature to me; I don't know how he appeared to everybody else. I could always sense that he had a depth of thought and knew exactly where he was going. But on the other hand he didn't convey this outwardly. He had eyes rather like a faun, which were very expressive and full of affection and delight. Delight, that is, when he knew things were going his way and the way he wanted them to go. I became rather like a doll in his hands. Something that he possessed, in a way. I was not quite real to him. I was something he liked dressing up. He took the trouble to make the belts that went with the clothes himself. He took my false hair and stranded gold that went through the curls. I found him enchanting to work with. He loved everything he was doing. He took a delight in it. It was part of his being, the things that he was creating on you. . . .

Oliver made a white dress for me with a blue sash worn like a halter, which he made from a wonderful material called *lisse*. It's finer than organza. This was a costume I wore when I represented the face that launched a thousand ships. I was standing on top of a rostrum in this white dress and its wonderful sash of blue. It was stunning. The material was plain and simple, and that is what he visualized. He had a sharp eye for what you were. He never overdressed me one iota. Not for a moment. And it was a complete sensation. It is still talked about to this very day. It is part of the history of the theatre.

Oliver went for simplicity. I know there was a great mind working behind the scenes much of his life, but he was delightful and very happy with his doll. He made me look a million dollars. He is the only person in the whole of my career who has ever had that privilege. I have never given it to anyone else.

The show was an unqualified success, but behind the scenes acrimony had existed between designer and producer. Cochran had commissioned Oliver to design the production without the precaution of a written contract, and Oliver, who was in some financial embarrassment (as he was to be for the rest of his career) pursued Cochran with demands never made hitherto by any designer in the world.

By now Oliver had moved to 16 Yeoman's Row in Chelsea and his life style there was proving costly. The following are exchanges of correspondence between Cochran and Oliver:

November 12th 1931

My dear Oliver

I am alarmed at the result of your conversation with Hal Lewis. Your demands are quite impossible for any production of the character I am undertaking.

It was, of course, wrong of me, as a business man, to allow you to proceed without entering into an arrangement, but as I intended to be liberal, I did not think we should have any difficulty.

Nobody has greater appreciation of your ability than I have, but if you were Michael Angelo, I could not afford to pay the terms you have suggested. They have, so far as I know, never been paid any theatrical production. In offering you the royalty I did, it is in excess of anything I have paid, except in the case of 'Cavalcade' at Drury Lane. I am prepared to give you the same terms.

I have tried to reach you by telephone this afternoon, without success, and it is essential that we meet without further delay. I could not afford to produce *Helen!* with your designs on the terms you suggest. It would not be commercial to do so, and they are out of all proportion to what I might reasonably expect. Should the play be a great success, I am perfectly willing that you should profit by it, and that is why I suggested a royalty.

I would like to settle the matter tonight, and shall be home from 7.30 p.m. Please 'phone me –

Yours as ever
Charles B Cochran

The telephone conversation took place and Cochran replied by letter:

20th November 1931

My dear Oliver

You are talking a language I don't understand. In my experience, I have not known any designer for the theatre being paid so much for certain territory. I

The opening scene of *Helen!*

have followed the usual custom in paying so much for my designs — in most cases, a lump sum, — outright.

When we finally agreed terms, which I confirmed by letter, I considered the matter settled. The figure I have had in my mind for this work is £1,000 [a considerable sum for those days, considering designers were paid as little as £300 for a production after the war, some 20 years later!], but I suggested in the first place ½% on the London run as a sporting chance of you getting more. As you preferred £25 per week, I fell in with your view, but in my wildest dreams I had never expected you would ask me to pay for the designs twice over, if I produced in America, or three times over if I produced in the Provinces.

The terms I am giving you have not, within my knowledge, been equalled for any musical production. What you say about the Folies Bergère is all nonsense. Miss Ada Peacock and others I have known working for the Folies Bergère get 25 to 50 francs a sketch. Professor Ernst Stern who has, I think, the greatest reputation among stage designers, asked me £500 for an entire production.

I have not modified my offer to you because your lack of knowledge of stage requirements and the restrictions of the theatre make it extremely difficult to carry out your scenic designs, and I and my staff have given you every assistance, but I take this opportunity of advising you to study theatre technique conscientiously for a year or so before you put yourself in a position to create an entirely new standard of payment for the work I have called upon you to do. There is no theatrical production which could carry the fees you now suggest. But for the fact that I hope to do the play in America, I could not afford to pay you the terms I have agreed upon during the London run. No American manager would consider the payment of a royalty for designs which had already been used in London. . . .

Cochran's letter continued for another page reminding Oliver that no other producing manager in London would have made him a better offer.

However, the matter was not to rest there. Oliver, determined to the end, replied to Cochran but when he failed to get a response from the great man, wrote again:

4 December 1931

Cocky Dear

I haven't yet had an answer to the note I sent by hand about a week ago about our financial arrangements. For in your letter confirming our verbal agreement you say that my payment finishes with the end of the run in the West End of London, to which I had never agreed. I put down what seemed reasonable should the show go to other countries and in proportion with what we had agreed and from which I could only profit in case of extreme success.

I see that you cannot pay out a sum to start with that would cripple a show, but I do think it only fair that if the show has chances in other countries I should also stand to win.

I would not worry about this so much if I were not in such depressing complications financially, and for five months from September to January I shall not have been able to make any other money.

If you disagree we must meet without delay (on very friendly terms) and talk it out.

love
Oliver

5 December 1931

Dear Oliver

With reference to your letter, I suppose we had better talk it over. I thought my last letter had settled the matter.

Nobody appreciates the merit of your work more than I, but I can assure you that your demands are in excess of those of any theatre designer in the world.

With affectionate regards

Yours ever

Charles B. Cochran

Oliver, of course, was clever as a box of monkeys, and before they met decided to create a model of the set for the famous bedroom scene in order to sway Cochran's judgment. But he needed to work speedily if he was to secure the contract, and enlisted the help of a young apprentice designer, Tony Harris. Harris worked for Alec Johnstone, who ran one of the leading scenic painting studios in London.

Tony Harris: I was only about sixteen at the time and met Oliver once or twice when he visited the studio to have backcloths made. I had been to secondary school and had no formal training as an artist, but I could take a set design and make a three-dimensional model out of it.

Oliver arrived in a flurry one day and asked Alec Johnstone whether I could help him out by making the model for *Helen!* – which he said had to be done in a hurry – and Alec agreed to let me go. So I went along to his studio in Yeoman's Row to make the model – and subsequently stayed on as Oliver's assistant to work on his next production, *The Miracle.*

Equipped with the beautifully made model of the set, Oliver set off for his meeting with Cochran – and so spellbound was the impresario with the art-work that he offered terms on the spot in line with Oliver's original demands, and wrote him afterwards to verify the arrangement:

11 December 1931

My dear Oliver

'HELEN!'

This is to confirm our verbal arrangement of this morning to the effect that I am to pay you as follows for your costume, scene and accessory designs and the supervision of the making and painting of same:-

£500 upon production

£250 two months after production, and

£250 four months after production.

In the event of the play not running four months, any part of the £1,000 above referred to which has not already been paid is to be paid at the end of the run.

Should the play be presented in the U.S.A. and Canada, I or any management with whom I make an arrangement for the play, shall have the right to use all the designs, without further charge, providing the play has not had a run of forty weeks in London. In the event of the play having run forty weeks or more in

London, you are to receive an additional payment of $2,000 U.S. if I use the designs for the American production. It is understood that I am not compelled to use your designs in America.

Yours sincerely
Charles B. Cochran

Oliver had finally won the day — albeit with reservations — but Cochran had the last word:

3 February 1932

My dear Oliver

I was overjoyed by your letter. I feel that it has been a great privilege to introduce you to the British public as a designer for the theatre. I have had the greatest confidence in you from the outset and one of the happiest memories of 'Helen!' will ever be that it has given you your proper place in the world of art.

If I might offer a word of advice, it would be that you made a serious study of stage techniques, which will help you tremendously with your designing.

With affectionate regards
Yours as ever
Charles B Cochran

In defence against Cochran's criticism of his lack of stage technique, Oliver later commented: 'In my time there was no training for theatre design. One trained as a painter. Today there appear to be millions of aspiring students of stage design, a discouraging prospect in the face of the diminishing number of theatres, or plays presented.'

Letters and telegrams poured in to Oliver after the openings in Manchester and the West End: Cole Porter, Francis Lederer, Cecil Beaton, Syrie Maugham, Douglas Byng, Daisy Fellowes and many others including Cochran himself. Oliver's mother wrote to him from Nymans:

I still feel as if it were all a dream and as if those exquisite scenes and dresses were part of a wonderful enchantment. I cannot tell you how thrilled I was from the beginning to the end: a sunny, lovely fold of drapery and a shade of silvery white, or the blaze of colour at the end made lasting pictures in my mind.

My darling, I think you knew all that I would say, but words fail me. Only, can I tell you how proud I am to be your mother? I shall always remember our little dinner in your studio before and your sweet thought in giving some of those lovely lilies which are with me here.

God bless you, my darling, and may your way be ever strewn with sweet and lovely things and may you still remain as you now are, quite unspoiled by all the admiration and praise which is showered upon you.

All my love
your devoted
Mother

A note of congratulations came from Peggy Wood, star of the original London production of Noël Coward's *Bitter Sweet*:

I cannot let the day go by without dashing off these few words to you about the decor of 'Helen!'

My delight may not mean much in your scheme of things but I shall intrude to the extent of telling you that I have never seen anything so ravishing anyplace — *never*.

I got a night off yesterday from rehearsals, and enjoyed myself as I have seldom done!

Sincerely

Peggy Wood

From Bobbie Andrews [Ivor Novello's life-long friend]:

My dear Oliver

I have *never* seen anything so beautiful as your work in 'Helen' in all the 40 years I've been on the stage!!

In fact it made me cry, it was so lovely.

A thousand congratulations

Yours

Bobbie

From Hugh (Binkie) Beaumont, who had succeeded to the H. M. Tennent theatre empire:

My dear Oliver

I know that I have no right to do this — but I must express my delight and deep admiration for your overwhelmingly beautiful '*Helen*'. Never have I seen in the world anything as perfect. It will take years for me to view a play without comparing it with your amazing spectacle — and even then nothing will ever be as good. I have always heard that one could be spellbound by beauty, and for the first time I was.

Do let's meet soon when you have a moment.

Ever

Binkie

A portrait of Cecil Beaton that was in Messel's possession

Cecil Beaton, a long-standing friend and contemporary of Oliver's (they were born a day apart) and later a neighbour of his in Pelham Place, London, had gone off to do some work in the United States. He wrote to Oliver from the Waldorf-Astoria in New York on 8 February 1932 saying how much he enjoyed seeing the designs for *Helen!* reproduced in the *Sketch*. The show had opened in his absence but he assured Oliver that he would be seeing it immediately on his return to Britain. He was, however, enjoying his stay in New York and particularly seeing the new plays as well as his visit to Radio City Music Hall — which he found 'heaven'. He was to leave for Hollywood within ten days but seemed more excited by the fact that Lil Dagover, the German film star in the Pola Negri mould, had lent him her house over there.

By the beginning of March, however, Oliver had failed to reply to this letter and Beaton wrote to reprimand him for this oversight. He went on to describe the pastel shades of the rooms of the Waldorf-Astoria and the comfort its environment brought him as he was beginning to feel 'pretty haggard' — not only because he had been working too hard, but because New York's night life and nocturnal trips to Harlem were beginning to tell on him.

Beaton finally received replies to his letters, whereupon he complained that he'd had enough of New York's racy tempo and was anxious to get to Lil

Dagover's red and white house at Malibu Beach. Dagover's successful personal appearances in the leading cities of America had delayed her departure for the coast and Beaton regretted that by the time he arrived there their mutual friend Syrie Maugham would have left for England. He was enthusiastic about the new films on release in the U.S.A. – particularly mentioning Marlene Dietrich whom he found 'ravishing' in *Shanghai Express*, and Garbo as *Mata Hari*. Signing himself by the pet name Oliver had given him – 'Tittywitten,' – he ended his letter by sending love to Oliver's sister Anne.

The effect of *Helen!* on the public was overwhelming. The creation of the white-on-white set Oliver had designed was later copied by interior designers, and none could have admired both Oliver and his work more than Syrie Maugham, who had taken to interior design. 'I am off to India,' she told friends, 'to paint the Black Hole of Calcutta *white*!' When she went to Hollywood, a friend told Oliver, 'and now she's white-washing the whole of the film colony!'

In between his work for the theatre, Oliver continued to paint portraits, and designed a book jacket for Cynthia Asquith:

> Adelphi Terrace House
> Strand, W.C.2
> Oct 27 1932
>
> Dear Mr Messel
> Just a line to say how enchanted I am with the 'Silver Ship' jacket. I think it's a most lovely design and can pass the day very happily just gazing at it.
> I'm afraid the contents of the book are scarcely worthy. I am so grateful to you for doing it so beautifully.
>
> Yours sincerely
> Cynthia Asquith.

In 1932 Max Reinhardt wrote to thank Oliver for a note of good wishes, and said that he hoped they might collaborate in some new work. They were, indeed, to work together again. Reinhardt had in mind an American production of his celebrated production of *The Miracle*, which C. B. Cochran was to produce for England. Lady Diana Cooper, who was destined to appear in the production on both continents, sent Oliver a postcard from the Central Hotel, Glasgow, on 11 November 1932:

> *R.S.V.P. please*
>
> Dear Oliver
> Let there be no excuses on the
> night of Dec 21st. I am giving a
> Christmas party at Gower Street
> [her then home] at 11 and I cannot
> do without you.
> Diana C.

A painting by Oliver Messel of Titania and Bottom (1937). Messel designed the sets and costumes for a memorable production in 1937 of *A Midsummer Night's Dream*, produced by Tyrone Guthrie

C. B. Cochran takes up the story, here quoted from his memoirs:

Set design for Act III, Scene 3 of the C. B. Cochran
production, *Helen!* (1932). Courtesy of the Victoria and
Albert Museum

Messel painting his model for the last act set of *The Sleeping Beauty* (1946). Courtesy of the Victoria and Albert Museum

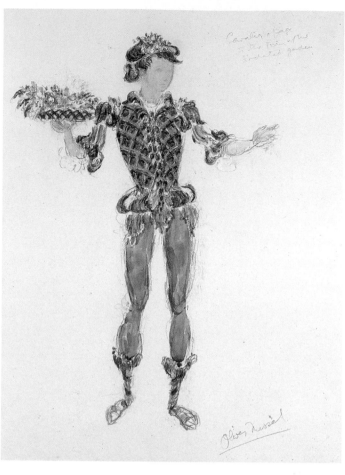

The Sleeping Beauty

Left above, costume design for the Cavalier of the Fairy of the Enchanted Garden. Courtesy of the Victoria and Albert Museum

Left below, costume for the Queen, Act I. Courtesy of the Victoria and Albert Museum.

Robert Helpmann as Carabosse, gloating over the outcome
of her wicked spell. Photograph by Frank Sharman of the
1946 production

A street in Bath; a drop curtain by Messel for the 1945
production of *The Rivals*

Opposite, costume design for the Glyndebourne production
of *La Cenerentola* (1952). Courtesy of the Victoria and Albert
Museum

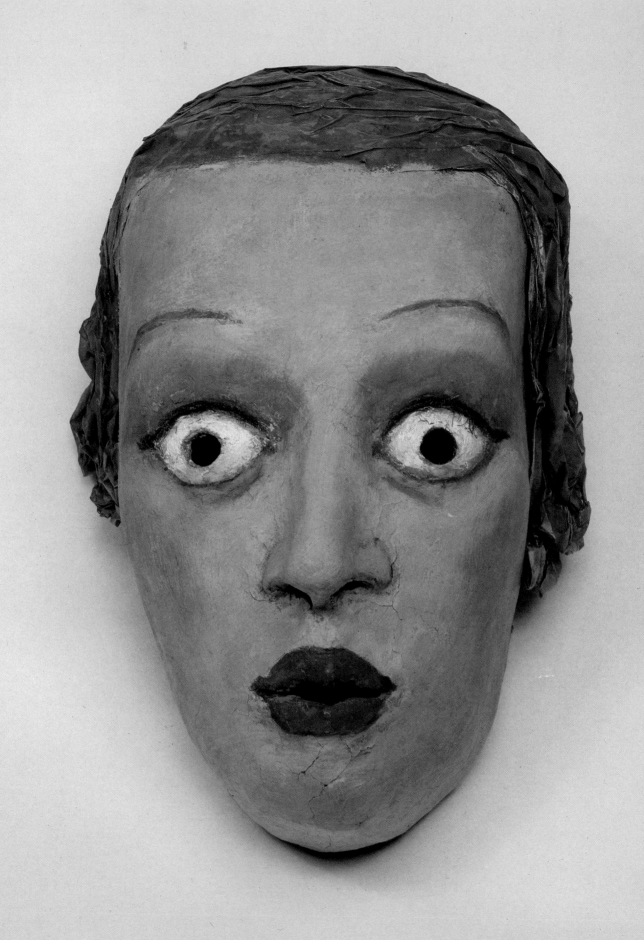

Cochran: Young Oliver Messel's exquisite costumes and scenes for *Helen!* were still a matter for theatrical wonder when I commissioned him to do the designs for *The Miracle*. Hardly had the critics exhausted their stock of adjectives in praising the beauty of Messel's designs for the Greek burlesque before they were forced to ransack the dictionary for new ones to greet his colourful reconstruction of the legendary Middle Ages. Reinhardt, who had never heard of him before, was overwhelmed by his work for *Helen!* and most anxious that I should entrust *The Miracle* to him.

The New York production of *The Miracle* with the Norman Bel Geddes setting, and my own revival at the Lyceum with the Strnad setting and the Oliver Messel costumes, were adaptations to the limitations of the stage of a spectacle originally conceived for a large arena.

(From James Laver's Introduction, pp. 33–35)

In *The Miracle*, Oliver was faced with an altogether novel set of problems. Here was no opportunity for witty comment on modern fashions; frivolity of any kind would have been entirely out of place. The dominant flavour was of necessity medieval, and although the banquet scene, the coronation scene and the scene in the forest gave plenty of opportunity for fantasy, it was fantasy of a more restricted kind.

The scenery for *The Miracle* was the work of Oskar Strnad and Felix Augenfeld, but the designing of the 750 costumes was entirely in Oliver's hands. Indeed, in the figure of the Madonna he may be said to have designed part of the scenery too, for Lady Diana Cooper was encased in a kind of hollow statue which remained *in situ* when the living figure descended to assume the garments of the nun played by Tilly Losch.

The cloak of the Madonna involved weeks of experiment in an endeavour to find some substance which would look sufficiently solid, would not crack, and would be light enough to open at a touch. It was finally made of house-flannel moulded to the folds of medieval statues and solidified with plaster. It was mounted on a hinged framework fitting exactly to the head and neck of the actress. The result was curiously convincing.

The figure of the Infant Christ was modelled with the help of Glyn Philpot, Oliver's early mentor, and Oliver himself made the crown in the coronation scene from wire, paper, glue and gigantic chandelier lustres giving the appearance of rock crystal. The coarse wire ends were tipped with gold, creating a very rich impression. All the head-dresses, made by Oliver, were remarkable.

When the nun became the mock bride of the mad king, Oliver was able to revert to his favourite scheme of white and made her costume of rubber sheeting, painted white to resemble porcelain. It was worn by Tilly Losch, standing on a red bamboo bridge against a misty sky. Oliver gave her a towering head-dress founded upon those of the mid-fifteenth century, but more lofty, more fantastic, with great loops of stiffened, transparent gauze built upon a steel framework and rising in double tiers to a height of more than four feet from the head.

The Miracle opened in London on 9 April 1932.

Anne: It was obviously a very important night for Oliver. He'd worked so hard on the costumes. He suddenly got a panic call from a friend of his who had been

One of Messel's masks for the Cochran revue of 1928, *This Year of Grace*. Courtesy of the Victoria and Albert Museum had up for something or other. He was at the police station and no one would bail him out, so although the curtain was about to go up, Oliver got hold of some money, jumped into a taxi and bailed the poor man out. Very few people who have anything to do with the stage would do *that* on a first night, but this illustrates Oliver's chivalry and caring for other people.

Brian Howard, Oliver's rather embittered friend from their Eton school-days, took a hostile view of the production in the *New Statesman*, under the title 'Miracles never cease; or *dommage à Diaghilev.*'

It is as the derisive and gangsterish funeral service of the Russian ballet, not an inspired blast of propaganda, that I view this remorseless production, the Lyceum *Miracle*, since, when we are not staring at processions of what seem gleaming debutantes disguised as nuns, supporting electric fixtures, and intoning they know not what, the stage is chiefly occupied with a series of ballets . . .

The chief pretensions of the production, naturally, are to be found in the scenery, costumes and choreography. Half the auditorium has been transformed into Hollywood Perpendicular, while the cathedral on the stage is more a triumph, possibly, of the parrot, than the Paramount, mind. The Forest scene, opening the second act, is conceived with that nice admiration of the natural and formal most detrimental to both, and succeeds in resembling an effeminate vegetable garden. . . .

As regards the dresses, there are two pages and some negroes in the coronation scene whose clothes are as beautiful as their *provenance* is suspect. For the rest I would like to remind Herr Reinhardt and Mr Cochran, that if they find Picasso or Chirico too highbrow, there are designers in this country who, although they might not be able to compete with Mr Oliver Messel on his own ground, might be accorded preference when there is apparent need for serious and original work. We can all remember Bakst for ourselves. . . .

Tilly Losch played the Nun in the Max Reinhardt production of *The Miracle* (1932), for which Messel designed the much-admired costumes. Here she is seen as the mock bride.

Opposite: Lady Diana Cooper as the Madonna, wearing the hinged cloak described on p. 73

Oliver could recall no reason for such animosity from an old friend: 'Brian was often capricious, and you never knew how he would take things — or write about them. He probably thought I needed taking down!' All was forgiven, however, when Oliver later accepted a commission to do a painting of Brian Howard's great friend Sam.

During the run of *The Miracle*, Noël Coward was introduced to Lady Diana Cooper. 'Didn't you write *Private Lives*?' she asked sweetly. 'Not very funny.'
Not to be out-done, he came back with the swift reply: 'Aren't you in *The Miracle*? Very funny, indeed!'

Oliver's career as a portrait painter was fast gaining recognition, and commissions were completed with concentrated intensity from his studio in Yeoman's Row. But he had been neglecting his health and it was suggested that he take a trip to a health clinic in Munich. There he met a young portrait painter, Derek Hill, who became a friend of his and Anne's. Nowadays living in Ireland, with periodic visits to his home in Hampstead, Hill has travelled the world in pursuit of his subjects, including Cardinal Heenan, Yehudi Menuhin and the Prince of Wales who became Edward VIII.

Derek Hill: In the early 'thirties, when I was 16 or 17, I was studying to be a portrait painter in Munich, and Oliver came there to see the famous Dr Martin who was a great curer of everything. Dr Martin ran a fashionable health clinic popular with the social set. That was long before health clinics were started in England. Oliver came over with Gerald Berners and we all went to the Oktoberfest together with Bob Boothby [now Lord Boothby] and then shared a splendid picnic together.

Twenty years older than Oliver, Berners was one of the most colourful figures of the period and among Oliver's closest friends. He was short, tubby, bald-headed and mustachioed — and wore an eyeglass. He was also rich (he had a house in Rome overlooking the Forum and another in Berkshire). A witty man too, Berners was a subject for the leading cartoonists and satirists of the day. Max Beerbohm drew an affectionate caricature of him and he appears as Lord Merlin in Nancy Mitford's *The Pursuit of Love*.
His name was Gerald Hugh Tyrwhitt-Wilson until 1918, when his uncle died and he succeeded to the 500-year-old barony. As the 14th Lord Berners he became acknowledged in Europe as one of the startling voices of the musical *avant-garde* and was simultaneously a composer, a novelist and landscape painter, as well as an attaché at the British Embassies in Constantinople and Rome. When Lord Berners was compared with Erik Satie, the French composer retorted rather aptly, 'He is a professional amateur,' a tag he was to carry to the end. Like Satie, he was dismissed by the establishment as eccentric, and indeed he was. He had a collection of strange masks that he used to wear when motoring, no doubt created for him by Oliver, and was rarely out of the newspapers; no English aristocrat who sat in the back of his Rolls-Royce as it purred its way through Italy, peering out from behind a werewolf mask while playing the clarinet, could avoid comment.
He designed and built one of the last British follies before the advent of planning legislation ended the rich man's right to express his individuality in

architecture. Faringdon Folly, in Berkshire, is a 140-foot tower serving no obvious purpose. Guests slept in crystal beds and sat by brick fireplaces in Hepplewhite chairs. Meals were served in one colour; if his mood was pink, lunch might consist of tomato soup, lobster and strawberries, while outside, a flock of pink pigeons might fly overhead. He had his fantail pigeons dyed all colours of the rainbow, so that they would fly over the countryside and arouse bewilderment in neighbouring farmers. They were treated with harmless cosmetic dyes. The composer Igor Stravinsky's wife, Vera, by way of a thank-you note for luncheon, sent a special powder from Paris to help Berners make blue mayonnaise.

Diaghilev commissioned him to compose *The Triumph of Neptune* for the Ballets Russes, with a scenario by Sir Sacheverell Sitwell, which emerged successfully as 'a mixture of naïve Victorian pantomime, Jules Verne and modern satire'. Another ballet, *Wedding Bouquet*, written with Gertrude Stein, survives in the repertoire of The Royal Ballet.

Among his intimates were Emerald Cunard, the Sitwells — and Lady Diana Cooper, who was a regular guest at Faringdon.

When Oliver and Berners returned to England in June 1934, Oliver wrote to his father explaining that Dr Martin had diagnosed his ill-health as the result of overwork (his childhood setbacks of tuberculosis had always left him weak in stressful situations) and suggested that, provided he had plenty of fresh air and rest, he should be fit again quite soon. His father replied: 'Your letter has quite cheered us, as it looks as if Dr Martin has found out what is the matter. As he says that you must be out of doors most of the time, probably the best thing you can do is to be at Nymans, and do a lot of out-door painting there.'

Derek Hill: I was introduced to Oliver by my sister-in-law, Sheila, who was painted by him. It was a rather strong portrait, rather like the one he did of Gladys Calthrop [designer of Noël Coward's stage and film productions]. I used to visit Oliver a great deal in Yeoman's Row and I remember the first time, when I was barely seventeen, drinking rather too much apricot brandy which was absolutely delicious. Oliver always gave the most splendid parties, and I would help him with them.

I also helped him with that marvellous mask of Queen Elizabeth which he did for himself.

Oliver was rated very highly at the time, largely because of his successes with the production of *Helen!* After that, everyone, including Syrie Maugham, used white for everything. He rather inspired her and they became devoted to one another.

Oliver's studio was white as well. There were two rooms: one was the studio and it led into his bedroom through an arch hung with a white curtain. There was the most marvellous fur bedcover.

Dorothy Ward, Britain's leading 'principal boy', whose son, the director Peter Glenville, was to become a companion of Oliver's, remembers the fur bedcover vividly.

Dorothy Ward: I used to see a lot of Oliver with Peter when he had 16 Yeoman's Row. He used to have some wonderful parties; you met everyone there — all sorts of different people. There would also be a pianist and somebody that would sing very well (Olga Lynn, on many occasions). There was a high society dame whose daughter ran off with a coloured person; that sort of thing wasn't done in those days. Oliver was always fond of coloured people and had asked him to the party. When he entered the room the old girl sat bolt upright, turned her chair around, and spent the rest of the evening with her back to him.

I remember staying at Oliver's house on one occasion. There was a priceless fur rug on the bed: a vicuna, I think. As I prepared to turn in for the night, I threw it off the bed and it landed on the electric fire! I said to Peter, 'What can I do to replace it?' He said, 'You can't replace *that*. Give him a present.' So we went out and I bought him an expensive tea-service and some other things to make up.

Derek Hill: Mrs Jenkins was his marvellous daily who came in and swept and tidied. She was a dear old Mrs Tiggywinkle with a rather high-pitched squeak of a voice. Oliver used to have violent fits of disliking people; he would make little wax figures of them and tell Mrs Jenkins to stick pins into them. He didn't like doing it himself, which was always part of the morning's work! I remember him saying, 'Oh, Mrs Jenkins, do stick another pin into Lady Colefax for me.' But I don't think it was done maliciously or viciously.

Lady Colefax had achieved a great reputation as a party-giver. She lived for many years at Argyll House, Chelsea, next door to another of her social rivals, Mrs Somerset (Syrie) Maugham, herself an energetic and talented hostess, destined in later years to compete with Lady Colefax as a professional decorator. (Colefax and Fowler remain one of the élite firms of interior designers, in Mayfair). In his book *Distinguished Company*, Sir John Gielgud recalls: 'Lady Colefax was a small woman, though not as small as Lady Cunard, who resembled a brilliant canary, with curiously chiselled pale blue eyes. Both ladies were restless and indefatigable. Lady Colefax would think nothing of spending a week-end in the Isle of Wight, driving from Southampton next morning to lunch in Essex, before returning to London to give a party in the evening of the same day. Her car was always full of new books and stationery, so that she could keep abreast of her reading, or scrawl letters and postcards to her friends, both in England and America, in her almost illegible handwriting.' She was said to have founded her career as a successful hostess by inviting H. G. Wells and Bernard Shaw (on postcards) separately, declaring that each was eager to meet the other.

Derek Hill: Oliver's sister Anne used to come very often to tidy up. They were so alike and worshipped one another. When I was staying with Anne and Michael [her second husband, Lord Rosse] at Birr, Oliver would telephone. The conversations were absolutely smashing: 'Oh, my darling brother, is that you? My beloved one, how lovely to hear you.' And Oliver was obviously saying exactly the same thing at the other end. This went on for five minutes and then they put down the receivers, having cooed at each other for the duration.

Anne: There was another daily who looked after Oliver at Yeoman's Row. A few days after he had returned from one of his journeys, he told me that he'd got bitten all over, and we couldn't think what had happened. So I went and made his bed, and found that the blankets were simply smothered with bugs. She'd had her gentleman friends in his bed!

Later my mother, who was so sweet, used to pay for a woman, who had been a lady's maid, to go and mend his things and to see that everything was all right. And then every weekend this maid would go down to my mother at Nymans, be given port to drink, and slowly, bit by bit, my mother would extract from her everything that went on at Yeoman's Row. It was so lovely!

Most of the fashionable people in London went to Oliver's parties and some of them were painted by him. Olga Lynn, who had been taught to sing by Jean de Reszke, was one of them. She had a rather sweet, pure little voice and was short and dumpy. She might be compared to the great party-giver Elsa Maxwell — but as a somewhat prettier, jollier version. It was said that 'Oggie' — as she was known to her friends — could easily have won the same international success as party-giver Elsa, and no doubt have benefited from it financially as her American social-climbing 'sister' did. She was inclined to get into situations with which she could not cope and was always being helped by her friends. Oliver was chief rescuer. When she was not engaged in giving singing lessons she could often be found singing to the guests at Oliver's parties.

Oliver excelled in mimicking his famous guests and none escaped his incisive observation. One of his chief targets was Syrie Maugham, whom he imitated in the most hilarious way, in a rather clipped high-pitched voice: 'Go and pick up those pelmets *at once*, please. They've dropped. Spanier, will you stop doing that! You've been writing for *hours*.' Didine (sister of Ginette Spanier, the *directrice* at that time of Balmain in Paris) was her secretary and always referred to as 'Spanier'.

The twenties and thirties were a golden age for party-giving. Fantastic sums were lavished on clothes and decorations. The Ronald Trees gave an extravagant party at their home in Ditchley, where they organized a huge tent of white muslin on the terrace. Oliver decorated it with Negro heads sporting feathered hats and ropes of pearls; and the flowers were arranged by Constance Spry. The evening ended with a magnificent fireworks display. Women were asked to wear red and white and Oliver arrived in a white suit with a red tie:

'Bugger ought to be thrown in the lake,' muttered an outraged peer.

Oliver: The last of the parties I remember involving The Bright Young Things took place at a respectable club at Henley on the eve of Lord Gavin Faringdon's wedding.

Ever since his Oxford days Gavin Henderson (before he became Lord Faringdon) had been the host of large and expensive parties which vied with those given by William Acton, Sir Harold's brother. When Henderson gave a bachelor's dinner party for thirty friends on the eve of his marriage in June 1927, Oliver and Brian Howard were among the guests. This party took place at the Phyllis Court Club near Henley. After dinner, some of the guests got hold of eight two-gallon tins of petrol which they proceeded to pour into the river — and then someone 'set the Thames on fire'. Although the host confessed to the deed, it was known that Brian Howard was the instigator.

In his biography of Sir Oswald Mosley and his first wife Lady Cynthia, their son Nicholas recalls another occasion in the late twenties when the 'older folk' set about amusing themselves:

One of the more bizarre activities that grown-ups liked to indulge in at weekends was to play practical jokes on one another. In the downstairs lavatory there was a box which held the paper and when you pulled, a snake jumped out: Olga Lynn had hysterics, and the door of the lavatory had to be broken down. Then there was a story of how my father once arranged to have soap on toast served to his dinner guests as a savoury: Oliver Messel was warned by Mabel, the parlour maid, and went behind a screen with a pack of cards which he let fall to the floor thus making a sound as if he were being sick. Nanny used to recount to us these stories: it seemed to be accepted that they were about just the sort of things that grown-ups did.

When Lady Diana Cooper was touring with the American production of *The Miracle*, she and her husband, Duff Cooper, corresponded almost daily. Duff Cooper reported to her from London: 'There was a fancy ball at Ava Ribblesdale's last night, and all the women looked 50 % worse than usual – S. as Little Lord Fauntleroy quite awful, P. as a street Arab just dirty. Venetia and I had been to Michael [Herbert's] where was Willie Clarkson with brilliantined beard and frock coat, his whole apparatus and a lot of French porters' clothes. Rosemary [Ednam] looked well in your "Artful Dodger". The rest of us were porters. We thought we were pretty funny all dashing into the room shouting, *"Porteur, porteur!"* Gerald Berners was good as a hunting man with a marvellously funny mask by Oliver Messel, who had announced his intention of going as Nurse Cavell but was dissuaded.'

Derek Hill: Oliver had more of that awful word, 'charisma', than anyone I've ever known. Cecil [Beaton], whom I met at about the same time, could be terribly spiky, but Oliver never was. To me, Cecil was a genius photographer, absolutely brilliant, and I think he was good with stage design, but I don't think he was as good as Oliver and I think the tragedy of Cecil was that he always wanted to do the things he wasn't made out to do. There was nobody as good as he was at that time in the world of photography, but then he wanted to be everything; a designer – a portrait painter – everything. But Oliver had this extraordinary colour sense which no one else but Bérard had.

In my opinion, there is no doubt that in the fashionable theatre in the Western world, Oliver and Bérard were the best. From the point of view of colour in clothes, neither Oliver nor Bérard ever went wrong. They'd know that if the dress was green you would have to have some purple velvet somewhere, and Oliver's sense of materials, fabrics, was superb. His clothes for the theatre were generally made by an exceptional Russian, Karinska. Between the two of them, however, striving for perfection, the costumes were invariably late, arriving after the dress-rehearsal had taken place!

Early in 1932 C. B. Cochran planned two productions for the autumn. One was *Nymph Errant*, a large-scale musical with Oliver and Doris Zinkeisen sharing the *décor*; but Oliver had a breakdown in health, and Zinkeisen took on the task unaided. The second was *The Winter's Tale* by Shakespeare, for which Cochran contemplated Dorothy Hyson as Perdita and Oliver as designer. Both Granville-Barker and Gordon Craig had quashed the idea of directing it, but John Gielgud showed some interest after a meeting with Cochran and wrote to him on 6 November 1932. Cochran sent the letter on to Oliver.

Dear Mr Cochran

I have read *The Winter's Tale* twice since I saw you, and I think I would like very much to have a shot at it. If you are still willing for me to do so, and if my ideas coincide at all with yours, and I am free at the time you want. It is possible of course that the two plays for which I am contracted with Mr Albery may have come and gone by the spring, but naturally I cannot possibly know for some time yet. Whether you thought it worthwhile to try and come to some arrangement with him to leave me free for at least three full weeks would be a matter to decide later on. I should imagine some time round Shakespeare's birthday would be a good time for the play, but of course I have no idea of your plans.

I wonder if Cedric Hardwicke would not perhaps be available by then if you could not get Charles Laughton, and how you would like the idea of Frederick Ranalow for Autolycus. Also I should very much like actors like Leon Quartermaine (Polixenes), Abraham Sofaer (Camillo) and Ernest Thesiger (Time, as Chorus – and the Lord who describes the long meeting in the last act). I believe men who speak verse so well as these and yet are good modern actors would be the types to get.

I also feel that the richest manner for the play would be Renaissance classical dresses and decorations – a great terrace and Veronese colouring in rich dark and tawny materials for the court scenes, then the pastoral could be light and delicate in contrast. Giorgione rather. But Oliver may not agree with such an idea. I certainly do not believe in any kind of Greek or Roman decor in the classical manner, as it would milk the play and ruin all its passion and sixteenth century character. The half-and-half business has never been done wholeheartedly – except of course, to some extent in *Helen!* and I believe carried out with richness and imagination it would be the best decoration for the play as well as helpful to the interpretation of it.

Perhaps you will ask me to come and see you again near Christmas, when our film and *The Merchant of Venice* are done, and we can talk more fully.

Yours very sincerely

John Gielgud

Sir John Gielgud: I well remember going to a party at the Cochrans' at that time, the only time I really met him – and Mrs Cochran, who was pissed, came running in saying, 'Two men called Kennedy and Black have just flown the Atlantic!' I thought they were probably a new pair of Americans whom Cockie had engaged for his new revue!

At the end of 1932 Oliver designed the rococo flat, set in Venice, for *Business with America*, a play by Jeffrey Dell from a book by Frank Hirschfield, and won praise for the production, which opened at the Haymarket Theatre with a cast headed by Madge Titherage and Clifford Mollison – and closed shortly after.

This was followed (on 27 January 1933) by another Cochran revue, *Mother of Pearl*, at the Gaiety with Alice Delysia in the starring role, music by Oscar Straus, and book by A. P. Herbert. For the first time Oliver received adverse criticism from the press: 'Mr Messel's scenes would be amusing if they were turned over in a folio,' said *The Sunday Times*, 'but gazed at for long periods they become strident to the point of quarrelsomeness.'

Not only Oliver suffered at the critic's hands: 'Mlle Delysia, with nothing to act and nobody to act with, had to be core and heart and soul of a piece which didn't exist, and half-a-dozen of our best English actors cluttered the stage woe-begone and sheepish.' These included Reginald Gardiner and Austin Trevor. 'Of the young actress who played Pearl I propose to say nothing, except that the audience sympathised with a little lady pitch-forked into a leading part without leading qualifications.' The actress was Sepha Treble, a young actress who had been promoted from the chorus of *Helen!*

The opening night audience included a fair number of distinguished personalities, and as *The Tatler* reported, they were 'justly enthusiastic. . . . Mr Oliver Messel and his lovely sister, Mrs Armstrong-Jones . . . sat in Mr Cochran's box. In the stalls were Princess Arthur of Connaught in her favourite shade of vivid emerald green, and Dr Malcolm Sargent, and Lord and Lady Queensberry. I also saw various members of the d'Erlanger family, Miss Gertrude Lawrence, looking brown and fit after her Swiss holiday, Miss Olga Lynn, Mrs Roland Cubitt, and the witty Mr Herbert himself, who was being congratulated on all sides.

'There is nothing in the setting of *Mother of Pearl* that is likely to rival *Helen's!* snow-white, swan-supported bed (I wonder whether the well-known "lovely" won her bet that she would get Mr Messel to design her an even more beautiful one before the end of the run?) but we all enjoyed the frescoes on the walls of the private room in the naughty Red Elephant restaurant.'

Oliver came in for criticism from his peers as well – one in particular, the Viennese singing star Lea Seidl, who had a considerable success in Berlin where she appeared in Reinhardt productions. She made her British *début* in *Frederika* composed by Franz Lehár, and in 1931 played Josepha Voglhuber in Robert Stolz's *The White Horse Inn*, which ran for almost a year at the Coliseum.

Lea Seidl: I met Oliver through a friend of mine, Madame Felicite Kachovska. She had studied singing in Vienna with me. She was a tyrant but a wonderful teacher. She was half Dutch and half American and had a house near Oliver's in Yeoman's Row. He came over to visit her one day and invited me to see his studio. I met him again in Berlin when Oscar Straus wanted me to star in the original production of *Mother of Pearl*. I didn't want to do it because it wasn't exactly to my taste and I felt that I was too young for the part. They finally persuaded Fritzi Massary to take over the role.

When I saw the subsequent Cochran production of *Mother of Pearl* in London, I disliked Oliver's designs absolutely. It was the story of a chorus girl who becomes a *grande dame* of the theatre. The lover who gives her an illegitimate child is unable to marry her because of opposition from his family. It is unthinkable for him to marry a chorus girl, so the family bribe her with a sum of money in order to let him go. 'I'll show them!' she vows bitterly, and works at her career, finally becoming a great actress.

The second act takes place in her home when the daughter is grown up. The scene was so elegant when Fritzi Massary played it in Berlin. It was a very cosy drawing-room with oak panelling. She had many lovers, and when she discussed anything with her visitors, she would open yet another panel from the wall and

Messel and C. B. Cochran photographed together in Messel's house in Yeoman's Row, off Brompton Road (1942)

take out love-letters and photographs of her past lovers. It was enchanting. But Oliver made that second act look like a cheap bordello, and unfortunately Delysia played it that way. Not like the *grande dame*, which Massary was. A great actress can have been a naughty girl when she was in the chorus, but as a *grande dame* she has allure, and surroundings in keeping with her status.

But I found Oliver himself to be the most charming of men. He was very modest, never bragged about himself and was always the gentleman. When you went to his studio he was the perfect host. I liked him enormously.

If Oliver's ego was deflated by the reaction to his work on *Mother of Pearl*, it was not for long. No better defence or finer tribute could have been paid him by anyone more fitting than Cochran, who wrote the following at the time:

(From C. B. Cochran's Foreword to *Stage Designs and Costumes*, pp. 1–3)

Genius is not a word I apply lightly. I prefer to reserve it for those who, in addition to high technical skill and knowledge, have an indefinable quality that seems to touch their work with an inspiration which comes from outside themselves, lending it a distinction which places it in a category of its own.

In theatrical criticism particularly, the word 'genius' is applied so freely that it tends to lose its meaning; leaving no appropriate word to describe the work of a Shakespeare, a Mozart, a Da Vinci, or a Rembrandt.

Of all the brilliant young men and women who have worked under me during my long years in the theatre, I would unhesitatingly single out Oliver Messel as the one artist who possesses the rare and precious divine spark. As a designer of scenery and decor for the theatre, Oliver Messel has already established a unique position for himself. That I was able to give him his earliest opportunity is an achievement of which I am intensely proud.

In the generosity of his nature he has given me greater credit for his success than I can possibly deserve, for even if it had not been my good fortune to employ his talents for the first time in a London Pavilion revue in 1926, and in several succeeding revues at that favourite theatre of mine, his work was far too vivid to remain hidden for long.

One of Oliver's chief characteristics is his modesty, and in the theatre and society there are few more genuinely popular figures. Among my many friendships, established during a long career in the theatre, I value none more highly than that of Oliver's with his great loyalty, and his equally great gifts as an artist.

I feel that even after *Helen!* – generally admitted from the visual point of view to have been one of the loveliest productions our stage has ever seen, he is only at the beginning of his triumphs.

. . . He dresses a stage for a play that is to be performed by actors, and he is swiftly and subtly responsive to the dramatic requirements of action and atmosphere.

In all the arts a man may find his more remarkable achievements under-estimated among his work, which only a fellow-craftsman can fully recognize and admire.

In *Mother of Pearl* Oliver seemed to me to reach, in another way, a pitch of perfection in design fully comparable with *Helen!*

Some playgoers complained that Pavani's boudoir was overdecorated and showy. Of course: it was meant to be. Messel set out to design just the room that rather flamboyant lady would have lived in. Similarly his little dining-room at 'The Red Elephant' was not an attractive room to look at. But it was the essence of all such rooms in all such restaurants all over the world, and a fine piece of comedy in design which filled out the very spirit of the scene which the producer and the actors were evoking.

Such an ability is as much, if not more, the true mark of the really first-rate designer in the Theatre as the ability to create stage pictures of a beauty which may be pictorially attractive but are detached from the drama to which they are a setting. With all his joy in beautiful creation, Oliver never forgets that he is serving a stage.

After *Mother of Pearl*, Oliver's output for the rest of 1933 was negligible. An inopportune illness prevented him from completing the designs for the Cochran production of *The Winter's Tale* which John Gielgud had planned to direct, and the idea was finally shelved.

Reinhardt, so ecstatic about Oliver's work on *Helen!* and *The Miracle*, now planned a tour of four plays. This was explained to Oliver in a letter from Iris Tree (Sir Herbert Beerbohm Tree's daughter, who became a theatre producer), sent from Austria on 8 October 1933:

> I was in London for a week and tried in vain to reach you with pleas and proposals as follows: Eleonore [von Mendelsohn] is arranging with Reinhardt a touring company to start in Vienna and go round the world, that is, England, France, Italy, Scandinavia, Holland and so on – later, America. The cast will

include Eleonore, Helene Thimig, Paula Wessely, Rudolph Forster, Max Pallenberg, Zokolov, and all the best actors who cannot and will not now act in Berlin. There will be, I imagine, a great deal of interest and sympathy for the venture for political reasons aside from Reinhardt's name, only it must be as perfect as possible; for this they are hoping that you would do the decorations at any rate for the first play which would start in December. They are probably going to do Tchekov's *Three Sisters*, Pirandello's *Six Characters in Search of an Author*, *Faust*, and Schiller's *Mary Stuart*.

Mary Stuart will be the first play with Eleonore as Mary, Thimig as Elizabeth, Forster as Leicester – the costumes must be exquisite, the scenery as simple as possible and as they do not want an extravagant beginning, not costing too many fortunes.

Reinhardt admires you more than any decorator and as you know, he is going through many difficulties and success means much to him now. Also, Eleonore is interested in the venture and feels that you would add enormously to the artistic importance. I was bidden as messenger to plead with you in English to take the idea to heart. I hope you will.

Lea Seidl: Eleonore von Mendelsohn and Francesco, her brother, were fashionable society figures in their late twenties at the time. One didn't take Eleonore seriously as an actress, because although she was a great beauty, she was not a great actress. They were extremely rich and helped to finance Professor Reinhardt's brother who was a financial wizard. This is why Reinhardt could develop so well; he didn't have to worry about money. His brother would say, 'You dream your dreams. Leave all the finance and worry to me.' And he did.

Reinhardt was a very modest man. I couldn't understand such a great artist having such an inferiority complex. When I saw *Helen!* in Berlin, he said, 'Would the people in London like it? Would Cochran like it?' He was the head of the German theatre. He was a god on the continent. There was nobody to touch him in Vienna, Salzburg and Berlin, but when he was outside his own environment it was as though the ground had been cut from underneath him. He was married to Helene Thimig, a noted actress in Germany. She came from one of the most distinguished theatrical families. They were like a royal family, the Thimigs, rather like the Barrymores in New York. It was considered a great honour for Reinhardt to be married to Helene. They had a beautiful castle in Salzburg.

Oliver went over to Salzburg to discuss the project with Reinhardt and before returning to England, received the following note from Francesco von Mendelsohn:

Darling Oliver

I just wanted to tell you that Reinhardt yesterday, after you had left, said the most marvellous things about you. That you were *der genialste Bühnenmaler und kennen das Bühnenlicht* [the most brilliant stage designer and lighting expert] and so on, and such *ein strahlender Mensch* (a radiant personality) and he went on for twenty minutes until nobody wanted to listen to another word about you. But he was terribly nice himself, loving you so much and I thought you would be pleased to know it.

Have a good trip and I hope *auf Wiedersehen* very soon

Francesco

But because of the Anschluss of Austria, the project never took place. Reinhardt, who was Jewish, and his wife Helene — who was not — fled to New York and Oliver lost the opportunity of working with Reinhardt again. The great director had chosen New York because he had several friends there, but despite his attempts at stage and film productions, he failed to repeat the success he had enjoyed in his homeland.

However, the acclaimed young designer, not yet thirty, was on the threshold of a remarkable career. Those who watched the readiness with which he grasped the expanding opportunities that had come his way, the steady growth of his power to grapple with them, looked forward with eagerness and confidence to his future as a designer for the stage. But his output was not to be confined to that medium. After a successful exhibition of his designs and *maquettes* at the Lefèvre Gallery that year, he was lured into the film world.

Alexander Korda had formed the film production company London Films in 1932, with the financial support of the banker Leopold Sutro. Sutro's son John, an old friend of Oliver's from their Eton days, had become one of the directors of the company, and suggested to Korda that Oliver might be suitable for the planned production of *The Private Life of Don Juan*, which was to star Douglas Fairbanks. Merle Oberon, his co-star, played Antonia, and other performers in the cast included Binnie Barnes and Benita Hume. A memo from Mr Cunynghame of London Films to Oliver, dated 16 February 1934, shows that the original estimate for the 232 costumes (to be made by the costumiers Simmons) was £3,301 — more than Korda had spent on either the successful *The Private Life of Henry VIII* or *Catherine the Great*. Drastic cuts were therefore ordered in the number of costumes to be made and the materials to be used; the remainder were to be hired. Oliver worked with Sophie Fedorovitch on the design of this production, set in seventeenth-century Spain, and they worked together again on the next Korda film, Baroness Orczy's *The Scarlet Pimpernel*, in 1935.

The Scarlet Pimpernel was mounted as another vehicle for Merle Oberon, who was later to become Korda's wife. Her co-star was Leslie Howard, with whom she was in love; their liaison, in fact, lasted until his tragic death in an air crash during the Second World War. *The Scarlet Pimpernel* was a first-class romantic adventure set in the early days of the French Revolution, with a splendid and animated plot, and strong characters played by Raymond Massey, Nigel Bruce and Bramwell Fletcher against a richly detailed historical background.

The costumes Oliver designed for Merle Oberon were daringly low cut, one of them virtually exposing her flawless breasts; they were fanciful, fairy-tale versions of Regency styles, infinitely flattering and captivating to the star, who took an instant liking to the designer. They met on several occasions when he visited Hollywood the following year to work on M.G.M.'s *Romeo and Juliet*, with Leslie Howard as Romeo.

Oliver: I had known Sophie Fedorovitch and admired her art since the mid-thirties when we had worked together on the film of *The Scarlet Pimpernel*. But it was really during those haunted, splintery days in wartime London that we became firm friends. We used to meet on my leaves from the army when I would dash to the heart-quickening playground of the Sadler's Wells Ballet like a story-book truant rushing to a secret stretch of river-bank. And there, invariably, one found her, almost — as it seemed to me then — one of the most enduring and welcoming of theatre fixtures. I can see her now, a small, inscrutable, but oddly stubborn little figure, glimpsed perhaps at some junction of those labyrinthine backstage corridors, almost certainly brooding on her latest project and very possibly torturing the minds of her devoted friends, the stage staff, by refusing to come to a decision about details. The choice of a material or the strength of a dye were always matters which she liked to leave until five minutes to twelve [an idiosyncrasy Oliver himself was to adopt].

Yet it was wonderfully reassuring to find her so very much herself, so very self-sufficient and secure in a world which seemed then of spectral impermanence. It was as if coping with disaster were second nature to her. It was also highly unlikely that the toughness of spirit which had once helped her to earn a living as a Paris taxi-driver would permit a lowering of standards on any such trumpery grounds as wartime or utility.

Like all one's most cherished fellow artists, she was as refreshing a friend off duty as she was stimulating in the role of a working colleague. After long bouts of work when both of us were deeply engaged on our separate projects, we would break our separate spells and go off to have a drink together. I remember her vividly at such moments, a small, rather amorphous figure perched on a bar-stool, wrapped in a short, somewhat nondescript, fur coat, her pale blue eyes burning intently as if fixed upon some far-off vision of her own creation. It was seated alongside her in such an attitude that one waited anxiously for her latest opinions on life, work and people. They would be expressed with the maximum of brevity and the greatest possible force. The shock value of these pronouncements, given in tiny mutterings between clenched teeth and uttered in the minimum of devastating words, was not infrequently delicious. Once, it was reputed, an incautious designer had asked her advice by imploring: 'Tell me, Sophie, are those columns of mine too thick or too thin?' The reply was characteristically succinct. 'Both,' she said simply.

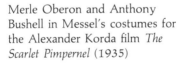

Merle Oberon and Anthony Bushell in Messel's costumes for the Alexander Korda film *The Scarlet Pimpernel* (1935)

Oliver Messel and his sister
Anne photographed by Cecil
Beaton in 1932. Oliver is
wearing one of the costumes he
designed for the role of Paris in
Helen!, which opened the same
year.

3 * Thirties revisited

THE PROCESS OF CREATION was always an almost insupportable agony for Oliver. He seldom began a piece of work until it seemed perilously near the time for its delivery, and the weeks between germination and fruition were governed by appalling mental strain. Then, when it seemed he could stand the pressure no longer, he adopted, as he always did under the stress of inspiration, the nocturnal habits of the owl, getting up at dusk, working alone through the night, and falling exhausted into his bed until his next appointment at the scene-builders or dressmakers. In this rapt state, in which panic, elation and insomnia all seemed present, he cherished a fancy that the mice might help him as they did the Tailor of Gloucester; but he worked meanwhile with feverish application and extraordinary manual dexterity, with hands that were possessed of finicky delicacy.

Because of this, his methods were unusual. According to Carl Toms, later to become one of his assistants, he did hundreds of small preliminary sketches on one of his favourite pads of blue-grey paper; but work entered its definitive phase only when he cut out the little paper figure of the hero or heroine of the play. This was the symbol of the 'human size' against which the designs were to be measured, and also the charmed mascot of the entire project. If, as was likely, the diminutive figure got buried from time to time under silks and papers, there could be no peace until it had been found.

After this, unlike some designers who put down their ideas in the form of a flat watercolour drawing, Oliver began working in three dimensions, straightway building up each scene as a little model, each part of which was cut out and coloured as he went along. When he found that he had returned to an idea or a set of shapes several times, he would start to make bits of model in a model frame — working very sketchily on pieces of cartridge paper with charcoal, snipped out with scissors and stuck together with brown gum strip paper, roughly bent and shaped. He never started with a ground plan — that evolved as he worked. He always tried to keep the rough model fluid — 'not cut and dried', Toms recalls his saying.

Not until after the models were complete did he finalize his flat-scale drawings for the scene-builders or begin work on the costumes and properties, and all the multifarious details of wigs and head-dresses, fans and slippers, frames and mouldings, lace-cuffs and cushions. Just as he would minutely supervise the painting of his backcloths, so he invariably made many of the properties himself. All his detail, whether of the embroidery on a waistcoat or the scroll-work on a rococo panel, was exceptionally delicate and refined, and he was characteristically inventive in the use of materials. If he insisted on the costliest of silks when they were necessary for effect, he was always ready to improvise with the improbable paraphernalia of the kitchen, the toolshed or the medicine cupboard. The fruit and flowers which bloomed within some tropic grove, or the

William Wycherley's *The Country Wife*, with sets and costumes by Messel, was a success at the Old Vic in London in 1936, with Michael Redgrave and Ruth Gordon. The production, with some cast changes, but with Messel's work intact, was taken over to Broadway by the impresario Gilbert Miller (see p. 105).

ormolu ornaments on a chimneypiece, were just as likely to be contrived from chicken-wire, gauze, dishcloths, pipe-cleaners and adhesive tape as from more conventional materials.

Though he appears so often to have been obsessed by his work, there was still plenty of play — and acute observation of all that went on about him in the social set.

Oliver: With the 'thirties came new phases and adventures. The madcap parties and high-jinks of the 'twenties were on the wane and were replaced by sophisticated parties thrown by rich Americans and titled English hostesses.

Cecil Beaton had acquired Reddish House at Ashcombe, Wiltshire, and I spent many hilarious weekends in this romantic setting tucked away in the downs. It had a kind of grown-up children's picnic atmosphere about it without the formality of organized entertainment.

One weekend we painted sections of Cecil's circus bedroom. A famous artist visitor returned a week later, uninvited, to find his cherished mural had been repainted by the rude but skilful hand of Rex Whistler.

The outlines of Cecil's friends' hands were traced on the walls of his bathroom rather like a wallpaper visitors' book. A famous American hostess, Mrs Corrigan, arrived unexpectedly to find the outline of her hand held in a grasped fist of Elvira Dolores Barney — who was under arrest for murder.

When Mrs Corrigan, who had a face like an enamelled nutcracker, gave dinner parties she distributed golden cigarette cases and other Cartier trophies to the highest ranking guests. Abroad, her one dilemma was to figure out the correct places at table for foreign royalty. On a trip to Rome, which she deemed a success, she explained to Henry 'Chips' Channon, 'The Colonnas had me, the so and so had me, the this and that had me — and the Pope could have had me, only he had me last year.'

Mrs Corrigan was a figure of fun and provided a fount of inane observations to the amusement of Chips Channon, an American who had become a naturalized Briton. He was the most successful collector of crowned and uncrowned heads, but not naïve — which Mrs Corrigan was. A connoisseur of mid-European palaces and art and the author of books about the Ludwigs of Bavaria, Chips was witty and relaxed, and achieved stardom as a host. He was like a Beau Brummel of today but without Brummel's vanity or failings.

The international set that he entertained were new to me, but I didn't take long to make friends. I wished I could have been as spontaneously witty as Fulco, the Duc de Verdura. His presence was a great delight, like that of any star comedian. In those days he was a playboy and rather hard up. A few years later his extraordinary talent was discovered and he developed into a designer of jewellery of exquisite taste and imagination.

Of the parties in London in the 'thirties, I enjoyed Syrie Maugham's the most. She had a pale, delicate complexion and boundless energy. The idea of eliminating colour, that I had featured in the all-white scenes in *Helen!* and in the earlier Cochran revues, was carried into the home by Syrie. The all-white era swept through the houses of the rich. Her special flair for interior decoration produced a recognizable style of her own. It was not based on exact knowledge, as many a priceless piece of gilded carving was cloaked beneath a skin of crackled white. Yet Syrie had a unique eye for discovering unusual shapes of furniture and creating an atmosphere of delicious charm and comfort. She had an individual way of entertaining, and the exquisite flower arrangements concocted by Constance Spry for every occasion made their first appearance in her house.

Syrie's parties had a glamour that others could hardly equal and when she had a party everything else had to be cancelled in order to be there. She had the secret recipe. All the most attractive and creative groups of friends were invited with no regard for social position. The stage was set with infinite care, so that as you arrived at the door it was magic. Small parties, big parties or weekends in the country – it was always equally delightful.

Lady Colefax, her deadly rival in the decorating business, lived next door to Syrie in the Kings Road. The party room in Syrie's house had high windows overlooking Sybil Colefax's garden – but before each party the windows were smashed as if by a phantom, and Sybil swore that she had nothing to do with it. The feuds reached the Capulets and Montagues extremes, but neither would give in. A high brick wall was finally erected between the two houses – and later they both sold their houses to Lady Crewe. Thus the rival establishments were joined into one.

Syrie was an amazing person who had strong likes and dislikes. Few people meant more to her than her adored daughter Liza, for whom she lived, worked and breathed. And for those lucky people she counted among her close friends, including Glyn Philpot and me, there was no limit to the trouble she would go to on any occasion if she felt her help was needed – as it often was.

Derek Hill: Oliver was a constant friend and in those days I used to go along to his studio in Yeoman's Row to draw some of his models. He had a model who was black – an actor, but apparently an obscure African prince as well. I remember painting him, because that brought me the greatest luck. Molyneux saw the picture, which had been bought in some students' exhibition by Lady Scarsdale, and he suddenly arrived one day at my studio in Paris. He said, 'You must give up stage design and take to painting. I've seen this portrait of yours and you can do it.' And so I did, because I was never very theatrically minded. I hate tantrums and first-night quarrels, and even the *Trovatore* I designed after the war at Covent Garden was fraught with drama. The soprano was terribly difficult and said she wanted a hat like the Merry Widow, and bare bosoms, and I said, 'There's only one thing you can be if you have bare bosoms!' And on the first night her Merry Widow hat fell off, and I clapped very loudly.

My whole career started through Oliver. Robert Irving, who became a well-known ballet conductor, wanted Oliver to do the sets and costumes for Rameau's *Castor and Pollux*, which was to be produced by the Oxford University Opera Club at Oxford. Oliver couldn't do it, because he was working on something else, so he suggested me. Robert came over, saw my work and asked me to do it. Oliver came to the first night and brought masses of his friends; Gerald Berners, Daisy Fellowes, Billy Clonmore and all that world, which fascinated me. It was produced by Violet Tree, and the present Duke of Wellington was Mercury dressed in nothing except a leopard skin. Beecham's mistress, Dora Labette, was a soprano and Barbara Ward, who became the well-known economist, played Venus.

And then Ivor Novello asked me whether I would do the sets for *Glamorous Night*. I'd had an exhibition at the Stornon Gallery; Oliver wrote the introduction in the catalogue. Then Syrie Maugham gave a luncheon party for me (I was only 17!) and said I could ask anyone I liked in London. Or Paris, because it was the same day Prince George and Princess Marina were showing their wedding presents at St James's Palace, so all their Paris friends had come over. Everyone glamorous in the world seemed to be there, including Ivor who then asked me to do *Glamorous Night*. But I simply couldn't. I was far too young and wasn't capable of doing it. I had only done *Castor and Pollux* and some study in Munich and wasn't experienced enough. And so Oliver did it.

Oliver, however, was no great admirer of Ivor Novello — or of his productions.

Oliver: I was working on designs for one of those ghastly productions by Ivor Novello for Drury Lane, *Glamorous Night*. I took it on gladly to gain experience in coping with a big-scale show with non-stop changes of scene, starting from the back streets of Brixton, with endless rows of aspidistras framed in lace-curtained windows, to the extravaganza of Balkan palaces. Everything happened, including the shipwreck and sinking of an ocean liner. It had palace ballrooms, gypsy encampments and a gypsy wedding, all to show Ivor's profile to advantage.

Leontine Sagan, who had just directed the film *Mädchen in Uniform*, had been engaged to direct this epic. She was a pretentious, wheedling, yet domineering, female. It was suggested that I should set off for Hungary to study, and if possible acquire any suitable authentic Magyar costumes. I suddenly remembered that she was Hungarian. How could such a project be contemplated without her as the one to accompany me? The key that could open all doors to her homeland. The school-ma'am personality soon earned her the nickname of Letty Saggybags. So we set off, an oddly assorted couple, on our journey.

On arrival in Budapest Oliver wrote to his sister Anne:

> The exciting adventure of the Orient Express was only slightly diminished by the ever-present bossiness of Saggybags. Enthusiasm of the things we had to see and do in her native land lost its magic as the Spartan governess-voice droned on. Wickedly, I had omitted to mention that I had one or two friends in Budapest.
>
> Although having sent Sauchi Woofner a telegram, I wasn't sure whether he had received it. Nearing Budapest, as the train slowly pulled in to the station, I hardly had a moment to wonder what lay in store before a group of beaming faces running down the platform boarded the train with porters and cameras and champagne to give us a dizzy welcome to Budapest. Saggybags' astonished face was a study worth waiting for. The cloud had lifted and the fun began for me.
>
> I deposited Saggy at her lodgings, and off we set with my little band arriving at this delicious hotel which you would adore. Nothing changed but the plumbing since the time of Empress Elisabeth. I have a little anteroom, bedroom, bath and sitting room. The walls are lined with red silk or damask, and the bed recessed in an alcove. The kind of Hungarian Rosa Lewis atmosphere but a bit grander and sexier with lovely mirrors reflecting any antics on the bed!!
>
> As I had slept a good deal on the journey, there was just time to have a bath and scramble into clean clothes before setting out for the evening. Saggybags had

Glamorous Night, written by
Ivor Novello, designed by
Messel, and starring Novello
and Mary Ellis, was one of the
London theatrical highlights of
1935. Above, Mary Ellis's
entrance in the palace; left, Ellis
and Novello in the gypsy
wedding scene

a headache, but took little persuasion to come out and get a worse one.

Sauchi had so kindly laid everything on with that amazing Hungarian hospitality. There was Gustav Olaf, who designed settings for the State Opera and ballet, and Count Duly Attiani, also an artist of considerable talent and from a distinguished Hungarian family. He reminded me of darling granny. It would hardly do to say 'You remind me of my grandma.' We were given a superb dinner at a three-star restaurant, my head reacting with the glorious wine and Tigonie's swooning violins and zithers. It was all too much for Saggy who became skittish and coy as we drank out of one of her slippers, which will never be the same again. This, I fear, goes for her too, as she never surfaced for the whole week which, fortunately, left me to my own resources.

How I wish you could be here, my darling. It's all crisp and wintry in the snow. Must rush off, so will write again immediately.

Devoted love

Oliver

P.S. All that wine and the continual toasts set my head spinning round and round. It's disgraceful; for the first time in my life I got disgustingly drunk. I fell unconscious and got terribly sick. Never again. Hope father never finds out of his son's erring ways.

A few days later he wrote again:

Quite recovered now from the worst excesses!

Old Sagan is still laid up. Count Duly Attiani arranged a fascinating excursion for me today. A longish drive through the flat snow-covered plains to a village where by far the most interesting national costumes are still worn to church on Sundays. I took a lot of snaps and made small sketches.

The girls' skirts are closely pleated and at the bottom swish out, being held by rows of twisted paper, which acts like horsehair braids. These are edged with coloured braids and give a really interesting distinctive line. All the embroidered aprons, jackets and head-dresses have woollen pompoms and long fringes like furs and give the most unusual and barbaric effect that I have seen.

Those in black are also stunning and the boys' fancy pleated linen skirts and embroidered aprons are very effective.

(Later) Sagan got out to some cheap theatrical costumiers and bought some copies of national dress peasant costumes of a kind hardly anything usable, so in the end I designed all the costumes from ideas seen in Mazoporechet.

Equipped with his designs for *Glamorous Night*, Oliver returned to London to supervise the making of the costumes and the construction of the sets.

Oliver: Mary Ellis looked splendid and sang away all the time to tremendous effect and applause. 'It's all so wonderful,' I remember her gasping in admiration of Ivor who was a mere boy of forty-three. At that time, in the nastiness of youth (I was a mere boy of thirty-one!), forty-three seemed to me about as mature as anyone could get. Only as the years spun by, the term 'mere boy' somehow became far more elastic.

A dear friend, Elisabeth Welch, had some wonderful moments in the show and she and I would sit together during rehearsals and sometimes get into hot water, not being able to contain our irrepressible giggles at the most toe-curling moments. Ivor himself took deadly seriously the corny concoctions that he produced, in spite of consistent criticism, derision and abuse from the press. The public continued to fill the theatre. Possibly the fact that no matter how naïvely he himself believed in every situation, however far-fetched, a certain section of the public, as with adoring fans of Liberace years later, were swept away under a kind of sugary hypnosis.

Ivor enjoyed being the centre of an adoring group of friends. The overwhelming coat of dandy sweetness always seemed a bit too artificial to be convincing to me. Some of his more caustic entourage, like Bobby Andrews, I somehow appreciated much more.

Through the auspices of the American showman John Murray Anderson [whose *John Murray Anderson's Almanac* first appeared at the Erlanger Theatre in New York in 1929], little Binkie Beaumont suddenly rocketed into the orbit of Ivor's group and was soon to become the guiding light of H. M. Tennent's and perhaps the most powerful impresario of the London theatre. Harry Tennent [whom Binkie Beaumont was to succeed] was still holding the reins at the time of *Glamorous Night*.

As I was not a designer of modern fashion, I suggested that Charlie James should design the modern dresses. Charlie was the most brilliant artist, the forerunner, one might say, of Dior and Balenciaga.

Derek Hill: Charlie James was an extraordinary character. He was American by birth and lived in England for many years. He had a studio in Bruton Street, which again was all white with dyed pampas grass in great vases. He was very slight and rather Japanesey – rather Eastern looking. He'd made my sister-in-law (the one Oliver had painted) her going-away dress, and it was the first-ever dress with a zip. It went around her like a bandage, and at the bottom he ended the zip with a little clasp. And Charlie gave my brother the key to the clasp as a wedding present!

Charlie was a genius. He had an exhibition in Paris after the war and every great designer came: Balenciaga – and even Vionnet came to pay tribute to him. Not one of his creations looked out of date. But he was always on his uppers because, rather like Mrs Patrick Campbell, he was exceedingly rude to the people who rescued him financially and so they naturally withdrew their support. Elizabeth Arden gave Charlie a great boost by starting a new dress shop entirely for him, as well as for her beauty products, in New York, and within the month he was saying, 'Oh, that old bitch. I can remember when she was hanging her washing up in a tenement flat in Biarritz.' And, of course, that was the end of *that*.

Oliver: Charlie was unpredictable, to say the least, and immediately bit the hand that fed him, insulted his most influential customers by telling them that their figures were lopsided and grotesque, or at a fitting he would cut through their underwear, leaving them naked, with their clothes in shreds.

His work, however, was so brilliant that a small group, including my darling sister and one or two others, determined to prop him up and try to help reorganize him. With buckets of soap and water we scrubbed his premises in Bruton Street while he constructed fabulous collections of dresses. The trouble was that the bailiffs were constantly at the door. There were never enough skilled

Messel's sister, Anne, wearing a dress designed by Charles James, photographed in Messel's 'white on white' drawing room in the Yeoman's Row house

hands available to help him stitch together the specially cut pieces ingeniously created by the master hand. As soon as Charlie had cut his patterns and fitted them roughly for Anne, she would snatch them away, and being immensely talented with a needle, she would finish them off herself superbly at home.

Like Dior's dresses later, Charlie's models were constructed on a boned corset foundation which held the diaphragm firmly in place and the gossamer fabric would be draped and secured to this base with fine silk thread. Some of his most sensational creations were designed for the spectacular American society beauty Millicent Rogers, and a great deal of his work is preserved in various museums in the United States.

After a good deal of persuading, I finally had my way, on condition that Cochran could come along to the fittings, having been assured that Charlie was to be reorganized in the most conventional way.

Shortly before the opening of *Glamorous Night*, Cochran, who had financed the production, complained that he hadn't yet seen the costumes and it was arranged that he, his wife and Oliver would visit Bruton Street, after the salon had closed, at midnight.

Oliver: As we approached the building, strains of music and billows of chiffon floated through the first floor windows. But it was Charlie who danced and modelled the dresses himself, insisting that the model girls didn't know how to move. And so the two girls sat huddled, quite nude, on a sofa, with some doves' wings loosely shrouding their two little 'darlings'. Charlie won out in the end and everything was ready on time and the dresses turned out a huge success.

Mary Ellis was Ivor Novello's leading lady in *Glamorous Night*. The range of her theatrical talent has been astonishing. While she was still in her teens, her exceptional singing voice brought her the 'young' roles at the Metropolitan Opera in New York, where she sang with all the great artists of the time, including Caruso, Scotti and Chaliapin. In 1924 she had a sensational personal success when she created the title-role in the *première* of Friml's *Rose Marie* on Broadway. In England, nine years later — to the amazement of London audiences who until then had seen her only in 'straight' plays — she triumphed again on the light musical stage when C. B. Cochran asked her to star in Jerome Kern's *Music in the Air*. Seeing her for the first time in that production, Ivor Novello was inspired to write his two biggest Drury Lane successes for her, *Glamorous Night* and *The Dancing Years* (1939) — with which her name will always be associated — and, sadly, the later failure, *Arc de Triomphe*.

Mary Ellis: Oliver Messel's genius for settings and costumes helped to create the magic of *Glamorous Night* — a shipwreck, a pillared palace, a gypsy encampment and a baroque stage within a stage — all this I am sure wove the spell. I shall never forget the lovely opera costume he made for me. It was the first time anybody had seen things like that, or seen scenery like that.

Oliver was the most enchanting, lovable, warm, sensitive person with a tremendous sense of humour and he was so lovely to look at! I used to just sit and look at him. He was lovely to work with. You never had an argument with him.

What he presented was always so perfect that all you said was, 'Oh, yes please.' And all the technical and mechanical movements of the scenery worked beautifully.

My first impression of him was of someone very beautiful. He was very sensitive, very quick, and I trusted his taste implicitly. For me he was better than Beaton, because Cecil was more an egoist. Oliver got fascinated and enchanted by what he was doing and that's why everything he did was enchanting. Of course, Oliver and Cecil were not alike in any way, because the thing that Oliver had was a human quality, a sense of communication. Cecil did lovely scenery and costumes for *Arc de Triomphe* but somehow there was no communication – no heart. Oliver had a certain individual quality for the theatre and he always reminded me of a painter instead of a designer. I suppose one could have compared him to Dufy.

Glamorous Night was one of my great magical moments. It was absolutely new. It was London's great magical moment too. Nobody who saw that first night will ever forget it. I swear that.

Leontine Sagan was the first woman producer at Drury Lane but her lack of charm, coupled with her *Gauleiter* methods of enforcing her will on the company, hardly endeared her to them. The result was enmity from beginning to end. Fortunately this did not flow over into the audience, and the production elicited a box-office guarantee of £100,000 after the rise of the first-night curtain on 2 May 1935. Novello was fortunate in securing Mary Ellis, supported by a strong cast performing on that famous stage, whose ingenious mechanical devices afforded the production a visual excellence comparable to Noël Coward's *Cavalcade*, which had scored a triumph there five years before. It was, moreover, a masterly achievement for Oliver, who had set out to learn the rudiments of a big-scale show, with many non-stop changes of scene, which proved to be one of the most difficult – if not unhappy – assignments of his early career.

Written and composed by Ivor Novello with lyrics by Christopher Hassall, *Glamorous Night* is a Ruritanian operetta set in two acts, concerning a young English inventor (Ivor Novello) who saves Militza Hajos (Mary Ellis) from political enemies. Swept away by the enchanting music and the outstanding stage effects – notably the scene of the shipwreck which brought down the first act curtain – most of the critics were content to forget about the improbable plot. The settings and costumes Oliver had created for the production were generally well received, although James Agate in the *Sunday Times* was chilling: 'Mr Messel's decor suggests that he has succumbed to the notion of designing down to a popular audience.'

The success of *Glamorous Night* meant that Oliver was more than ever in the public eye. Since his sister had divorced Armstrong-Jones and become engaged to marry the Earl of Rosse, their names and photographs were continually in the press.

Sir Harold Acton: Of course I had been up at Oxford with Michael [Rosse] and knew him for years, but his meeting Anne wasn't really anything to do with me or Oliver, who had also known him from the early days. The beautiful Mrs

Armstrong-Jones was at every party and every ball. And I think it was because of everybody knowing everybody that they were bound to meet. She was photographed by every society photographer; *Vogue* and Cecil Beaton — the lot.

It took them a little time to get together, though, and fortunately, since Colonel Messel and Linley were very close to Armstrong-Jones, there was no animosity and it proved to be a most favourable match for all concerned.

Oliver was unable to attend the wedding, as he had been called away to Hollywood for talks about a projected M.G.M. film.

With the advent of her daughter's birth, Norma Shearer had faced a long absence from the screen. Her husband, Irving Thalberg, the Boy Wonder of Hollywood, who in partnership with Louis B. Mayer had transformed M.G.M. into the greatest film factory in movie history, decided to bring Shearer back with a role that would display her beauty and refinement to best advantage, and chose for this purpose *Romeo and Juliet*. Mayer was violently opposed to the idea, because he felt not only that Shearer, at past thirty, could not possibly play a fourteen-year-old, but that the masses did not understand Shakespeare. He was therefore convinced that the picture would be a failure. However, Mayer's opposition merely strengthened Thalberg's resolve to proceed with the project and he cast Leslie Howard as Romeo and John Barrymore as Mercutio.

Thalberg engaged George Cukor to direct the picture and Cukor approached Oliver to design the sets and costumes, giving him a broad canvas together with a substantial budget as added inspiration.

On Oliver's departure, *The Daily Express* reported on 19 July 1935:

Expensive young man to interview is artist Oliver Messel, who sailed for the United States yesterday. To talk to him for one week only, on their home ground, is costing the Hollywood film company nearly £1,000.

They are paying him £300 a week for the three weeks he will be away from England. Also all his expenses (suite on *Berengaria*, airplane across America both ways). In September Messel will return to Hollywood to do some actual work. They will then pay him £250 a week for at least five weeks, probably more.

Such payment, to a man chiefly known as a designer of elegant stage settings and costumes for West End revues, is remarkable. It is justified by Messel's unquestionable talent, his flair for starting rather than catching up with vogues, his dazzling yet solid success.

Oliver: It was quite the most interesting work I had yet undertaken. I paid a four-days visit to Hollywood and returned to England. I then went all over northern Italy by car in search of authentic colour. In a library in Verona I found the coats of arms of the two families concerned in the romance upon which Shakespeare is believed to have based his play. These figured in the film.

By the time Oliver returned to Hollywood the following year to supervise the making of the costumes and the constructions of the sets he had designed, he found that Irving Thalberg's top designer, Adrian, had already designed the costumes. All the studio wanted was for him to vet them and put his name to them. Oliver, however, turned on his well-known charm and diplomacy, and persuaded the director George Cukor to throw all Adrian's designs into the waste-paper basket. He then sat down to earn his salary (£250 a week) in the old-fashioned way — by doing exactly what he had been contracted to do.

ROMEO and JULIET
by
William Shakespeare

Messel's first Hollywood experience centred round his commission to design the sets and costumes for M.G.M.'s production of *Romeo and Juliet* (1936), with Norma Shearer and Leslie Howard as the young lovers. Right, the balcony scene

Being one of the first English designers to be asked to Hollywood he naturally found his position challenged by the existing contract staff.

Oliver: Cukor wanted a fresh outlook on Hollywood. That was why I was invited. Another reason was, perhaps, the fact that I had been brought up on Italian art and travelled to Italy over several years.

I sat for two months in an office by myself drawing my designs and when these were passed by Thalberg and Cukor, I set to work buying all the materials. There was a wonderful shop over there called Dazian's that sold every kind of material ever made. But Hollywood was like that. You could buy anything there.

I bought every yard of material personally and I supervised every stitch that was put into the costumes. I used no patterned materials at all. All flowered and patterned costumes seen in the film were painted by hand, and every piece of embroidery was worked by hand as well.

Some 500 girls worked for six solid months. I was in the workroom at 7 every morning and worked there until very late every night. People worked much harder in Hollywood because it was possible! It had the ideal climate. Not like England where it was sheer misery to put your nose out of bed in the morning.

The sets and costumes Oliver designed were sumptuous. A large, decorative tapestry filled with Elizabethan figures came to life amid a flourish of trumpets, and a herald described the two households and the star-cross'd lovers whose tale comprised 'the two hours' traffic on stage'.

The balcony scene alone was filmed in a garden that occupied the whole of huge Stage 15. Thirty arc lamps were required to light the set, and Cukor shot the scene for days, focusing from a variety of angles. However, although the balcony scene was imaginatively staged and the actors brought a freshness to the time-worn phrases, something seemed to detract from the scene's effectiveness. Perhaps it was the enormity of the set, and the length of the journey by which Romeo had to pass through the garden and up the walls to come within a few feet of Juliet.

Hollywood gossip had it that Adrian had walked out at M.G.M. because Norma Shearer wore the costumes Oliver had designed in preference to those he had created. Never since she first became a star had Norma Shearer worn any but Adrian's clothes. But Oliver himself had not heard this rumour. 'We all worked in peace and harmony,' he explained. 'It was natural that the studio people wished to do the costumes and sets themselves — but director George Cukor wanted me, so I went. I saw no signs of jealousy and no "temperament". It was hard work, but pleasant. Norma Shearer was the most beautiful woman I saw in Hollywood, but the truth is that you never see a plain woman there. It would be almost a relief if you did!'

Romeo and Juliet was premiered in New York on 20 August 1936 amid much fanfare, and the critical reception was mostly favourable. Frank Nugent of *The New York Times* called it 'a jeweled setting in which the deep beauty of

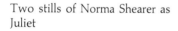

Two stills of Norma Shearer as Juliet

[Shakespeare's] romance glows and sparkles and gleams with breathless radiance.' Nonetheless, Louis B. Mayer was proved right; the movie audience wasn't ready for Shakespeare and the public reaction was temperate. The film drew receipts almost equal to its cost of over $2,000,000, but because of distribution and other expenses this represented a loss of almost $100,000, making it the only substantial deficit ever sustained by a Thalberg film. However, Thalberg declared that his intention was not to make money with the picture but to provide his wife with an elegantly romantic vehicle.

On Oliver's return from Hollywood on 4 June 1936, his sister met the *Berengaria* boat-train at Waterloo Station. He received a rapturous welcome from a phalanx of fashionable women friends and family. 'Lipstick marks still covered his face as he laughingly told of his experiences,' the *Daily Sketch* reported.

While mounting an exhibition of masks, film sets and costumes at the Leicester Art Gallery in London (it opened in July 1936), Oliver worked on the designs for *The Country Wife*, which was to open at the Old Vic three months later.

'In his designs for costumes and sets for the Hollywood film of *Romeo and Juliet*, which are now on view at the Leicester Galleries,' *The Times* reported, 'Mr Oliver Messel had the wit to feed his imagination on the early Italians generally. The result is an appropriately "young" production, not based upon any artist in particular but with apt allusions, as to Duccio in "The Funeral Procession" and to Botticelli in the costume design, No. 2. With the prevailingly youthful atmosphere there are the right touches of sophistication, recalling the dandy pages in "The Story of Griselda" in the National Gallery. The personal accent of the artist is one of lightness and elegance, well seen in the two settings "Juliet's Garden," and "Sycamore Grove". "Juliet with Gazelle" is a very charming invention.'

The Country Wife, with sets (eight in all) and costumes designed by Oliver, opened at the Old Vic on 6 October 1936 with Ruth Gordon, Edith Evans, Michael Redgrave, Alec Clunes, Freda Jackson and Ernest Thesiger. In his memoirs *Stage Directions*, Sir John Gielgud recalls how the production came to be staged both at the Old Vic and in the United States.

Sir John Gielgud: In 1934, at Sadler's Wells, Tyrone Guthrie directed *Love for Love* in the season in which Charles Laughton and Flora Robson starred, and two years later he also directed Wycherley's *The Country Wife* at the Old Vic, though the governors were hard put to it to persuade Lilian Baylis that such a pornographic piece was suitable to enliven the boards of her famous, but strictly moral, theatre. Miss Baylis was a great realist, however, and since the magnificent scenery and costumes (by Oliver Messel) were to be paid for in advance by Gilbert Miller, who proposed to transport the production afterwards to New York, and Edith Evans, always a tremendous favourite at the Old Vic, was to play Lady Fidget, she finally agreed to the revival.

Gilbert Miller had explained to Oliver that, as he had not become a member of the Designer's Union in New York (for which he would have had to go over

The New York production of
The Country Wife

and sit an exam) his designs, but not his name, could be used for the American production. This naturally upset Oliver but Miller managed to get round the Union restriction by presenting the production at the Old Vic and then taking over most of the company to New York. The Broadway production opened on 1 December of that year with the British contingent consisting of Roger Livesey, Irene Browne and Anthony Quayle, and the rest of the characters played by Americans, including Ruth Gordon.

The American press were unanimous in their praise of Oliver's work. The New York *Wall Street Journal* said, 'The key for the performance is clearly set by Oliver Messel's settings and costumes, which are at *once* stylized and fanciful, artificial and amusing'.

With a steady run of stage and film successes behind him, Oliver now turned his hand to commercial interior decoration and for his first commission redesigned the interior of the fashionable San Marco Club in Devonshire House in London. His murals consisted of the Rialto Bridge and the Piazza San Marco in Venice, in sharp contrast to other wall designs in the Surrealist style, which included meticulous examples of beasts, birds, fruit and flowers. London's social elite lunched at the San Marco where, instead of Italian fare, they were served

The ballet *Francesca da Rimini*, designed by Messel in the busy year of 1936

liver and bacon, and by night enjoyed a simple but excellent supper followed by cabaret.

Later that year Oliver returned to the fine arts to design the sets and costumes for the ballet *Francesca da Rimini*, choreographed by David Lichine for Colonel de Basil's newly formed Ballets Russes company (later known as the Ballets Russes de Monte Carlo), in succession to the late Diaghilev's company.

In the programme notes for this new production, it was explained that Michael Fokine had taken the theme for the ballet, first performed in 1915 at the Maryinsky Theatre (now the Kirov) in Leningrad, from Dante's *Divine Comedy* and arranged the choreography to Tchaikovsky's *Fantasia for Orchestra: Francesca da Rimini*. Based on Canto V of the *Inferno*, it begins in Hell with a flight of carnal sinners being tossed about by ceaseless winds. Dante and Virgil look down on this scene from a height, and two lovers approach to tell them their story. The tale unfolds in flashback, danced in a series of short episodes on different parts of the stage brought to life, under pools of light, in medieval Italy.

This new production opened the Covent Garden season on 15 July 1937 with Tchernicheva, Danilova, Riabouchinska and Baronova in a dazzling production, and was performed three months later at the Metropolitan Opera House, New York, to mild reviews.

The programme continues with a synopsis. Francesca (Lubov Tchernicheva), the Lord of Rimini's daughter-in-law, is seen with friends in her garden. The scene changes and she is revealed reading a book. Presently, her husband's handsome brother Paolo (Paul Petroff) brings her flowers. They read together, look up and kiss; she tries to escape but he follows her into her bedroom and declares his love. Clad in full armour, Francesca's husband (Marc Platoff) returns and is enraged when he learns from a spying servant of his wife's infidelity. He enters the lovers' room and slays them both. The action reverts to Hell where Francesca and Paolo conclude their story — and the ill-fated couple soar again into their world of torment.

The ballet enjoyed a revival at Covent Garden the following year, when Oliver scored over the performers, as reported in *The Times* on 23 June: '... when it is over the chief remaining impression is rather of the prettiness of Mr Oliver Messel's *décor* than of a completely integrated ballet, in which the drama, the decoration, and the music have been caught up in terms of dancing and so welded together.'

Oliver: I worked myself into a frenzy of despair over *Francesca da Rimini* and was quite ill. David Lichine arrived at Yeoman's Row in a fury, to be told by Mrs Jenkins, my daily, that I was ill. 'He may *die!*' he screamed, 'but only *after* the ballet!'

Karinska made the costumes and was equally desperate over finishing them on time. As the curtain rose on the opening scene of the ballet at Covent Garden, some of the costumes were still being loaded into taxis from Karinska's workshop off Long Acre!

Some of the details never reached the dancers, but the rest were so well executed that no one but I knew.

The ballet was financed in touching tribute to Tchernicheva through the life savings of a great fan of hers called Miss Parish — whom nobody had ever heard of before, and afterwards, at Boulestin's, we all drank champagne out of Miss Parish's shoe.

The next play Oliver designed was the Tyrone Guthrie production of *A Midsummer Night's Dream*, which opened at the Old Vic on 27 December 1937 for the Christmas four-week season. It featured Vivien Leigh (Titania), Ralph Richardson (Bottom) and Robert Helpmann (Oberon); and Ninette de Valois was the choreographer.

Sir Robert Helpmann: When Guthrie decided to do *A Midsummer Night's Dream* I auditioned for him and got the part of Oberon and to my delight the designer was Oliver. Funnily enough, the costume I wore was much more beautiful than the design; much more glamorous and wonderfully made. Maggie Furse made it, or rather *created* it, because it needed creating. He supervised everything, though, fitting after fitting.

I think I had more laughs with Oliver than with anybody else. I met him long before I did anything in the theatre with him; at a party. Everybody knew him — and he knew *everybody*. The great thing I adored of his mimicry was the one he used to do about the whore in Venice. 'My Venetian Idyll,' he called it. Oliver would leave the room and all you'd hear was what happened there. He used to do the woman and the man who picked her up. The man was frightfully English and you'd hear this pompous voice, 'I say, *regardez mon pince-nez — regardez!*' 'Ooh, la, la!' she'd reply in a high pitched voice. And then the rough husband came home and you'd have sworn there were three people in that room. And he'd have a basin of water and do it with terrible water effects.

'Tyrone Guthrie's version [of *A Midsummer Night's Dream*] is as enchanting and as fresh as if the play had been neglected for a hundred years,' J. E. Sewell wrote in *The Daily Telegraph* after the revival at the end of the following year, when there was another four-week Christmas season. 'With Oliver Messel to

The first scene of Tyrone Guthrie's production of *A Midsummer Night's Dream*; opposite, Robert Helpmann as Oberon

help him he has translated the "Dream" into an early Victorian fantasy. The scenery is delightfully formalised, the Athenians wear neat little side-whiskers, and the fairies, in white muslin, wear delicate chaplets of flowers, coyly tilted.'

Earlier in 1938 Oliver received a cable from the American producer Vinton Freedley, followed by one from Cole Porter, about a new musical comedy called *Leave It to Me*. This had a book by Bella and Samuel Spewack, the husband and wife team who wrote several Broadway plays and over twenty screenplays — mainly for M.G.M. The music and lyrics were by Cole Porter, and the show was scheduled to open at the Imperial Theatre in New York on 9 November of that year.

> Would you be interested designing scenery and costumes for musical show Cole Porter score scene laid in American University transatlantic plane and Greek islands stop. Believe would give you great scope for imaginative design stop. Please cable Vintonfree New York will then write full details
>
> Vinton Freedley

> Vinton Freedley is cabling you about a new show please be efficient and reply promptly love from us both address me Waldorf
>
> Cole

However, given that the show would require an out-of-town tour before the Broadway opening, Oliver realized there wasn't enough time to make a good job of it, and politely refused the offer; he was, moreover, planning another exhibition of his *Romeo and Juliet* film designs — together with some portraits — which was scheduled for a two-weeks showing at the Carol Carstairs Gallery in New York from 19 to 31 December, a commitment he couldn't cancel.

At the beginning of 1939 after the New York exhibition, he returned to London, where he continued his theatre work and undertook to design some of the costumes for the new Korda film, *The Thief of Baghdad*, starring Conrad Veidt, Sabu, John Justin and June Dupre. It won two Academy Awards after it was released the following year.

When *The Tempest* was offered him by the Old Vic, he seized the opportunity. With a star cast including John Gielgud, Jessica Tandy, Alec Guinness, and Jack Hawkins to play Caliban, it seemed that the production, directed by Marius Goring (who played Ariel) and George Devine, couldn't go wrong. But it did.

The critic Herbert Farjeon reported:

> How to conjure up the miracles conjured up by Prospero [John Gielgud] between his strange fits of perturbation. To answer this last question, Mr Oliver Messel, most brilliant of all stage designers, has been called in. He achieves many near-miracles by a careful and sensitive consideration of gauze and effect. But miracles they aren't, and that is a worry. You can't reproduce Prospero's magic one hundred per cent. — and since you can't, wouldn't something more formal, leaving something more to the imagination of those who have got any, serve the purpose better? If the sound of *The Tempest* is the sound of a shell, might not the formality of a shell, with its exquisite and finely-defined convolutions, serve as the best guide for an artist in this case? Mr Messel's costumes are unexceptionable. And given the approach he has chosen, I know of no other artist who would have got nearer the goal. I question, however, whether the approach is the right one. The attempt to make the pageant really insubstantial is too challenging.

It opened on 29 May 1940 and was Oliver's last production before joining the army; but he was given leave for a few days later that year to put the final touches to the Cocteau play, *The Infernal Machine*, in which Jeanne de Casalis played Jocasta, Leueen McGrath the Sphinx, and Peter Glenville the vain, egotistical, petulant young Oedipus. Oliver appeared in subaltern's uniform on the first night of this highly modernized version of *Oedipus Rex*, on leave from Aldershot where he was stationed. It took place on 5 September — the night of the first big air raid on London.

Oliver had formed a close friendship with Peter Glenville, the handsome young son of the Irish comedian Shaun Glenville, and it was from Yeoman's Row that Peter wrote the next week to Oliver in Aldershot about a bomb that had caused considerable damage to the house.

> Last night an incendiary bomb fell on the studio next to mine and burned a hole through the floor above your bedroom. Reeves are putting the whole thing right and are renewing the glass above both studios and (rather quaintly) are painting the outside of both houses.
>
> Fire incendiaries fell in Yeoman's Row and several high explosives round Montpelier Square. Katina Paxinou has been sweet. She is staying at the Ritz and she has asked me to go and stay with her every night in the shelter there. It is very gay (with King Zog in person) and you don't hear a thing (so far!).

Peter Glenville

The Old Vic production of *The Tempest* (1939), with Messel designs. John Gielgud played Prospero and Jessica Tandy was a young Miranda.

She wants to get a good play for both of us and go to America with it. Whether or not that is a sensible idea or not I do not know.

After you left on Sunday I dined with Elinor Smith [The Lady Elinor Smith, who wrote a popular novel about gypsies called *Caravan*]. We were caught in the most terrific barrage so we chased back to her place, opened a bottle of champagne and talked the whole night about theatre, Byron, etc. It was rather fun. Still no gas, but my electric heater has been attended to so that I can bath.

Warners are, I hear, doing three films so that I may hope to be in one of them. I hope your work won't be too exhausting.

I met Michael [Rosse], Harold [Acton] and little Anne at the Ritz last night.

Write and tell me about your work.

love
Peter

4 * Regal rôles

Oliver: I was stationed at Norwich as Camouflage Officer to two Corps. Although the headquarters were at Newmarket, Norwich (at that time preparing against invasion) was considered a more practical centre.

I started in some old sheds and an old house in Bishopsgate by the river. I was then asked by Eastern Command to find premises for a camouflage school; this, of course, was all done in dead secrecy for security reasons. While I was exploring around the many interesting byways of Norwich, an old Georgian building standing forlornly off the road behind some nice old brown gates caught my eye. The building looked derelict and the door was open, so being interested in all old buildings I walked inside and found the rooms stacked to the ceiling with crates and boxes, and the beautiful plastered ceilings and walls festooned with cobwebs.

The Assembly Rooms had been the scene of all the most important social functions of Norwich for the past 120 years; tea, wine and cards were available to visitors, and there were also morning concerts at which the music gallery was kept 'entirely for the gentlemen who choose to sit there'. It was owned by Mr H. J. Sexton, who turned it into a girls' high school and now planned to give it to the city as an arts centre. But it was requisitioned for war purposes. It was a stroke of exceptional good fortune that it came under the control of a branch of the Service in which Oliver served. He was quick to recognize the beauties of this magnificent example of eighteenth-century architecture and enlisted the help of skilled plasterers on the staff who, in their spare time, did careful repairs to the plaster work on walls and ceilings, and restored paintwork. It was handed back to the city after its function as the camouflage school ended with the war.

However, Oliver's war effort wasn't confined to the Assembly Rooms. He disguised some pill-boxes as Gothic lodges and others as caravans, haystacks, ruins and wayside cafés, always with his meticulous attention to detail. 'Plant some old-man's beard here in the spring,' he would instruct his work-force, or 'Paint a pot of flowers in that window.'

Lord Snowdon: When Oliver was a captain in the Camouflage Corps in Norwich, he was designing frightfully pretty baroque pill-boxes and also had wonderful parties. At one time he did have to go square-bashing and stood there on the quadrangle with the Sergeant Major bellowing his head off. The general came up, and Oliver, instead of saluting, clasped him with both hands and said, 'Oh, how wonderful to see you.'

He then took the general by the hand and, as they walked through the ranks, said, 'You must come and meet dear Smith who is being so kind and looking after me,' and introduced his batman to the general. The general sweetly went along with it; fortunately he knew Oliver very well.

overleaf
Messel's famous production of *The Sleeping Beauty*, mounted in 1946 for the grand re-opening of Covent Garden. In the Royal Box (second from stage, middle tier): King George VI and Queen Elizabeth, Princess Elizabeth and Princess Margaret

114

Captain Oliver Messel at the Camouflage Unit in Norfolk (1942)

Lady Rosse: That dear general was Sir Gerald Templar, who admired Oliver tremendously for saving the Assembly Rooms at Norwich. Oliver had got all the men in the unit to do the things he wanted them to do. I remember years later dining with Sir Gerald at a charity function. He spoke so charmingly of Oliver; he was such a sympathetic person and allowed him to do exactly what he wanted to do to save these things at Norwich.

Many years later Sir Gerald wrote a most touching obituary of Oliver to *The Times.*

Oliver's posting was of a somewhat rare nature, for even while serving as Captain in the Corps, he was granted leave to design for the theatre. Charles B. Cochran wrote to him on 12 September 1941:

> Would it interest you, and would you have time, to design scenery and costumes for Shakespeare's *Antony & Cleopatra.*
>
> I need hardly tell you that the scenery must be of the simplest character, and the costumes should be made in the wardrobe, from your designs of simple material and, I should think, hand painted. You could put somebody (Honoria Plesch, for instance) in charge of the wardrobe to work under your supervision.
>
> The proposal, if it comes off (it is not quite definite) is to get to work at once.
>
> Please give me an immediate reply.
>
> Robert Atkins, who will produce the play with Clare Luce as 'Cleopatra', suggests that you might like to do it in the fashion of the Elizabethan masque.

Oliver, however, had agreed to design the ballet of Milton's *Comus* for the Sadler's Wells Company at the New Theatre, with choreography by Robert Helpmann to music by Purcell arranged by Constant Lambert, and for lack of time declined the offer to do *Antony and Cleopatra.* This news sent Cochran into an unreasonable temper, since he was anxious to receive the costume designs he had commissioned from Oliver for the 'Flamingo' sequence in his forthcoming revue, *Big Top*. He wrote on 26 November 1941:

> Honoria [Plesch, set and costume designer] frightened me today by saying she didn't think you would be able to let us have any designs to get on with until after the production of *Comus*. This isn't so, is it? Because that would be impossible.
>
> Obviously, Andrée Howard [the choreographer for *Big Top*, a former ballerina with Ballet Rambert] cannot start to rehearse without knowing all about the costumes, and in about ten days time I shall have no work for Mrs Kelly and she would have to disband her sewing women.
>
> Please don't think I don't know how difficult it is for you, but I thought you had nearly finished with *Comus*.
>
> If all your chorus designs are to be different it will be lovely, but we must have plenty of time. I find from the time we get the designs it takes now, with the coupon difficulties, two weeks to get the material, and I am hoping to produce the last week in January.
>
> It will be a terrible disappointment to me if you cannot do the numbers, but it would be better not to attempt it unless our costumes can be well in hand within two, or at the latest, three weeks from now.

Despite Cochran's pleas and consternation, Oliver could not undertake *Antony and Cleopatra*, but he assured Cochran that the designs for *Big Top* would be delivered on time. He was given seven days' leave from the army in Norwich to visit London where he supervised the completion of the scenery and costumes for the *Comus* company, headed by Robert Helpmann and Margot Fonteyn.

Sir Robert Helpmann: The basic premise of *Comus* is the Milton masque. Having played Oberon I was anxious to speak again, so I spoke the two big famous speeches of Comus about night and about magic; the orchestra would stop for this. Constant Lambert had arranged a wonderful score. He had played the music to Oliver when he started designing it. Oliver was given leave from the Camouflage Unit to supervise the costume fittings, and we only met twice because we were on tour. He kept sending me the designs and the whole thing was that I was frightfully nervous about the men in the production. There are no 'lifts' in the ballet at all. There was only myself as Comus and the two brothers. All the rest, although they were dressed as men, were women under the masks Oliver had designed.

Margot Fonteyn, who danced the role of The Lady, was taken ill prior to the London opening and Beryl Grey stepped in for her. One of Britain's most accomplished prima ballerinas, Beryl Grey won a scholarship to the Sadler's Wells Ballet School when she was nine, and at fourteen joined the Sadler's Wells Ballet Company. She celebrated her fifteenth birthday by dancing for the first time the rôle of Odette/Odile in the full-length version of *Swan Lake* and shortly afterwards made her first appearance in the title rôle of *Giselle*. Later she became the first Western ballerina to dance at the Bolshoi Theatre, Moscow.

Beryl Grey: It was the first time I ever understudied Margot. I was still only fourteen and Margot was ill in Oxford and I danced the rôle of The Lady. The

Robert Helpmann in the ballet
Comus, based on the masque by
Milton, a production designed
by Messel during the war
(1942)

costume was absolute hell to work in because it was prickly. It had a marvellous effect but the tight bodice was made of terribly coarse horsehair. It was beautiful, though, with minute dark red birds *appliquéd* onto the bodice. It had a light, wispy skirt. I had a small hairpiece with five little curls that swept across the top of the head and then fell down into ringlets. It was simple, but very effective.

The Sabrina costume was in flowing blue, and we had lengths of blue material that represented the sea. Six attendant sea nymphs entered on their knees — one of them making the noise of a frog!

The entire cast were women, dancing the men's parts, except for the two brothers and Bobby [Helpmann], who had a wonderfully flamboyant costume that simply flowed with his every movement.

Margot Fonteyn and Oliver worked together again later when he designed his celebrated production of *The Sleeping Beauty*.

Oliver: It would be impossible for me to attempt to add to the innumerable eulogies that have been written about the superb artistry of Margot Fonteyn. But what has perhaps struck me more than anything else is the way in which the rare

117

integrity of her character is projected through her every movement on the stage. Her selfless dedication, superb manners, and modesty, found only in the great, have placed Margot on a pedestal to be adored by everyone who is near her. By her example, Margot has set the highest standard and is the inspiration for the whole ballet world to follow.

The rose that she gave me from her bouquet on the stage of the Metropolitan Opera House in New York at the opening performance of *The Sleeping Beauty* is one of the things I treasure most of an unforgettable evening.

Fortunately Cochran and Oliver did not fall out over the *Antony and Cleopatra* affair, and when Oliver returned to Norwich he completed and delivered the designs for *Big Top*, which was to feature Beatrice Lillie, Madge Elliott and Cyril Ritchard. During preparations for the production, Oliver renewed acquaintanceship with his old friend Rex Whistler – the last time he was to see him, for Whistler was later killed in action in Normandy. Whistler had designed a cloth of a boulevard café for *Big Top*.

Despite the inordinate amount of talent that had been poured into the show, there was no shortage of problems. Sensing one of them, Oliver sent a telegram to Cochran in Leeds where the show was stretching its wings prior to a London opening. He suggested that Tyrone Guthrie be brought in to light the 'Flamingo' sequence, which was built around the exotic dancer Yoma, whom Cochran had discovered and promoted as the most beautiful woman in the world. On 28 April 1942 Cochran replied to Oliver from the Queens Hotel, Leeds:

> Your wire received, and of course I should welcome Tony Guthrie's assistance if you can persuade him to offer it.
>
> I wish it could be possible for you to come to the lighting rehearsal, and I know you will if you can. Although the scene gets applause every time it is shown, we have not got it right yet. I visualise something which I just have not been able to achieve – I think what I visualise is what you would like.
>
> Failing Tony Guthrie, is there anybody else in whom you have sufficient confidence to entrust the lighting of your scene? It is so important to me that you are pleased.
>
> Yoma will be lovely in 'Flamingo'. Andrée is doing it beautifully.

However, Guthrie was unavailable; but even if he had been free, this revue, the last Cochran was to produce, was not likely to have succeeded. It opened at His Majesty's Theatre on 8 May 1942 and Cochran reported to Oliver five months later:

> After its triumphant tour, *Big Top* flopped badly in London, which did not surprise me very much, as I knew it was not a good show, but I could not get it right. Bertie Farjeon [Herbert Farjeon, author of several witty revues] was very obstinate and wouldn't help us at all to remedy the bad spots, which were so obvious, even before the production at Liverpool. He concentrated upon his own little show, which fared rather worse than *Big Top*.
>
> If you are in town for a day or two, wouldn't you give me the pleasure of having luncheon with me; I don't like the thought of your passing completely out of my life.
>
> Noël Coward has pulled off a huge success with his picture [*In Which We Serve*]. I

expect you have seen it. If not, you ought to. It is a tremendous effort without a tinge of cheapness.

Although heavily committed with his work in the camouflage unit, Oliver received many offers: from the BBC to give a talk, from the Slade Society in Oxford to lecture on a subject of his own choice, from the Manchester Ballet Club for a sketch of his for their forthcoming exhibition, and from the Sadler's Wells Opera:

18 March 1943

Dear Mr Messel

We hope to produce an opera by Tchaikovsky called *Pique Dame* [*The Queen of Spades*] and I am so dreadfully anxious that you should design it for us. Is there any possibility of your doing so?

The first performance will be in early autumn in London, and Tony Guthrie will, I hope, be the producer.

I have made plans so far ahead in the hope that you will be free to squeeze it in for us *somehow*.

We will give you every possible assistance if you will consider this.

Most sincerely yours

Joan Cross

Director of Opera

However, he was not able to accept any of these offers until he was released from the army in 1944 in order to undertake the mammoth task of designing the new Gabriel Pascal film, Shaw's *Caesar and Cleopatra*.

The fee he asked for was £10,000, and he unwisely sought the council of his arch-rival Cecil Beaton. 'Do you think it's too much?' he said. 'After all, it will involve a year's work and I shall have to make all the jewelled head-dresses myself and provide a great many of the "props" which will have to be specially made.' Beaton told him his fee was perfectly reasonable, and then prepared similar designs himself and offered them to Pascal at a lower fee. Later, when Oliver discovered Beaton's devious ploy, instead of being angry or reproachful he just giggled. He could afford to do so, as he had won the contract himself after all.

Oliver was also asked by H. M. Tennent to design a new production of *Lady Windermere''s Fan*. As managing director of H. M. Tennent, Ltd, 'Binkie' Beaumont had become an extraordinarily powerful theatrical manager. Tyrone Guthrie once said that Beaumont, more than any other single individual, could make or break the career of almost any worker in the British professional theatre. Before the days of the big subsidized companies, he dominated the London theatre with his unique talent for producing brilliant shows that were both critically and commercially successful. By the time of his death in 1973, a full list of his productions required four columns of *Who's Who in the Theatre*.

On 30 January 1945 he wrote to Oliver:

I had a visit today from Mr Norman of Simmons [the costumiers] and it seems to me that it is getting rather serious about the actual time for making of clothes. From what I can gather, Norman could do *Lady Windermere's Fan* for us, if we definitely

Sheridan's *The Rivals* was produced by H. M. Tennent's in 1945 with sets and costumes by Messel. Audrey Fildes played Lydia Languish (opposite) and Edith Evans was a memorable Mrs Malaprop (right).

settle to produce the play at the end of April or early May. As you know, I have held up and not worried you until the Pascal film was finished, because I knew you were far too occupied with finishing that to start designing *Lady Windermere's Fan*, but do you think that now you could find time to have a conference to discuss the whole thing?

Because of the film, Oliver could not undertake *Lady Windermere's Fan* for Beaumont (in the event it was successfully done by Cecil Beaton), but when he became available later that year, he agreed to design a revival of *The Rivals*. Beaumont wrote on 29 May 1945:

> This is just a little line to remind you (which I am sure is quite unnecessary!) about *The Rivals*, because I am sure that in the next ten days we must start laying out with the contracts the full details. Although, of course, I realise that you couldn't have the designs completed in that time, by now I presume, with half an hour's discussion, we could find out the number of costumes both for men and women that will be required, and the amount of scenery involved, so that we can get the contractors to commit themselves to lay aside the necessary period for the work to be carried out.
>
> I am sorry to keep on nagging about this, but I know how vitally important it is, particularly as we hope to rehearse about July 16th, and whilst it seems there is quite a lot of time, there is not enough of it.

The reopening of the Criterion Theatre after the war on 25 September 1945 was marked by the production of Richard Brinsley Sheridan's *The Rivals* with Edith Evans playing Mrs Malaprop, Anthony Quayle as Jack Absolute, Audrey Fildes as Lydia, Jean Wilson as Julia and Peter Cushing as Faulkland. 'Mr Oliver Messel has the proper sense of the old comedy', *The Times* headed its review the next day — even before mentioning the cast; 'His settings are elegantly and amusingly in keeping with the plot, which is brilliantly ingenious but seldom altogether artificial, the most absurd situations seeming to follow naturally from the characters which take part in them. His decorative artificiality has, in short, style, conviction. It is precisely the quality which the revival as a whole lacks.'

Caesar and Cleopatra (1945) was the third Bernard Shaw play to be filmed by Gabriel Pascal. Messel designed lavish sets and costumes, and the stars were Vivien Leigh and Claude Rains.

Three months later the £1,000,000 film of *Caesar and Cleopatra* was released: 'The most expensive film ever made', *Picture Post* declared. Stephen Watts in the *Sunday Express* reported on 16 December: 'For the work of Oliver Messel who designed the clothes and sets, and for the Technicolor photography I have nothing but praise.' 'I think it's the best work this brilliant young designer has done,' said *The People*, '— breathtakingly beautiful. He was released from the Royal Engineers to do this job.' *The Daily Telegraph* was even more impressed: 'The sets are gigantic. Oliver Messel's *décor* and costumes are richly imaginative in Technicolor, for once agreeably restrained. Made though it was in difficult war-time conditions, *Caesar and Cleopatra* is as spectacular as anything the screen has ever given us.'

Vagn Riis-Hansen, photograph
by Snowdon

The making of the film had not lacked stormy incidents; indeed, Oliver threatened to quit the production during actual filming. The producer, Gabriel Pascal, took a dislike to a long black wig which Oliver had designed for Jean Simmons. Pascal strode on to the set, snatched off the wig, grabbed wigs worn by other girls in the scene, and tried them on Miss Simmons.

Oliver, green with exhaustion after an all-night designing session, watched in horror. He ran along behind Pascal, pleading with him to put the wigs back. When arguments failed, he announced that he was walking out of the production. Gathering up some ornate fans which he had lent from his parents' famous collection, he turned to leave. Vivien Leigh stepped into the breach. 'If Oliver goes', she said firmly, 'so do I.' Pascal gave way. Oliver stayed. So did Vivien Leigh — and Jean Simmons played the scene in the black wig.

By the time the war was over, Oliver met the man who was to become his life-long companion and administrator, Vagn Riis-Hansen. He was born in Jutland, the part of Denmark that was the setting for many of Hans Christian Andersen's imaginative tales.

He had started by opening a dress shop in Copenhagen in partnership with another Dane, and spent much time in Paris, London and America selecting clothes for the shop. He married a young Scottish actress, Zoë Gordon, whom he met when she was appearing in Noël Coward's production of *Bitter Sweet* in the early 'thirties. During the war he fought in the Danish resistance and three times escaped from German concentration camps. 'Rather like the Scarlet Pimpernel', Oliver recalls, 'he continued to assist Jewish families or war prisoners to escape from the Nazis to safety.' After the war he returned to the England he loved, and became a British subject. His wife had died tragically of a brain tumour, and he settled down with Oliver, sharing a relationship that endured for thirty years, until his death.

Derek Hill: I first met Vagn very early on when I was at school, at Marlborough. In 1932 a cousin of mine, Nancy Tennant, met him on a boat going to America. He hadn't got his papers in order and was refused entry into America. He was sent to Ellis Island, and Nancy, feeling frightfully sorry for him, paid for his fare back to England — and so he returned to England under the auspices of my cousin. As he had no money and had nothing to do, she employed him to come and produce a children's pantomime.

He had gone to a fancy dress ball given by Diana Guinness at Bidston as Voltaire, in a magnificent wig made out of string by Robert Byron — the sort of thing Oliver would do — and as I was to appear as Prince Charming in this pantomime which was in a village called Ugley, for the Ugley Women's Institute — Vagn lent me this wig. Nigel Gosling was in it too, together with his brother and Margaret Watney, whose father was the brewer — and Vagn produced it.

I never saw Vagn again until after the war. I heard vaguely that Oliver had a Danish friend who was his manager and general factotum. Next time I went to see Oliver, the door was opened by Vagn whom I had first met twenty years before.

Oliver was rapidly becoming the highest-paid theatre designer in Britain, if not in the world. He was the first designer ever to demand — and receive — a box-office percentage. This enabled him to move from Yeoman's Row to fashionable Pelham Place, in South Kensington. He bought a house there, and then a little later the house next door, knocking the two into one. Here, he lived in what became a select community that consisted of Cecil Beaton, Emlyn Williams, Margot Fonteyn, Peter Ustinov and Mary Ellis.

Mary Ellis: There were evenings when Oliver Messel, Peter Ustinov and Emlyn Williams came and had coffee — Oliver giving a very funny performance as a Peruvian lady; Peter was more operatic than any opera singer, turning himself into a cello or a trombone; Emlyn reading aloud the lesson-book on *How to Play the Recorder* and making it unspeakably funny. And there was open house at Christmas — warmth, friendliness and happiness.

Emlyn Williams: Our house in Pelham Cresent had been badly bombed. My wife and I were living elsewhere and were resigned to never getting it back. I met Oliver outside. 'I've moved to 17 Pelham Place round the corner,' he said. 'It had been blitzed but they've put it to rights. Why don't you do the same with this?' And we did. We moved back, and we were all neighbours for about twenty years, until Oliver moved to Barbados.

During that time, the four of us became the closest of friends; both Oliver and Vagn had a spontaneous and enduring affection for my wife, Molly. Oliver knew that she had a passionate interest in what are called 'the visual arts' and he had a touching habit of taking her arm excitedly, like a child with another child. 'Darling, I've just finished my model for the play at the Globe and I do think it's rather beautiful' — and he would whisk her into his studio.

Whenever either house gave a biggish party, the other would send somebody scuttling round to borrow plates and knives and forks. Oliver and Vagn were perfect foils for each other, and their parties the best ever — Vagn the expansive host, seeing to every practical need from the Danish *slivowitz* onwards, and Oliver the quietly convivial welcomer: the one a Rabelaisian Danish Bacchus, the other a deceptively shy enjoyer of company.

The other guests could be either friends we had not lately seen, or people we'd never met, or celebrities, often a mixture of all three. One night it would be Marlene Dietrich, another Christian Bérard, Elisabeth Welch, Ava Gardner, Louise de Vilmorin — you never knew. You just knew it would be fun, in warm candlelit rooms, romantically sumptuous and yet unaffectedly intimate, the guests at their best.

There was once an unusually large party (with most of our kitchen staff commandeered) for a visiting Spanish dance company; I left at one a.m. to go round the corner to finish some work, and when I returned at three the rout was still at its height.

Sometimes, especially later on when there were only three or four of us, in the middle of an animated conversation Oliver would gently slip to the floor and lie on his back; nothing was interrupted. Then Vagn would say gruffly, 'Oliver, you silly bugger.' He was a Dane who did not mince his English. 'You've been overdoing it again, are you all right?' 'I'm fine, Vagnie dear, just relaxing.' Those were the only times you knew he was in constant and great pain: arthritis.

He seemed always to have been fascinated by facial masks: certainly by 1928, when his creations for the chorus in the number 'Dance Little Lady' created a sensation. Over the later years, he must have sporadically made more masks, and one night around 1948 he produced a batch: extraordinary faces, alive with character, beautiful, or funny, or hauntingly macabre – A drooling old man, an exquisite black teenager, a guilt-ridden half-witted young man staring open-mouthed, a tight-lipped harridan, an ancient duchess whose head was half-face, half-skull. Oliver persuaded me to put a mask on, he put on another, and I found myself exchanging outrageous impromptu dialogue with him.

This was quite unlike me, who was used to playing parts, in plays, most carefully rehearsed; and I found that through 'hiding' behind a mask I felt unselfconsciously free to characterize all sorts of voices, men's and women's. And I realize now that when, two or three years later, I embarked on a one-man show 'as Charles Dickens', I was learning (from Oliver's masks) to hide behind the Dickens beard and undertake impersonations of which I would have been very shy if I had been appearing as myself. So I have a professional debt to Oliver, on top of the incalculable one of friendship.

Later, Barbados. Happy days, and nights . . .

Despite the fun and games, Oliver continued to work through the night until morning, when everyone had gone to bed.

Oliver: I've always lived in London, and while living there, I lived like a hermit in the country, locking myself in my studio where I worked alone, with cups and cups of black coffee. I always found it difficult to make myself work. Before any production or anything that I was embarking on, I would always say, 'Oh, God, this time I can't do it. I can't bear it this time.' I was going through absolute agony. And the more I went on, the more things I did, the miracle was that I eliminated a great deal. I'd say to myself, 'You can't do that, because it's got to be like this or like that; you're in danger of repeating yourself.' Each time I had to dig out something else. And each time it became more and more difficult.

Snowdon: I remember first working for Oliver when I was six, making *papier mâché* masks. At Covent Garden just after the war he made the head-dresses for *The Sleeping Beauty* out of pipe cleaners. Ballet has always been part of my life since I was introduced to it early on by Oliver.

He taught me to use my eyes, to look at detail. We used to walk all night together, just walking, walking, walking round and round Venice which he loved so much. He was a great scholar in the history of art and had an impeccable sense of colour and taste and shape. Wandering in Venice, he'd just point out the odd proportion of a cornice of a building. Most people don't look up, and miss a lot. He had a marvellous sense of humour that made it fun to learn.

In spite of finding work increasingly difficult, Oliver persisted and brought continual surprise and awe to his designs, notably at Covent Garden. The fate that had befallen the Opera House during the war was as hideously conclusive as if one of Hitler's bombs had flattened the place. Disguised as a commercial *palais de danse* catering largely for servicemen on leave, the beautiful old building could doubtless be said to have 'done its bit' – like a *prima donna* gallantly tackling 'Roll Out the Barrel' in the N.A.A.F.I. But it was painful to think of that acoustically perfect interior, which once echoed to the voices of Patti, Melba and the de

Reszkes, insulted year after year by the graceless monotony of quickstep and rumba.

The choice of production for the reopening of Covent Garden was *The Sleeping Beauty*, the masterpiece of ballet in the grand romantic style, designed on elaborate lines and demanding a large cast of first-rate dancers. The Sadler's Wells Ballet Company began rehearsals with Robert Helpmann as Prince Charming and as Carabosse the Witch, Margot Fonteyn as Princess Aurora, and Beryl Grey, Moira Shearer and Pamela May.

Oliver was commissioned to design the production, and on the night the curtain rose, 20 February 1946, he was still onstage putting the final touches to the scenery as the Royal Family entered the theatre.

The King and Queen, Queen Mary and Princesses Elizabeth and Margaret attended the reopening of the historic theatre after its seven years service as a dance hall. Their presence, together with that of the Prime Minister and Mrs Attlee, Members of the Cabinet, Diplomatic Corps, the House of Commons, and the House of Lords, made this the most glittering social event in the theatre since its pre-war international seasons.

To patriotic ballet fans, however, the significant fact was that a British company occupied the stage on this notable occasion; the Sadler's Wells Ballet Company had been transferred to the new Covent Garden Opera Trust for an initial period of four years with this production, and gave the most sumptuous full-length version of Tchaikovsky's lovely ballet since Diaghilev had presented it almost twenty-five years before.

The Bluebird costumes Oliver designed for *The Sleeping Beauty* have gone down in the annals of ballet design and have been repeated in productions on both sides of the Atlantic for the past thirty years.

Sir Robert Helpmann: They were wonderful. They gave the impression of being birds. Of course, the ballerina was a Princess and her partner was the Bluebird, but Oliver wanted them both to be dressed as Bluebirds, and he was right.

The highest compliment I can pay Oliver is to say that he had the most exquisite taste of anybody in the theatre that I know, not only about designing but about people's performances. He was infallible in his judgment of people's talent.

The worst thing I can say about him was his irritating stubbornness. I don't know whether that's a fault but that used to get me down a bit. But on the other hand, he was right in nine cases out of ten.

Beryl Grey, who danced the role of the Lilac Fairy, recalls the events that led up to the first night curtain:

Beryl Grey: We rehearsed on the stage every day, instead of in rehearsal rooms, and we had this marvellous array of costumes (some 208) in every part of the Opera House for the four weeks before we opened. Oliver was always there, saying, 'We want this here. We want this there,' and looking at the costumes in relation to the people who were going to wear them. But even so, not one costume was finished by the last day of the opening night! Mine certainly wasn't. I was sewing little lilac flowers into bits of net on the shoulder and round the bodice of my costume almost until the curtain rose. I was disappointed when I

first saw my Lilac Fairy costume because it was white. I had a lovely skirt which was white — but my overskirt, which was satin and wider, was also white. I thought it ought to have been lilac, but Oliver said, 'It can't be all lilac because it won't give the right impression. It will only work if the costume is white with lilac trimmings.'

Oliver's designs gave you the concept of what he had in mind, but when they came out they were all better in their realization. They were extraordinarily functional. The interesting thing about his designs, compared with later designers in the theatre, was that he used materials that would work and that would last. He had so little choice in those days because of rationing, yet he knew what to get — and how to get it — and his costumes lasted for *years*. We had come out of those very sparse war years, when we just about made ends meet. We had only enough material to get the right effect, then suddenly, thanks to Oliver, we were getting all these little extras onto the head-dresses and earrings: gorgeous trimmings that you could dance in — that didn't weigh you down and didn't pull you back when you turned. So often you get dresses that look lovely, but when you move in them — when you turn — they turn after you, stopping your pirouettes. But never Oliver's! Nowadays, by the dress-rehearsal costumes are all ripped because of the materials chosen. Oliver dyed materials a lot. A great deal of dyeing was done in those days — but with vegetable dyes, not chemical dyes which are used now and which are harsh.

That first production was what everything should be if it is perfect — and almost never is. His costumes were very 'dance-able-in'. He *cared* if you were comfortable. His production had all the richness, all the grandeur that you expect with that wonderful period, but at the same time he captured the magic and made a statement of royalty, elegance and good taste. He also managed to express a spirit of mystery as well as magic. Designers nowadays attempt to achieve something by precision, whereas Oliver had inspiration and worked from that together with his intrinsic knowledge. I felt that he'd got some sort of inner meaning from the fairy story that somehow came through all the gorgeous magic he created; I suppose he was influenced by the Opera House.

He made a great deal of use of the levels of the stage. [He designed four sets, gauzes and drop curtains.] In the Prologue my entrance was made from the foot of a ramp at the back and I gradually came up to stage level. I remember Carabosse [Helpmann] going down through trap doors. Oliver had these beautiful transformation scenes, which have never been bettered. At the beginning, when the Princess falls into her deep sleep, transparent curtains with trees painted onto them rose up from the stage, giving the impression of the forest growing. Some curtains came down at the same time — and others criss-crossed. I — the Lilac Fairy — moved slowly backwards calling them up and across — and that was magical. The most beautiful scene besides that one was The Awakening, with the spiders and cobwebs painted onto gauzes. Then you had Carabosse followed by the Prince through these different drop cloths with spotlights highlighting their movements. As I took Carabosse back across the stage — banishing him — one gauze flew up and he would follow me; and then I went by the next gauze and it flew up — and then the huge cobweb at the end went up as the Prince kissed Princess Aurora, and she awoke. It was pure magic.

Oliver's production of *The Sleeping Beauty* reopened the Royal Opera House after the war and I shall always remember it as the best production I have ever seen.

Robert Helpmann and Margot Fonteyn as Prince Florimund and Princess Aurora in Messel's *The Sleeping Beauty* (1946)

Philip Hope-Wallace, writing for *Time and Tide*, reported of this production, 'Bakst's costumes and those old baroque sets take some expunging from the mind, but Messel's new setting, refulgent, plumed and gauzy, imposes itself as a proper match for Tchaikovsky's pulsating and romantic grandeur. The wonderful array of costumes blend and "move" (one of the hardest problems) in a way which calls up the discretion and taste of the illustrations to a French story-book (whose name escapes me). It is a vast improvement on the former Wells setting. Such a splendid mounting of this sumptuous piece is indeed a sight for the sore eyes of Londoners.'

Despite the generally favourable press reception for *The Sleeping Beauty*, there was a discordant note. Oliver was indignant at Cyril W. Beaumont's review in *Ballet* magazine, edited by the author and critic Richard Buckle, and asked why Buckle had not written the notice himself. He resented comparisons with *The Sleeping Princess* (the title used for the production at the Alhambra Theatre in 1921 designed by Léon Bakst for Diaghilev): 'Mine is better,' he declared.

Sir Robert Helpmann: Bakst's costumes were absolutely undanceable. They were heavy and unwieldy. They were wonderful to look at, though. I knew Sokolova and Lydia Lopokova who danced the role, and they used to complain about Bakst's costumes.

The Bakst production came to be called *The Sleeping Princess* because of Lydia Lopokova who was the darling of the British public. Olga Spessivtzeva and Tamara Karsavina were popular but the public loved Lopokova. When she ran away with her first husband it made headlines. It was a tremendous scandal at the time.

Richard Buckle was finally given the opportunity of producing his retrospective opinion on the occasion of the exhibition of Oliver's life-work at the Victoria and Albert Museum in 1983. It was an assessment Oliver would have respected. Buckle had, through the years, been a great admirer of Oliver's work and wrote informed criticism of his output on many occasions. He added his comments to Oliver's original 1946 production, explaining how Oliver and Bakst had arrived at their individual conclusions for *The Sleeping Beauty*.

Richard Buckle: Both Bakst and Messel looked back towards the seventeenth and eighteenth centuries: both borrowed as much as they have invented. Alexandre Benois thought Bakst was shaky on architecture and perspective: I thought Messel even more so. Each designer sought inspiration from the fantastic palaces conceived by the Bibiena family of stage decorators, who, in the words of A. Hyatt Mayor, 'at their drawing boards, unhampered by the need for performance, the cost of marble, the delays of masons, the whims and deaths of patrons, in designs as arbitrary as the mandates of the autocrats they served, summed up the great emotional architecture of the baroque.' Both Bakst and Messel mixed the periods of their costumes. Each had an overall vision which transmuted borrowed themes into personal statements. While Bakst aimed in his court scenes at the utmost splendour of colour and grandiloquence of baroque design, Messel's opalescent fairyland was seen through the dewy eyes of a love-sick poet.

The Prologue (Christening Scene) of *The Sleeping Beauty*. This photograph is of the touring company in 1959.

Buckle's retrospective identifies the sources for Oliver's inspiration; 'the flattened arches and banded columns of Oliver's prologue, *The Christening*, through which could be seen a feathery park, were taken from Watteau's painting *Les Charmes de la Vie* in the Wallace Collection,' for instance, and the trees in Act I were 'unreal like the later Gainsborough's.' Buckle was none too pleased with Oliver's interpretation of the second act scene which ends with the Prince's Vision of Aurora. Again comparing Oliver's designs to Bakst's, he says: 'Messel tried to be different. His gloomy grotto might have been acceptable, but its distant view of bleak hills was not. He had dared to invent a landscape and failed,' but adds that *The Awakening* was, 'from the point of view of design and lighting, the most beautiful moment in the ballet.'

Richard Buckle (continuing his retrospective criticism): It was easy to spot Messel's favourite among the dancers of the *divertissement* at the Act III *Wedding*: on the tunic of Florestan, who danced the swinging *pas de trois* with his two white-clad Sisters, the designer had lavished his favourite discord of orange-vermilion and cyclamen pink. As one fairy-tale character succeeded another Messel's fancy never flagged. . . .

131

Messel's set for *The Magic Flute* (opposite), produced by the Royal Opera, Covent Garden, in 1947. Above, the costume for Monastatos

Paint-brush in hand, with a mouth full of pins, begging, borrowing – for clothes coupons were scarce in 1946 – badgering and bullying, Oliver Messel had done his conjuring-trick. The Royal Opera House was open again. Our Ballet, soon to become Royal, was installed there in fitting splendour.

When Oliver's production of *The Sleeping Beauty* opened at the Metropolitan Opera House for a season three years later in 1949, Margot Fonteyn wrote of her first night: 'In the audience, applause greeted the Oliver Messel décor before anyone danced a step. When I ran out to the stage there was a burst of sound. It drowned out the music and also some of my mind, for I have never been able to remember anything between those first minutes of deafening applause of my entrance and the incredible reception after the third act *pas de deux*.'

If it seemed that Oliver, his taste, his industry and his unquestioned artistry had reached a peak, there were still other heights, other acclaims and greater successes in store for him. His next production, in 1947, was the Covent Garden *Magic Flute* for which he received unprecedented reviews: 'An austerely mounted *Zauberflöte* would be an absurdity, and Oliver Messel's decor is sumptuous, extravagant, fantastic, and for the most part appropriate,' the *New Statesman* announced. 'By what will the 1947 production be remembered?' asked *The Daily Telegraph*. 'First of all by Oliver Messel's decorations which – though too rich and fanciful, save for those who regret the severity of the 1939 scenery – are surely as beautiful as any there have been in 150 years of *Magic Flutes*.' And *The Stage*: 'The true hero of this production is Oliver Messel, whose scenes have a beauty, dignity, and spaciousness that have surely seldom been equalled – at least in opera. Indeed, their magnificence is sometimes to put the general ensemble out of joint by slightly dwarfing the singers. Only protagonists and superhumans could fitly grace these pictures. There is nothing superhuman about our native singers and Mr Messel has put them under severe obligations by paying them such a handsome compliment.'

There now followed other opportunities to design for the movie medium. In 1946 he designed Sally Gray's costumes for the Two Cities film, *Carnival*, based on Compton Mackenzie's novel, and the following year Anatole de Grunwald commissioned him to design the production of *The Queen of Spades*, which was to star Anton Walbrook and to give Edith Evans her first opportunity to appear in films. (He designed the opera production of it three years later at Covent Garden.) Oliver worked in close collaboration on the film with the art director, William Kellner:

Oliver: I first met William Kellner after I had been released from the Army to undertake the designing of *Caesar and Cleopatra*. William Kellner was assigned to assist me in translating my designs for Cleopatra's elaborate palace in Alexandria into plastic form in scale models and plans.

His architectural knowledge and meticulous eye for detail at once won my appreciation, and, therefore when embarking upon the designs for my next film production, I was anxious to secure his services – this time in the capacity of art director.

If I make a design I discuss it with Kellner and have complete confidence that he will help me put it into practical form exactly as I would wish. At the same time, without in a selfish way imposing another viewpoint, he will give his suggestions and 'fuse the work', as it were, with his own resources of architectural knowledge and practical experience. While seeing the atmosphere that I have drawn come to life, it is often my delight to be surprised with some beautifully executed detail which has automatically taken shape under the guidance of his watchful eye.

We worked on *The Queen of Spades* at Welwyn Studios, an Associated British-Anatole de Grunwald production, adapted for the screen by Rodney Ackland and Arthur Boys, from the short story by Pushkin. It was directed by Thorold Dickinson.

The story is macabre, set in St Petersburg in the early nineteenth century. The dramatic atmosphere is heightened by touches of the supernatural.

The strong contrast between the extravagance of the aristocracy and the squalor of the serfs afforded Oliver particularly varied scope as a designer. There

Contessa
visiting Conte di German

Philip Mercer

Messel's costume design (left) for the Countess as a young woman in the film of *The Queen of Spades* directed by Thorold Dickinson in 1948, starring Edith Evans. Right, one of the sets devised by Messel for the film

were scenes in the palace of the old Countess which, in the story, had remained unchanged since the days of her youth. The gilded, rococo elaboration of her state apartments was mellowed under the dust and patina of years, and the vaulted hallway and great staircase of stone struck a more sombre note. There were scenes in a dazzling ballroom introducing the quite different style of architecture which developed under the influence of the Empress Catherine — classical columns of marble as in a Greek temple, standing in a forest of candelabra, formed a background to a lively mazurka.

After filming had completed, Oliver began work on two more stage productions. One, for Cochran, was *Tough at the Top*, destined for the Adelphi Theatre; and the other, *The Lady's Not for Burning* by Christopher Fry, produced by H. M. Tennent, with a cast which included John Gielgud, Pamela Brown, Claire Bloom, Richard Burton, Esme Percy, Nora Nicholson and Harcourt Williams. It became a memorable success both in the West End and on Broadway.

The Lady's Not for Burning, by Christopher Fry (1949), was remembered for the performances of John Gielgud, Pamela Brown and Richard Burton, and for Messel's designs. Photograph by Angus McBean

137

5 * From Fry to fantasy

THE ACCLAIM Oliver received for his work on *The Lady's Not for Burning* followed the pattern of most of his previous productions: 'Oliver Messel's scenery and costumes help to weave a spell of enchantment such as we have not experienced in the West End for many a season,' *Theatre World* reported. And *The Guardian*: 'Mr Oliver Messel's settings and costumes contribute very largely towards the pleasure of the evening.'

He was inundated with congratulatory telegrams: 'They tell me the decor is not for burning. Caryl Brahms.' 'Darling we hope it is a huge and wonderful success for you. Stop. Looking forward to seeing you tonight. Love. Larry and Vivien.' 'My sincerest and deepest thanks for your brilliantly wonderful production for which I am more than grateful. Binkie.' And from the author: 'With all my best wishes and love and deeply felt gratitude. Christopher Fry.'

Sir John Gielgud: The audience liked the romance and colour of *The Lady's Not for Burning*; there had not been a costume play in London for a long time and Oliver Messel had done a most beautiful decor for it — a little too beautiful, I thought afterwards. I had an idea that if it had been staged in modern dress perhaps the meaning of the play would have been clearer. Christopher Fry had been a conscientious objector and his views were reflected in the character I played, a soldier returning from the war, wanting to be hanged in his disillusionment. I thought that if he had come back in battledress, the disowned son of a gentleman who had joined up in the ranks, the message might have been clearer.

Christopher Fry agrees with Sir John that the set might have been a little overwhelming for the subject:

Christopher Fry: I had been given the good fortune of Oliver Messel's designs for *The Lady's Not for Burning* in 1949. The set was enchanting; the inventiveness of it stays in the mind — the hanging birdcage, the shelf behind Tyson's desk, the way to the garden, the feeling of spring. It was all a bit grand and ecclesiastical for an impecunious mayor of a small country town, perhaps. But the charm of it, and particularly the space of sky, by sunlight, rainlight and moonlight, outweighed any such reservations.

After *The Lady's Not for Burning*, Oliver suffered a mild setback. C. B. Cochran's runaway success with the musical *Bless the Bride*, by A. P. Herbert and Vivian Ellis, prompted him to stage another show using the same formula, with Wendy Toye again as director. He chose *Tough at the Top*, his 127th production, which opened at the Adelphi on 15 July 1949. It was the story of a Ruritanian princess who comes to London at the start of the century for the Coronation of

The stars of Christopher Fry's verse play

King Edward, and falls in love with a prizefighter. The princess was played by Maria d'Attili, the petite opera singer from Puerto Rico who had a glorious voice; the boxer by an American star new to Britain, George Tozzi (later he became Giorgio Tozzi — a star of many productions at the Met), who combined a magnificent voice with a physique that any middleweight might have envied. Once again, the laurels went to Oliver, as *The Stage* reported:

Oliver Messel's decorations are of the most handsome order. Pomania (the country in which the story is set) though precariously situated at the turn of the century between those ancient enemies France and Germany, must have been a lovely country to live in. Its little court, too, was maintained on the grandest Ruritanian scale.

The show failed completely to repeat the success of *Bless the Bride*, but Oliver was in greater demand than ever. During the 1950s he undertook so many commissions that he may well have set a record. There were over seventy,

One of Messel's most typically inventive designs was for Act III of *Ring Round the Moon*, by Jean Anouilh (1950). Opposite, Claire Bloom as Isabella

including plays, operas, ballets and interior design. It is little wonder that his health should have been affected, particularly since he had a history of illnesses since the time of his tuberculosis in childhood.

His first work in 1950 was to design the sets and costumes for the H. M. Tennent production of Jean Anouilh's *Ring Round the Moon*, translated by Christopher Fry. It opened at the Globe Theatre on 26 January 1950 and was one of Oliver's favourite creations. Its cast included Paul Scofield, Margaret Rutherford, Claire Bloom and Mona Washbourne.

Christopher Fry felt that if Oliver's set-designs had not been tethered by practical commonsense they might have lifted off the stage altogether. This was certainly the impression given by the design for *Ring Round the Moon*, the most successful of his three collaborations with Fry. His Muse or Genius seemed in this instance to have appeared on the stage without human aid. The delicacy, wit and 'visible music' of his art seemed quite effortless, both in the set and in the costumes.

Ring Round the Moon was directed by Peter Brook, with whom Oliver was to work again later on three other productions — *The Little Hut*, *The Dark is Light Enough* and *House of Flowers*.

Oliver: I loved working with Peter Brook because he and I worked in absolute sympathy with one another. He is wonderfully sensitive. I am an absolute bundle of nerves on starting on any new project and feel, 'Oh God, nothing is good enough. Nothing is going to be up to the standard that I want it to be.' I need help and encouragement because I deflate myself terribly. Peter Brook is wonderfully susceptible to that. He flatters and cajoles, makes everyone feel, 'This is going to be splendid.' And then he eggs one on. Instead of trying to clip your wings and come up with something less imaginative, he likes to turn one inside-out and do something that's a little bit stranger and more exaggerated — to me, of course, that is more fun. He sees the whole story in a visual way. He will see everything I have done in drawings — and then agree when he feels I am in accord with his own vision of the piece. I know that he would light everything to perfection even if I wasn't there. He gives one a secure feeling. It's not a battle, trying to urge your opinion against someone else's.

The setting Oliver designed for *Ring Round the Moon*, recalled as an emblem of absolute fantasy, culminated in a memorable, magnificent fireworks display. 'Mr Oliver Messel's exquisitely arranged winter garden, though little changed from scene to scene, never wearies the eye', *The Times* reported, 'and seems indeed to be completely refreshed by the charming display of fireworks which serves in the end the purpose of wedding bells.'

The actual construction of the set, which was intended to suggest an extremely delicate conservatory, presented a basic problem. According to Peter Glenville, the scene builders first approached insisted that it should be constructed of wooden hoops, whereas Oliver felt that the effect he desired could only be achieved with metal. 'His persistence won out. He discovered a new and little-known scene builder who was willing to carry out his idea. The result was a classic — a triumph of elegance and originality.'

It was also an innovation. Years later, Sean Kenny used the same kind of steel structure in his set for the musical *Oliver!*, and designers to this day rely on the device Oliver worked out for his superstructure.

It was described as the prettiest thing Oliver had ever designed. He had rarely had such universally favourable reviews, and it was not surprising that the production ran in London for eighteen months.

At this time he also undertook his next interior decoration commission. On 9 March 1950, the King and Queen were hosts to the President of the French Republic and his wife, Madame Auriol, at a ballet gala performance at the Royal Opera House, Covent Garden, and Oliver was asked to design the Royal box for the occasion.

He first conferred with Norman Hartnell, the royal dress-designer, in order to make sure that the curtains of the Royal box and other ornamentation of the house should not clash with the dresses worn by the Queen and the Princesses. The French Embassy was consulted about the gown to be worn by Mme Auriol.

The Royal Opera House had rarely presented as sumptuous an appearance as on the occasion of that Royal Command ballet. In the entrance hall, the tent-

Messel's design for the gala programme at the Royal Opera House on 9 March 1950 during the State Visit of Vincent Auriol, President of France, and Mme Auriol. Overleaf: Messel's decoration of the Royal Box for this state occasion

ROYAL OPERA

COVENT GARDEN
Thursday March 9th
1950

drapery in white and pale blue, and the splendid banks of camellias on the staircase, were temporary; but much of the decoration of the foyer was to remain. The walls, formerly cream, had been repainted pale blue and white, the pilasters had been marbled with gilt capitals, crimson curtains had been introduced, and the lighting greatly improved. The magnificent chandelier was not only cleaned, but its illumination so rearranged that it actually glittered for the first time. The wall brackets, previously black with discoloration, were regilded and fitted with burnished steel mirror backings, so that, almost unnoticed before, they were now seen to be very handsome objects.

Much excellent furniture, *objets d'art*, and pictures, lent by the Victoria and Albert Museum and by a number of collectors, gave the foyer an unusually well-furnished appearance. One of the light fittings of a gold-cage with an exquisite ornamental bird inside, made by Oliver, so captivated the Queen in the Royal box that Oliver presented it to her. She has it to this day.

A huge crowd cheered the royal party as they arrived at the Opera House. Inside, the stalls were ablaze with diamond tiaras. The Duchess of Westminster was there, wearing two diamond wings in her hair, and a magnificent emerald necklace. Lady Diana Cooper wore pink flowers in her hair, and a pink-and-black dress with a blue fox cape. Oliver's sister, the Countess of Rosse, wore the famous Womersley emeralds, left in trust to the Earl of Rosse's family: of tiara, necklace and earrings — probably the finest in the world.

As for the programme itself, leading dancers of the Royal Ballet performed divertissements. Among the artists were Beryl Grey, who recalls the event:

Beryl Grey: Among the dancers were Elaine Fifield, Margot Fonteyn — in the middle — Rowena Jackson, Nadia Nerina, Svetlana Beriosova — and Philip Chapfield who was my partner. Oliver had designed the costumes with a lovely long line to the bodice reaching down to very, very long tutus. The bodice had elastic which helped to retain its long line. I had an exquisite head-dress complemented exactly by the replica of its design in the necklace — and long earrings. Of course, at the dress-rehearsal all the jewellery went swinging around! When you swung one way, the necklace went the other way, for instance. But he resolved the problem by fixing the necklace onto flesh-coloured mesh in time for the actual performance.

Despite the West End success of *Ring Round the Moon*, the New York production that opened in autumn 1950 at the Martin Beck Theatre did so without Peter Brook's direction or Oliver's enchanting scenery. The original jewel-like set had been made stodgy; the Dufy backdrops were charming but somewhat irrelevant.

Gilbert Miller, who presented the play on Broadway, had written to Oliver earlier in the year:

> I find to my great regret that you have still not joined the Designers' Union in New York. This means that I could use your designs here but would have to give the credit for them to another designer who belonged to the Union, and even this would have to be done somewhat *sub rosa*, as a member of the Designers' Union here is not supposed to use the designs of another who does not belong to the Union.

Miller went on to explain that he could not get around the ruling in the same way as he had done fourteen years before with *The Country Wife,* since he had already contracted American artists for his forthcoming production. Furthermore, if Oliver wished to have his name among the credits, he would have to leave for New York immediately and become a member of the Union. This would require his taking an examination for which the lists were to close within four weeks. Oliver declined the invitation, but was somewhat mollified by another production of *Ring Round the Moon* at the Folke Theatre in Copenhagen the following year — with his set, and with his name as its designer.

At about this time he became involved in another *contretemps* with the Americans. For nearly fifty years, George S. Kaufman matched his phenomenal talents as playwright and director with the genius of people like Marc Connelly, Morrie Ryskind, Edna Ferber, Moss Hart, John Steinbeck, Ben Hecht, and Charles MacArthur to bring the curtain up on such hits as *Dinner at Eight, You Can't Take It with You, Of Mice and Men, The Man Who Came to Dinner,* and *The Front Page.* Another great success, *Guys and Dolls,* opened at the 46th Street Theatre on 24 November 1950; it ran for 1,200 performances and made a net profit of almost two million dollars — excluding film rights.

Two young American producers, Cy Feuer and Ernest Martin, presented *Guys and Dolls,* based on a short story by Damon Runyon — and Kaufman directed it. When the show was being prepared for its projected London opening at the Coliseum, Martin and Kaufman went to see Oliver whom they wanted to design the West End production. They knew that Oliver was highly placed socially and a friend of the royal family — and they also knew that he could be inflexible about his own ideas for work he undertook. On the way to see Oliver, Kaufman kept reminding Martin to be as agreeable as possible, but it was Kaufman who objected when Oliver wanted to retain a scene which Kaufman had cut, because Oliver thought it would make a 'great' set.

'You want me to leave in a bad scene,' Kaufman asked, 'just so you can have an excuse for a set?'

Needless to say, as Oliver could not get his way, he refused their offer.

Before he embarked on his next production for 1950, he undertook a couple of private commissions. He set about the decorations of his sister Anne's bedroom at Birr Castle, containing a gold 'gothic' fourposter in white and gold, and orange walls. The ballroom he decorated for Lady Marriott's party in London involved his connecting the back of her house and the sides of the two neighbouring houses, giving it a tent-like effect with silk hangings concealing the outside walls, and chandeliers adding a soft glow. Lady Marriott was the daughter of Otto Kahn, an exceedingly rich New York banker. Known as 'Momo' to her friends, she married Major General Sir John Marriott, who came from Stowmarket in Suffolk. Although Momo was considered to be basically lazy, she gave elaborate parties which were attended by London's social figures.

His next assignment was for the Edinburgh Festival, where he designed the Glyndebourne production of Richard Strauss's *Ariadne auf Naxos* which ran from 21 August to 9 September 1950. Under Professor Carl Ebert's artistic direction and conducted by Sir Thomas Beecham, the opera proved to be one of the most exciting events of that year's Festival. It was a hopeful sign to audiences at Edinburgh and Glyndebourne that a theatrical designer of taste and experience had been discovered; in the long run, his arrival on the scene at Glyndebourne appeared to be of more significance than the conducting of Sir Thomas Beecham.

Derek Granger, theatre critic, former literary adviser to the National Theatre and subsequently television producer (notably of Evelyn Waugh's *Brideshead Revisited*) contributed to the 1955 Glyndebourne Festival Programme Book an assessment of Oliver's value:

Oliver had done little for opera until Glyndebourne asked him to design *Ariadne auf Naxos* in 1950. The decision to accept faced him with a series of new artistic problems, but it may well have seemed inevitable that one day Messel and Glyndebourne should find and adopt each other. Here, on the one hand, the designer who in another age would surely have been the engineer of Pageants and Triumphs, Court Masques and *Fêtes Galantes* — who, even in these cramped times, could turn his hand with equal facility to the decorations of a Royal box or a worker's canteen. Here, on the other hand, the rural Opera House, still subsisting miraculously on private patronage, still showing itself proud enough to aim only at perfection, even sometimes suggesting, on a fair summer night, a touch of some orderly and very English *fête champêtre*.

Oliver: My first introduction to Glyndebourne was through *Ariadne auf Naxos*. Audrey and John Christie came to see me. They had just arranged with the great Sir Thomas Beecham to conduct the full original version of the Strauss opera. Sir Thomas was a three-star delight, endless fount of knowledge and non-stop entertainment. I couldn't bear to miss any rehearsals — they were always full of incident and often outrageous scenes. Although he was particularly averse to directors, he was wonderful to me, thank God. On occasion he would pitch in mercilessly to Carl Ebert, which I sometimes couldn't help enjoying, for although I was fond of Carl, he had that certain Germanic humbug which could be quite maddening at times.

In 1934, when Fritz Busch agreed to take charge of the first Glyndebourne Festival productions (a fortnight's season of two Mozart operas, *Figaro* and *Così Fan Tutte*), he asked Max Reinhardt to mount the productions. Reinhardt's fee, however, was out of all proportion to the small budget of the new Festival Opera, so Busch recruited a Reinhardt disciple instead. This was Carl Ebert, who, like Busch and for the same reasons, was now in voluntary exile from Germany. Ebert, whom Busch described as 'a big man of handsome appearance, not unconscious of this quality', was then 47; he had enjoyed a successful career as an actor before his appointment in 1927 as Generalintendant of what one might call the 'dual purpose' Hessische Landestheater in Darmstadt brought him into close professional contact with opera as well as drama. As an actor in 1922, his experience in the part of the Narrator in the first German production of Stravinsky's *L'Histoire du Soldat* had first made him think of becoming an opera producer, but it was not until he had been at Darmstadt for a couple of years — learning while earning, so to speak — that he finally had the chance to direct *Figaro* as his first opera production.

With the exceptions of John Gielgud's production of *The Beggar's Opera* in 1940 and Eric Crozier's of *The Rape of Lucretia* in 1946, Professor Carl Ebert had produced all the productions for Glyndebourne by the time Oliver was commissioned to design *Ariadne auf Naxos* in 1950.

Oliver: Carl Ebert opposed my ideas all the time — then later blindly claimed

Ariadne auf Naxos, the opera by Richard Strauss, was produced at the Edinburgh Festival with Messel designs in 1950.

them as his own. Something of a friendly war ensued between us, but led us to a successful partnership in the years to come over many productions all the same.

The *Bourgeois Gentilhomme* introduction to *Ariadne* gave great scope for an endearing performance by Miles Malleson, who also adapted the Molière play.

I couldn't claim or consider myself to be musical at all, and have little musical knowledge or coherent memory for music, yet somehow it is music and working for operas and ballets that I have most loved. From the start, the time spent with the conductors has been something that has remained in my mind and that I have appreciated so much: those hours with dear Fritz Busch, Sir Thomas Beecham, Constant Lambert, Robert Irving, for instance. I think of the conductor Vittorio Gui in the candlelit room and cosy atmosphere of my home in Pelham Place as he played through the scores of Rossini's *Cenerentola* and *Le Comte Ory*. The music seems to help by forming pictures, elusive as in a dream. These I try to capture long enough until they can materialize, however vaguely, as a scribble on paper.

Oliver had been developing a penchant for creating exotic 'garden' designs of Caribbean, desert island fantasy, and this flair could not have been more aptly displayed than in his settings for his next three-year run in the West End. This time the play was André Roussin's *The Little Hut*, adapted from the French by Nancy Mitford, and again the director was Peter Brook.

There was some anxiety on the tour, however, when the production reached Glasgow, and Peter Brook wrote to Oliver on 1 August 1950:

For the past week I've been to every performance of *The Little Hut*. The play is going extremely well, and, I think, improving the whole time. Anyway, we're rehearsing very hard. Also I've had the opportunity of watching the set and every prop very closely. As you know only too well, there is an enormous amount of work

Messel's drawing for the monkey costume in André Roussin's *The Little Hut*, translated and adapted by Nancy Mitford

to be done by everyone before the set begins to recapture the enchantment of your model. As it stands at the moment, there are so many crudities in the building and painting and so many things unfinished that I am very glad we are so far from London. Thank God, there is little chance of anyone we know seeing it before we've been able to get it completely right . . .

I can't stress too much how many things need your attention and how little time we have left. Can you come and see the show again, either this week, or alternatively come with me to Newcastle at the end of next week. I'm very sorry to worry you with all this when you have so much on your mind [preparing forthcoming productions for Glyndebourne and Covent Garden]. But with *Ring Round the Moon* as a standard of comparison only two doors away I am desperately jealous for your reputation. Whether your success is maintained in this or not depends solely on how exquisitely you get your craftsmen to put their finishing touches. The least tattiness or lack of finish, and the whole show is down the drain.

Oliver responded to Peter Brook's call and set about the adjustments with his usual, meticulous care, supported by two craftsmen, Hugh Skillen and Stanley Hall of Wig Creations.

Stanley Hall: One of the great influences in my life was Oliver. I had been very lucky working at Denham Studios in the 'thirties, the halcyon days of Alexander Korda films, creating make-up and wigs for those wonderful period films *Rembrandt*, *Victoria the Great*, *The Thief of Baghdad*, and films with Indian and African settings and international stars. The fabulous days I enjoyed so much ended when I joined the army.

After the war I met and worked with Oliver on many productions. He followed every design through the laborious stages from sketch to fully dressed achievement and knew exactly how materials behave.

His talents amazed me and his artistry helped me to bring an added dimension to my own endeavours. He was only satisfied by the ultimate, and although his attention to the smallest detail may have meant remaking a wig or costume or head-dress three times over (which naturally didn't endear him to some of the craftsmen; they weren't paid any more either), he improved each small detail and the final result made all his work force very proud of their achievements. We sat back in the theatre or cinema with a satisfied feeling and were proud to have had the opportunity to contribute to his magnificent efforts.

He could make or 'mock up' anything from wigs to costumes and sets, and in this way he helped and encouraged his workers and taught them how to extend their potential. In wig-making one uses a block — a formless head — but Oliver made up heads and shoulders with faces, a complete bust in *papier mâche* so that one could see the final effect of the wig even before fitting it on the artist.

The Little Hut ended with an amusing monkey, played by William Chappell, climbing down a palm tree on the stage. Oliver asked me to make a monkey mask and this I created in life-like animated rubber. Hugh Skillen was the most wonderful maker of head-dresses and stage jewellery, and Oliver always insisted on working with him on productions. He liked to have the same work force around him, tried and trusted friends who were prepared to work with him, often in the realm of his wonderland.

He had asked Hugh to make the monkey costume but when he saw my mask and the Skillen costume, Oliver decided that Skillen and I should change roles and so I made the costumes by having hair 'knotted', or 'woven', into a leotard and Skillen made a *papier mâché* monkey mask which just stared at the audience, not like the realistic one I had made. Oliver was right — he didn't want a 'real' monkey but a fantasy one which rounded off the witty play as the curtain fell.

The first official mention of Hugh Skillen as assisting Oliver in his capacity as a maker of masks and head-dresses was in connection with the production of *Comus* (1942). He was also involved in a number of Messel's commissions in later years, including *The Sleeping Beauty*, *The Queen of Spades*, *Ring Round the Moon* and *The Little Hut*, and his creations, while recognizably Messel's in style, showed Skillen's own ingenuity and skills. His head-dresses were so light and so excellent in construction that artists found them comfortable and even exciting to wear. For Oliver's production of *Der Rosenkavalier* (1959) he made the exquisite Silver Rose, used in the 'presentation' scene in the second act; he highlighted it with gold and sequins, creating an impression of dew on the rose-petals.

At the end of 1950, Covent Garden presented its first ever production of Tchaikovsky's *The Queen of Spades*, directed by the late Michael Benthall, a prolific theatre director with many West End successes and several productions at the Old Vic to his credit. As Oliver had designed the sets and costumes for the film version of this Pushkin story the year before, he was the obvious choice for the opera version. The costumes were made by Olivia Cranmer, and the wigs and make-up were created by Stanley Hall.

Edith Coates sang the role of the Countess, played on the screen by Edith Evans, and the part performed by Anton Walbrook was sung by Edgar Evans.

The tale revolves around the old Countess Ravevskaya who, as a young and beautiful woman, had been betrayed and, in order to raise the money to cover up her indiscretion, sold her soul to the devil in return for a secret of winning at cards.

Herman, an army officer of slender means, reads the fortunes of a Countess in a very old book of strange happenings and immediately relates this in his mind to the Countess Ravevskaya. In order to gain access to her household, he successfully courts her young companion, and arranges with her to enter the house at night. But instead of going to her room he finds his way into the bedroom of the old Countess, whom he implores to give him the secret of the three winning cards. This she cannot do, because her very existence depends on her keeping the secret. Herman persists with entreaties and promises, and finally threats; but still she will not give in. When he becomes violent she dies of shock, without having spoken a word. In his demented state he hears a ghost voice which seems to be hers, giving him the secret of the three cards.

In the following scene he excitedly plays the three cards in a game with his fellow officers, and wins repeatedly. He amasses a great fortune and gambles this on a last throw, but when the third card comes up, to his horror it is the dreaded Queen of Spades — and he loses everything. The ghost-voice of the dead Countess is heard cackling with glee in the knowledge that her secret is safe.

The most significant scene, that of the Countess's death, was a masterly conception; Oliver placed her in a giant armchair, thus creating the illusion of her shrunken image.

The Royal Opera production of *The Queen of Spades*; Messel's design for Act I, Scene I

Opposite, Olivia de Havilland in Peter Glenville's short-lived production of *Romeo and Juliet* on Broadway (1951). Messel, a long-time friend of Glenville's, was responsible for the sets and costumes.

Stanley Hall: I loved working with Oliver on the film of *The Queen of Spades*: he created such a wonderful atmosphere with the sets and costumes, which were exactly right for this powerful and dramatic story. I was therefore very excited to work on the opera at Covent Garden, because in this vast auditorium it was a challenge to be able to exaggerate the details. Edith Coates, the Countess, was a large, 'comfortable' opera singer and one needed to give the impression of a very old and shrivelled woman. Oliver designed her clothes so that she looked absolutely weighed down by them and I made her wigs so vast that you felt she could hardly support all these trappings — a just punishment for having sold her soul to the devil! The make-up, which had to be heavy to be effective from the back of the Opera House, was white and cracked. I mixed an almost purple shadow so that I could shade her face away to look like a skull, and applied a large false nose to reduce the size of the rest of the face, and painted and shaded the muscles and sinews on her neck, and even emphasized all the ribs which could be seen because of the low-cut dress. I fixed long witch-like false nails and made up the hands to look like old claws. As I was doing the make-up for each performance, I had a pair of flesh-coloured net gloves made in order to save time. On these I painted the craggy 'claws' and attached the fingernails to the gloves so that she could just peel on the ready-prepared old hands.

Following an exhibition at the Redfern Galleries entitled 'Designs for a Cochran production', Oliver set off for New York to work on a new production of *Romeo and Juliet*, which opened at the Broadhurst Theatre on 10 March 1951 with Olivia de Havilland and Douglass Watson. Although the production did not catch the public's fancy, Oliver's sets added to his reputation. The production was directed by Peter Glenville, who felt that Oliver had used his great taste and flair to bring to life the 'fair Verona where we lay our scene' in the spirit of Benozzo Gozzoli and other painters of the Renaissance, but that he had also kept

Messel's model for the 1951 production of Mozart's *Idomeneo* at Glyndebourne

in mind the swift-moving action, the upstairs gallery and the forestage of the Elizabethan theatre to which Shakespeare moulded his dramatic technique.

In order to be able to design these sets directly for the Broadway production, Oliver submitted to the examinations required by the Designers Union for membership. Though he jibbed at some of the tasks involved in this process, there was never any doubt of his being passed for membership, and from then on he was free to exercise his art and crafts in the United States without any hindrances. Indeed, as Peter Glenville put it, 'The Union and its President generously and rather proudly welcomed Oliver into their fold.'

On his return to England Oliver cemented his connection with the Glyndebourne Festival Opera company by designing a new production of Mozart's *Idomeneo*. This was planned for Glyndebourne's twelfth Mozart season (summer 1951), and the repertoire included three other Mozart operas, *The Marriage of Figaro, Così Fan Tutte* and *Don Giovanni*.

Oliver: In designing for the theatre I divide myself in two. One half has to visualize and plan out the creative part and produce the designs; the other has to elaborate in detail and invent new ways to interpret those designs.

I have almost always gone through an agony like childbirth in the first capacity. The greater the experience, the worse it can be each time to attempt not to repeat what has been done before. A straightforward realistic setting, of course, does not have half the appeal or challenge of something intangible.

I had to design two of the operas at Glyndebourne for that season, *Idomeneo* and *Don Giovanni*, at the same time, but because of illness I had to give one up. I decided to do *Don Giovanni* in preference to *Idomeneo* for the reason that, having survived so successfully, it must be the better. Fritz Busch, however, changed my mind by telling me that *Idomeneo*, Mozarts first *opera seria*, was nearest to his heart, on account of certain handicaps in the rather stilted book, which required many changes of scene. When first produced it had failed and it had been regarded ever since as unproduceable. 'If you could work out some solution to the scenic problems, so that the music could flow without interruption and make the opera a success', Busch said, 'it would be more rewarding than to design one more production of *Don Giovanni*.'

And so I set to work on *Idomeneo*, for which the main simplified settings were built in slight relief, using steep perspectives as in Palladio's Teatro Olimpico in Vicenza. Echoes of Veronese and Tintoretto, but seen through eighteenth-century eyes.

I was devoted to Fritz Busch and he played the score through to me when I was in New York working on *Romeo and Juliet*. It was one of those evenings that stand out in my mind. Its special atmosphere made complete concentration on the music possible, and somehow I was then able roughly to plan out the production in that one night. The superb cast included the exquisite artistry of Sena Jurinac, Richard Lewis, and the first appearance in England of Birgit Nilsson as Electra.

Messel's design for Lady Diana Cooper's costume as Tiepolo's Cleopatra, worn to the Bestegui ball in Venice (1951)

Later in 1951 Oliver was once more enticed back to his beloved city, Venice. The millionaire Don Carlos de Bestegui was planning 'The Party of the Century' at his newly restored Palazzo Labia, which boasted some of the finest frescoes by Tiepolo. For a month Venice became the gayest city in Europe. The guests, including Oliver, arrived at the house-warming by gondola on the Canareggio, and supped on caviar, lobster and champagne. Outside the Palazzo, Bestegui provided free wine and salami for the native population of Venice, along with a greasy pole which they could climb up in search of prizes. There were reports that the fountains were filled with wine.

Lady Diana Cooper, acting as hostess for Bestegui, received his guests in a Cleopatra costume of delicate silver-blue with panniers of old rose, designed by Oliver in the style of Tiepolo, and a wig created by Stanley Hall. The Aga Khan, wearing the robes of an Eastern potentate, was the escort of Princess Radziwill. Princess Aspania of Greece, mother-in-law of ex-King Peter of Yugoslavia, arrived in costume, and Oliver attended in a rich red velvet uniform coat which had once belonged to a Bohemian prince.

The party, as expected, went on until dawn.

A new play, which was to be one of Oliver's favourites (though not one of his successes), was planned for an opening early in 1952 by H. M. Tennent's. This was *Under the Sycamore Tree*, by the American playwright Sam Spewack. His comedy took place in the throne room of a queen ant, and with all Oliver's inventiveness of decor and costumes, the imagination of Peter Glenville's production and delicate performances by Alec Guinness, Diana Churchill and Clive Morton, it could scarcely fail to arouse interest. When the curtain rose at the premiere, there was spontaneous applause at the brilliance of the scene framed in the twisted roots of a tree. Here a colony of ants have been dwelling in happy accord until a scientist (Guinness) comes among them and persuades them to imitate human beings.

A costume design by Messel for the play *Letter from Paris*, by Dodie Smith (1952)

Messel putting the final touches to the decor for a function at the Dorchester Hotel. Photograph by Snowdon

Peter Glenville: The play was a satire on the human condition. The action was described as taking place in the maze of rooms and corridors of a vast and modern hotel. The *dramatis personae* were a swarm of ants behaving more or less as ants could comically be perceived to behave. The text was funny and imaginative. I discussed a possible production with Oliver and he agreed to work on the play if, instead of a hotel, the action could take place in a real ant colony below ground; and if all the characters could be dressed to suggest humanized ants; and so it was done – naturally with the author's consent. Alec Guinness was a splendid hero, and the final visual effect was a feast of fancy and of wit.

However, *Under the Sycamore Tree* did not fare well, nor did Oliver's next assignment, *Letter from Paris*, an adaptation by Dodie Smith of Henry James's novel *The Reverberator* about the snobbery surrounding the marriage of certain Americans into the best French families. Set in the 1880s, Oliver's costumes were somewhat reminiscent of Manet and Renoir and found favour with the *Daily Mail* who reported, 'I suppose the real star is Mr Oliver Messel who did the dresses and decor. He smothers the inadequate action with his astonishing sets.'

Undeterred by the fate of the play, Oliver gave a sumptuous party at his Pelham Place house, and flew six flamenco artists in from Spain to be his guests of honour. He decorated the interior of his house in the spirit of Spanish Carnival and his guests included Godfrey Winn, Emlyn Williams, Cecil Beaton, the Spanish Ambassador Duke Primo de Rivera and virtually anyone of note who was in London on that date. He had become well-known for his parties, and this one was considered to have topped the lot,, with Pastora Imperio (the Pavlova of flamenco) and her team entertaining the guests all night.

The Victoria and Albert catalogue tells of Oliver's widening range of interests at this period. Having become much sought after for the design of plays, ballets, opera and films, Oliver, who had a feeling for grand occasions like the gala evenings at Covent Garden, lavish marriage receptions and balls, enjoyed dressing such settings with some form of tenting to disguise the customary lines and accentuate the new figuration with flowers, special lighting effects, and festooned fabrics. When he decorated the American Ambassador's house in Regent's Park he spent a great deal of time in Kensington Church Street hiring as many chandeliers as he could. He fitted these with candles, creating an unusually glittering effect.

His other work in the decorative arts included the design of textiles, furniture and metalwork. He received his first commission for textile design in 1952 – the printed silk scarf designed for Cresta Silks to commemorate the Coronation of Queen Elizabeth II. It was printed in gold; and for the Silver Jubilee, twenty-five years later, he used the same design printed in silver for Berne Silks.

In the early 'fifties, Oliver began an association of several years with the silk-making firm, Sekers, of Whitehaven, Cumberland. According to Lady Agi Sekers, her husband Miki (the late Sir Nicholas Sekers) had studied textiles in Germany and was in charge of a silk-mill in Budapest before he accepted the offer of the British government in the 1930s to set up a mill in West Cumberland. Hungarian experts trained the unemployed in a disused undertaker's shop while the building went up, and by 1939 these men and women were weaving the finest parachute silk for the RAF. Meanwhile, Sekers experimented with the use of nylon and became the first to develop drip-dry easy care fabrics with a sumptuous

appearance ideal for the theatre and ballet. He was a great supporter of the theatre and regularly supplied Covent Garden and Glyndebourne with fabrics; it was at the Glyndebourne Festival Opera that he and Oliver met.

Sekers had established the Friends of Glyndebourne in the early post-War period and Oliver gave luncheon-parties to a mixture of would-be patrons — friends, industrialists, music-lovers and socialites. He garlanded the tables with fresh flowers, antique china, glass, silver and a selection of foods from many countries to meet the tastes of the international visitors.

Having seen some of Oliver's striking stage designs, Sekers believed that Oliver could provide him with world's most glamorous silks and asked him to work for the firm. 'It's no use,' Oliver protested. 'I know nothing about weaving or materials.' But Sekers, knowing all about such matters, persuaded him to tackle the job. They planned to make their work the big surprise of the Coronation year (1953) spring collections, and the couturiers John Cavanagh and Worth designed the dresses. The colours chosen by Oliver turned out to be breathtaking — the most delicate pink-golds, blue-golds, oyster-silvers — in fabrics which were equally beautiful on both sides. He gave the designs easily remembered names: *Jewels, Scattered Leaves, Miniver* and *Twigs* — perfectly describing the patterns. He turned out designs fit for a Queen — and the Queen's designer, Hartnell, began using them.

Messel, Graham Sutherland and Cecil Beaton examining Messel's 'Coronation' silk design at the Seker Exhibition in London, 1959

A Seker's fabric promotion
designed by Messel

The firm of Sekers was also involved in Oliver's largest decorative commission in London, undertaken for the Dorchester Hotel. This has been described in an article by Marjorie Lee:

His brief was to build a luxury apartment, one which he himself would be happy to live in. The suite he created was named after him and has become world-famous. It was opened in 1953 in time for the Coronation and is still as designed by him.

Consisting of one large sitting room, one double and one single bedroom and two bathrooms, the suite has a balcony all around the outside wide enough to take garden furniture, tubs and window boxes of flowers with climbing roses and other climbing plants to cover the trellis work which surrounds the outside walls of the suite. . . . Above the fireplace [in the sitting room] is a

The garden balcony that forms part of the Penthouse, designed by Messel at the Dorchester Hotel in 1953

seventeenth-century mirror, and against the wall between the smaller french windows stands an ornate eighteenth-century Italian gilt marble-topped table. . . . On the walls hang two of Oliver's own paintings depicting seventeenth-century garden scenes, set in cleverly latticed frames with mirror glass behind the lattice which he designed specially for the room. . . .

The main bathroom is mirror-lined and all the fittings are in gold plate. He used lighting pictures which hang in the bedroom are his original designs for *The Sleeping Beauty* at Covent Garden. He was, much later, to recreate these designs for the ballet when it was put on in New York in the 1970s. Unfortunately he had forgotten that his original designs hung in The Dorchester, otherwise he would have saved himself a lot of work in redoing the sketches.

The main bathroom is mirror-lined and all the fittings are in gold plate. He used lighting fittings made in shell-like shapes and a shell cover for the loo seat.

The party suite Oliver created on the eighth floor known as the Penthouse, he designed for luncheon or dinner parties of up to 18 guests with a miniature garden balcony and pool with playing fountains and Leda and her Swan as the centrepiece. Two cherubs sit on either side of the pool holding urns out of which more fountains play. . . .

The Penthouse itself is a beautiful room designed as a decorative arbour of interlaced branches and leaves, painted light blue and gold on a background of mirrors which reflect the pool and fountains outside. Half birdcages were used for lighting fittings on the walls, which when switched on give the impression of full-rounded birdcages. The door handles are gold-plated birds on twigs and above the fireplace hangs Oliver Messel's own sculpture of Bacchus. . . .

The sitting room of the Oliver
Messel suite

Messel working at the model of
the suite at the Dorchester
which bears his name

The exterior of the Dorchester Hotel was decorated by Messel for the Coronation in 1953

The Penthouse has an adjoining reception room with two lovely mirrors which originally came from the old Assembly Rooms in Bath. . . . In one corner of this room is a Victorian decorative blind which is lit from behind and makes a pleasing contrast to the green moire silk on the walls. . . .

So popular did the Penthouse become that it was decided to ask him to design an additional room which could be used either as a drawing room or a larger dining room to accommodate about 30 people seated or 60 for a reception. Thus the Pavilion Room was added in 1956. Oliver Messel designed an ornate room with all the doors and cupboards painted by himself with *The Magic Flute* as its theme. Mirrors in this room and in the foyer to the suite are framed with leaves which he made from molten rubber on steel wire. When asked why he chose this method, he said he thought it would be cheaper than having the frames carved. 'They turned out to be more expensive,' he confided afterwards.

At that time the Oliver Messel Suite at £25 a day was one of the most expensive to rent in London — equivalent to £500 nowadays. One of its first guests was Marlene Dietrich while she was appearing in cabaret at the Café de Paris, followed by Bob Hope, Danny Kaye, Walt Disney, Elizabeth Taylor and Noël Coward.

Coward, who was a great friend of Oliver's, stayed in the Suite on a number of occasions and in June 1957, when he too was appearing at the Café de Paris, wrote in his diaries, 'I am home in England again installed in the somewhat excessive *luxe* of the Oliver Messel Suite. Apart from the highly coloured decor the rooms are full of flowers from loved ones and outside, London stretches from Hyde Park to St. Paul's. I can see across the grey roofs, green trees, the thick towers of the Chelsea power station, the tall red pencil of Westminster Cathedral, the Abbey, and Big Ben, all glittering in the smokeless air.' During an interview at the time, he remarked as he gazed around at the opulence, 'All this is terribly exotic, but it is not me. Still, I shall try to rise above it.'

At the same time as he was working on the decoration of the Oliver Messel Suite and the Penthouse, Oliver was asked to decorate the exterior of the Dorchester for the Coronation. He designed the front of the hotel as though it were the interior of a theatre, with the bay windows at each side draped like boxes, and the balconies resembling the dress circle and balcony of a theatre similarly draped.

He had been given *carte-blanche* by the builder and proprietor of The Dorchester, Robin McAlpine, who laid down no budget limitations. This may have been an uncharacteristic error of judgment, for Oliver exceeded expectations of expenditure on the various projects by a large margin.

Oliver: After the excitement over the exterior decorations for the Coronation at The Dorchester, the dear scion of the McAlpine family sent for me and explained that, had he been on the spot, he would probably have stopped Robin's extravagance of embarking on such a costly fantasy! However, he told me how pleased he was that Robin had carried the operation through to such spectacular effect and acclaim — and all was forgiven!

The rooms Oliver designed at the Dorchester are still very popular and much in demand. They were lavishly restored in 1981 by the Dorchester (whose

Messel decorating the Pavilion Room at the Dorchester

management were financial backers of the 1983 Oliver Messel exhibition at the Victoria and Albert Museum). All the fabrics Oliver had used in the Penthouse were duplicated and the draperies in the Oliver Messel Suite were substituted with Fortuny fabrics.

Oliver: The whole experience of the work that I did for the Dorchester has been for me one of the happiest memories, entirely on account of all the kindness and consideration that was shown me on all sides. The last frantic week I had to sit up each night without any sleep, but was sustained through the thoughtfulness and hospitality of the management, which was relayed on all sides through the entire staff. Dishes of the rarest caviar and other fortifying delicacies appearing as if by magic, and every possible gesture of hospitality and interest gave help and encouragement over the last finishing touches.

Though Oliver was an unusually assiduous worker, he was unable to cope with the volume of commissions he accepted at this time without help from one or more assistants. His first had been Tony Harris, who worked with him at Yeoman's Row and assisted in making the models for *Helen!* Others were John Claridge, who readily admits how much he learned from Oliver; Desmond Healey, who has become a noted theatre designer and whose work shows a distinct 'Oliver Messel' romantic influence; and Carl Toms, who went to work for Oliver originally for three weeks, and stayed for six years from 1953 to 1958, finding it one of the most rewarding experiences of his life.

Carl Toms had gone to art school in the Midlands and won an entrance to the Royal College of Art when he came out of the army. He went to the Old Vic School for a while when it was run by Michel Saint-Denis, George Devine, Glen Byam Shaw and Margaret 'Percy' Harris, and then on to the Merton Park film studio for a year as a junior art director. This led to an abortive project with Orson Welles, after which he received a telephone call from 'Percy' Harris saying that Oliver needed an assistant for the work he was to do on the Dorchester Hotel and arranged an interview. 'But there was no question of an interview,' Carl Toms says. 'He just started me there and then. He wanted me to make the models for the Dorchester Suite, which I did.' He went to work with Oliver on ballets, operas, plays and musicals, both in Britain and the United States. 'In the process Oliver taught me more about painting, architecture, furniture and costume than I had ever learned before.' Oliver's influence on Toms was most significant, and shows in Toms' work to this day.

Carl Toms: When I have a problem I still find myself wondering what Oliver would have done about it. . . . He had an amazing sensitivity and perception which wasn't in any way intellectual. Oliver could not, and would not try to explain why he had designed a show in a particular way; his language was entirely visual. . . .

He seemed to find his way to the style of presentation of a piece of theatre very tentatively; an outside observer would have got the impression he didn't quite know what he was doing. He would endlessly discard what would seem like brilliant ideas to try yet one more, in case it was better. Books were pored over in a search for things to spark off his imagination. It would often be something unexpected — a corner of a painting, the design on a piece of china, a strange piece of architecture (like for instance the Portuguese railway station which inspired *Ring Round the Moon*) or the postcard of a Raoul Dufy painting (which became the basis for *House of Flowers*). . . .

When the rough model seemed to be what he wanted we would start to make a finished version, replacing the rough pieces with carefully made ones so that it transformed slowly into the finished design. He would draw out each piece on scaled tracing paper, always by hand — he hated rulers, set squares and compasses. This design was then transferred to paper which he then painted in water-colour or sometimes even in oil paint. I then made it into a sturdy piece of model with details like furniture and set dressings — all half inch to one foot scale. I think that this freehand technique was what gave his work that special elusive quality, and a direct freshness, individual to him. This process could be achieved quite rapidly in days or it would take weeks and no one was allowed to see it until it was finished. He had to have total conviction in himself *before* it was presented to the director or the producer. . . .

Although his beautiful costume designs would seem to be, on face value, somewhat vague, he knew exactly what they were to be made of, how they should be cut, and he would choose all the details very carefully. He often made head-dresses, jewellery and masks himself, exquisitely.

Work was interrupted only by the arrival of one of the many celebrities who formed Oliver's circle; at that time it would be Ulanova, Tyrone Power, Eartha Kitt, Lauren Bacall and many of the early Hollywood stars including Gloria Swanson, Charles Chaplin, Marlene Dietrich — and Garbo. Cecil Beaton tended to be rather offhand with Garbo when they met at Oliver's, as he resented her devotion to him. He would vie with Oliver for her attention, snapping and yapping at his host.

Oliver's most admirable quality was found to be his total artistic concentration. When he was engaged in work only the best would do from both himself and his workforce. He found it vital to achieve the highest possible standard and it had to be higher than anyone else's.

Carl Toms: The maddening thing about him was his self-delusion; he had some false values about himself. He believed that he was all sweetness and light and that he was a paper saint — that he couldn't hurt anybody. In fact he thought he was perfect. He couldn't bear any form of criticism and took it rather badly if it had anything to do with his work. I remember saying to him how important it was to know one's own limitations and he said, 'But I haven't got any limitations.' I replied, 'Oliver, that's nonsense. Everybody's got limitations,' and he said, 'Yes. But I haven't.' This would often happen late at night when he would talk the truth but if he had an audience one would never get the truth from him; he did a pretty performance for other people. I preferred that gritty side of him.

He didn't like competition. He hated the thought of being put on one side or forgotten. He had a faultless instinct. When he knew somebody was wrongly cast he would agitate until the management got rid of them. He also believed in

Mock-up of Messel's workroom, made by Carl Toms for the Messel exhibition at the Victoria and Albert Museum in 1983

Jewish flair, and he certainly had it in abundance. He used to say to me, '*You* must have some Jewish blood in you too because you have emotional flair.' I don't know whether I have, but I always had a slight suspicion about my grandfather.

'I don't really care about money,' he would say, but he wanted to be offered enough to flatter himself into believing that he was good. 'They paid a lot of money and that shows they appreciate me.'

Although he would presumably have succeeded all the same without money, because he had built-in determination and his God-given talent, it made a considerable difference having an allowance from a rich family in the early days of his career. Unlike many young designers nowadays, it gave him the chance to educate himself by travelling a lot.

Carl Toms: He used to say to me, 'When I was young I only needed to do one show a year and then go and spend the rest of the summer in Italy.' He stayed with Cole Porter in Venice or with Harold Acton in Florence.

He got to know Marchesa Casati in Venice who became a good friend. When she lived in London later on I said how much I would love to meet her. 'Can't you ask her to tea?' I implored. 'I don't think so, Carly,' he replied. 'I really don't think I could. Hugh Skillen asked her for tea once and she stayed for three days.'

Oliver continued to live in Pelham Place, a haunt of retired colonels and their widowed sisters, in the two adjoining houses. The twenty-four rooms were barely enough to contain his accumulation of Regency furniture, baroque chimney-pieces, model theatres, Egyptian head-dresses, chandeliers, antique costumes, reference books, flowers, Aubusson carpets, portraits and *papier mâché* busts wearing wigs. There were twenty chairs and two sofas in his studio but nowhere to sit. Every seat was piled high with books and cardboard boxes overflowing with feathers, gauzes and sequined materials.

His collection of china and porcelain appears to have been one of the most individual in London. There was Meissen and Minton, Copenhagen and Worcester, Crown Derby and Rockingham. Some were gifts from friends, others family pieces, and some he had found himself in junk shops or at sales. Everything — the seventeenth- and eighteenth-century furniture, the massive gilt looking-glasses, the paintings, the *objets d'art*, the curtains — had a look of great opulence.

Yet in all this profusion financial crises were by no means unknown. During one of the most acute of these a friend opened a drawer in his studio and found it stuffed with unpresented cheques — over £2000 worth. Vagn frequently weathered difficult moments with finds made in the outside pockets of Oliver's jackets; it seemed that as soon as his stiff terms had been accepted he gave no further thought to money, lavishing his time, skill and possessions in a single-minded effort to achieve perfection.

The door at 17 Pelham Place was answered by a smiling, handsome young Dane in a blue striped butcher's apron. He was Leif Hansen who had come from Denmark to work for Oliver and Vagn. When he first arrived at Pelham Place there were six on the permanent staff, and three of them — all Danes — lived in.

An interior view of Messel's home in Pelham Place, London

Mrs Poulson, the Danish housekeeper affectionately known as Polly, had a room next door to the kitchen downstairs and the butler and Leif had rooms on the top floor. The full-time handyman, gardener and general factotum, Mr Potter, also helped with moulding and constructing set models. 'Mr Potter! Mr *Potter!*' Oliver would call in high-pitched panic when needed. Carl Toms and the secretary, Brenda Haydon, both worked long hours, far beyond the call of duty, and escaped to the sanctuary of their homes in the early hours – if they could. When the butler left, Leif took over his duties. *Ad hoc* helpers came in when productions and parties were in full swing.

Leif Hansen: My duties started at eight when I served breakfast but Mr Messel had his around two p.m. – toast, marmalade and tea. He never went to bed until five or six in the morning. On my days off, when I stayed out overnight, I would see his light on when I returned in the morning. If he heard me creeping up the stairs he would call, 'Leif, is that you?' 'Yes, sir.' 'I'm dying for a cup of tea.' 'Yes, sir.' And I'd crawl downstairs to the kitchen trying not to disturb Mrs Poulson.

It was great working there in the beginning, even though the hours were very long and the pay wasn't all that good. When I first went into the house I thought, 'Oh!' It was all a bit dull to me. I was young and not that keen on the Messel taste at first but the longer I stayed and the more I got to know him, the more I learned to appreciate it.

His sofa was like Cleopatra's and he used to lie on it rather like Shirley Bassey in her television shows!

Everyone was treated as an equal and there was no 'upstairs-downstairs' feeling in the house. When Oliver went away to Venice and later on to Barbados, Mr Potter would say, 'Right. The paint work has got to be done,' and the staff scurried around under his direction. The walls and ceilings were scraped, washed and repainted.

Leif Hansen: It never occurred to me that Mr Messel was the boss and I was the butler. There was no division — and he was never familiar with the staff. His irritating qualities came out when he was tired and heavily involved in new productions — if I put a foot wrong he would scold me, but a few minutes later he'd come back and say, 'I'm sorry. I didn't mean it. Forgive me.' He had his ups and downs, but I never actually saw him lose his temper and mostly he was kind and understanding.

Vagn was over six feet tall, heavily built, with blue eyes and fair, greying hair. He was an attractive man with immense charm, and, rather like Oliver, could twist one round his little finger. When Anne and Michael Rosse visited, they would ask, 'Is the Great Dane behaving himself?' They knew that he could be overly assertive at times. As manager and administrator, he was responsible for the outgoings and kept a firm grip on Oliver's income. 'You can't ask that much money for this production,' Oliver might say, realizing all too well that it was the figure that he himself had set, and Vagn would reply, 'It's just too bad because it's what we need to run this household. If they want you, they'll have to pay.'

When the house was sold, he was able to repay the mortage.

Leif Hansen: We were normally paid on the dot but in later years one was aware of the financial difficulties. I often saw Vagn biting his nails and then he would say, 'I've got to go and see the bank manager before lunch. Mix me a drink.' However, once or twice I was asked whether I could wait until the following week for my wages. But it was really Vagn and not Mr Messel who wanted the extravagant parties; the grander the better. He wanted to establish himself as the 'Great Dane'.

Mr Messel would have been happy to live on scrambled eggs, which he loved. He didn't smoke or drink but might have the occasional Dubonnet. On Fridays Vagn would give him a certain amount of money and he'd say, 'That's unfair. It will never see me through the week!' 'Well, it will have to do because it's all you need.' Then he would sulk a bit and Vagn would give in. 'I'll let you have a bit more, but don't spend it all!'

They usually dined together but sometimes Mr Messel would have a meal alone in his studio. Dinner was always at nine o'clock but Vagn was invariably late, which meant that by the time we cleared up there wasn't any spare time left for ourselves. A quick wash and to bed was the order of the day. Vagn was very fond of television and as it was downstairs in the staff room it was difficult to talk among ourselves because he was always there.

Of course I enjoyed meeting all the famous people who came to the house, particularly Princess Margaret.

The Royal Opera House celebrated Coronation Day, 2 June 1953, by mounting a new ballet by Frederick Ashton, happily entitled *Homage to the Queen*. This provided an opportunity for the four principal ballerinas to make their characteristic contributions to the occasion as queens of the four elements, earth,

Homage to the Queen, the ballet by Frederick Ashton, was designed by Messel and given its first performance on Queen Elizabeth's Coronation Day at the Royal Opera House.

water, fire and air — a motif popular at the Court of James I. The Opera House had commissioned Oliver (for a fee of £550) to design the sets and costumes. He evolved a new shape for the ballet tutu — a short depth in the front and, from the continuation of the bodice below the waist, a wide pannier effect — the 'Infanta Line'. Special colours and rich iridescent golden threads had been woven for the ballet by Sekers' West Cumberland Silk Mills. The Sadler's Wells Ballet Company excelled in the *divertissements*; Nadia Nerina danced the Queen of the Earth, with Alexis Rassine as her consort; Violette Elvin was Queen of the Waters, with John Hart; Beryl Grey was Queen of Fire, with John Field; and finally Margot Fonteyn was Queen of the Air, with Michael Somes.

Richard Buckle reported: 'Oliver Messel, an artist in the great tradition of Inigo Jones, adept at producing effects of splendour, fantasy and romance, was

Decoration of the Royal Box at Covent Garden by Messel for the Coronation premiere of Benjamin Britten's opera *Gloriana*

the obvious choice as a designer. Personally I prefer his sets when there are more architectural bones to them; this one, all blue-grey gauze and candles, is so delicate in its wispy *rococo* that it seems to be swooning away into a nostalgic pastel mist. The dresses are rich and imaginative; but as the Air ones are so white, I should have made the Water ones bluer to heighten the final colour-scheme.'

For the Gala Performance six days later of Benjamin Britten's *Gloriana*, composed to celebrate the Coronation, Oliver decorated the Royal Box at Covent Garden. It was the first time in two hundred years that royalty had attended the premiere of a new opera, and Oliver's participation stamped him as 'decorator laureate'. Under his direction, a new Royal Box with twenty-seven seats was built in the centre of the grand tier over three days. Supported on the centre archway, in the form of oak trees in green and gold, he slung a canopy of gold and lined the box with cloth of pale gold, woven especially for the occasion as a gesture from the West Cumberland Silk Mills. He festooned the four tiers of balconies with green garlands and transformed the approach to the box with a garden consisting of masses of summer blooms brought from Nymans. With the Queen were the Duke of Edinburgh, Queen Elizabeth the Queen Mother, Princess Margaret, and also the Princess Royal, the Duke and Duchess of Gloucester and other members of the Royal Family, together with the Crown Prince and Princess of Norway.

Coronation Year turned out to be auspicious for Oliver: the Glyndebourne season that year included his sets and costumes for *La Cenerentola*, *Idomeneo* and *Ariadne auf Naxos* in a season of revivals.

But that year also brought grief upon the death of his father. His obituary in *The Times* concentrated on his horticultural achievements:

The news of the death of Leonard Messel comes as a great blow to those interested in gardening. His father, L. E. W. L. Messel, founded the garden at Nymans. He was a man determined to grow everything that could be grown in the Sussex climate where he lived, and he made a remarkable garden, with many plants in it that no one thought could have survived in the open in that part of England.

His son, Leonard Messel, whose death we now deplore, succeeded his father in 1915, and had the same energy and persistence. The old plants grew apace under his care, and newer plants were added to the collection as they reached this country.

Even when the great disaster overtook Nymans in the burning of the house, rebuilt with taste and care by Leonard Messel, the garden hardly suffered, although the owner had to live in a house close by. In the house, before the fire, there was a wonderful collection of gardening books — old historic volumes being finely represented. They all perished. The taste and knowledge that went to forming the collection of books, and were present in the rebuilding of the house, could be seen throughout the garden.

Leonard Messel was a most generous friend, and anything that he could give to another good garden from his treasury of plants, he gave generously and willingly. He was a man of very many interests, and one who will be greatly missed by many friends in many circles.

Colonel Messel left the gardens of Nymans to the National Trust, together with an endowment of £20,000 for their upkeep. Deputizing for David Bowes-Lyon, the chairman of the joint Gardens Committee of the Royal Horticultural Society and the National Trust, Victoria Sackville-West, owner of the equally famous gardens at Sissinghurst, performed the opening ceremony which was attended by Oliver, his brother Linley and their sister. Anne, Countess of Rosse continues to live at Nymans, between visits to the estates of her late husband at Birr Castle in Ireland and Womersley Park in Yorkshire.

The end of Coronation Year brought with it a minor storm of controversy. King Frederick, the Kabaka of Buganda, had been deposed by Her Majesty's Government on the grounds of his refusal to cooperate with the British Parliament over serious issues concerning his Kingdom, a British protectorate. Oliver, a friend of the Kabaka since school days, abhorred this decision and put into motion steps to have the matter investigated. He also caused a rumpus when the flat he had rented on behalf of King Freddie in Mayfair was suddenly made unavailable to the deposed visitor: a clause in the lease prohibited black tenants. Oliver mustered all possible support from friends in high places and showed the tenacity of which he was capable in a matter of principle.

Model of Messel's exotic
setting for *House of Flowers*,
which opened on Broadway on
30 December 1954

6 * Foreign features

ON THEIR VISIT TO LONDON, the official Buganda delegation issued a statement, copies of which Oliver sent by hand, together with letters of his own, to three Members of Parliament:

Dear Lord Salisbury

With reference to Buganda

I have been asked to send you a copy of a statement which has been made to the press today by the delegates from Buganda.

Being very anxious to cause no possible antagonism, they wish to make clear their views simply so that something can be known of what they are here about.

I would appreciate greatly when you are better to be allowed to tell you some more of the circumstances.

With all wishes to you and Lady Salisbury

Yours sincerely
Oliver Messel

My dear Alan [Lennox-Boyd]

Thank you so much for telephoning this morning when you have such an enormous amount on your hands.

I enclose a copy of the statement issued to the press last night by the Delegation from Buganda in which they wish without causing any possible antagonism just to make clear what they are here for.

All very best wishes

Yours sincerely
Oliver Messel

My dear Bob [Boothby]

I have been asked to send you a copy for reference of a statement which the delegates from Buganda have made today to the Press.

While being most anxious not to cause any possible antagonism they would like to make their views clear in order to illustrate the purpose of their visit here.

All thanks dear Bob for all you are doing to help bring about a settlement satisfactory to all parties.

Ever
Oliver

P.S.   Our Government may find it easy to get rid of the Royalty in Buganda but once the precedent's started, what's to stop them trying it here?

Letters were sent to the Archbishop of Canterbury, Anthony Eden and many others, including Lady Churchill, who replied that she felt great misgivings about the Kabaka, considered that the matter had not been well handled, and assured Oliver that the facts he had put forward to her in his letter would be looked into.

Messel's portrait of the Kabaka of Buganda

Unfortunately there was little anyone could do. The Colonial Office issued a statement of its own, and wrote to the Kabaka, who was staying at the Savoy Hotel, informing him that the Government of the Uganda Protectorate intended to pay him an allowance of £8,000 a year as an *ex gratia* allowance, which would not be liable to income tax in the United Kingdom. It went on to warn him that should he, at any time, take up residence in or visit any part of Africa without securing the prior consent of the British Government, or should he intervene in any way in the affairs of the Uganda Protectorate, then the Government would be obliged to terminate the allowance. The letter assured him that there would be no interference with the Kabaka's private estate, and advised him to appoint trustees to manage it.

The Statement began: 'The Secretary of State for the Colonies has today informed Kabaka Mutesall that the decision of Her Majesty's Government to withdraw recognition from him as Native Ruler of Buganda cannot be altered.' And ended: 'The decision is final. It in no way alters the determination of Her Majesty's Government to further by every means the work now going forward for the well-being and progress of the people of Buganda.'

Thwarted on this issue, Oliver entered the fray concerning the flat he had rented for the Kabaka and appealed to the press for publicity on what he considered a gross injustice to the Kabaka; together with the deposed monarch, he called a press conference at his Pelham Place home. The house was jammed with reporters to the point where Oliver had to sit on the floor beside the Kabaka, who was seated in an antique chair. One report in a national newspaper upset Oliver and he complained to the editor in heated terms:

Dear Sir

Apparently a painting of Vivien Leigh as 'Titania' and a few antique chairs present to your reporter a scene of unusual exoticism.

I only wish that I possessed more of these chairs. As had that been the case, I would not have felt obliged, as host, to seat your reporter and his colleagues in precarious comfort upon them while I had to sit on a rug.

This courtesy, it seems, gave your reporter the inspiration for his flamboyant headline DESIGNER LIES AT KING FREDDIE'S FEET. I cannot object too seriously to the skittish and fanciful description of your reporter's visit to my house, where a press conference was being held to discuss the fact that at the last minute admittance to a flat in Park Lane was refused to the Exiled Kabaka of Buganda on racial grounds. I would like to point out that no personal implications were made and it is now understood that the chairman of the property firm owning the block of flats in Park Lane is himself opposed to colour discrimination.

It was made clear to the agents from the beginning that the flat was for the Kabaka. It was only on the day that he was to move in, by which time all arrangements had been completed, that he was laid open to this further embarrassment on account of his race. That is why I objected so strongly.

The dilemma is that the Kabaka is not permitted to return to his own country and is deprived of his throne against the wishes of his people. He is, as well, mourning the death of his sister. I should have thought that this is neither a matter for facetiousness nor merriment.

Lady Rosse: I remember the rage Oliver flew into when he took King Freddie to a restaurant because King or no King the manager wouldn't let in a black. It got to the point when a question was asked in the House of Commons about the insult.

The window display of Justerini and Brooks, Bond Street, devised by Messel

In 1954 Oliver took on again an unusual kind of assignment: the window display and interior design for the champagne and wine merchants Justerini and Brooks in Bond Street. The idea he had for the windows was the symbol of his favourite theme: figurines in the shape of enchanting and immaculately dressed monkeys similar to the ones he had made for the Sekers' silk promotion. Inside, customers sailed in through doors of Regency prettiness, and on into the salesrooms where the carpets were coloured the delicate shade of just-pressed grape juice, and the walls were hung in claret velvet. Wine was tasted in little rooms lit with white chandeliers, and cheques were signed at windows draped in tasselled white chintz. 'We had to curb Oliver in expense a bit,' complained one of the firm's partners. 'He would dash in and say, "I've found the cheapest line in gold door knobs – and only £50 apiece." We had to break it to him that we could only run to brass. I know it wasn't what he wanted, but we had to draw the line somewhere.

'Some of our old boys thought the place was a nightclub and they expected to see a girl in every cubicle. But our American clients loved it, and we had a spreading export business in the States.'

After work at Justerini and Brooks had been completed, Oliver embarked on the set and costume designs for Christopher Fry's new play, *The Dark Is Light Enough*, which Tennent's were mounting as a vehicle for Edith Evans.

The setting of the play was appropriately romantic for Oliver's style – a Countess's baroque country house in the Austro-Hungarian Empire, but the place now crumbling in the wake of the Hungarian revolution of 1848. The countess, a woman of great intuition and compassion, has given sanctuary to Richard Gettner, a deserter from the Hungarian rebel army. When Colonel Janik, a Hungarian officer, pleads with her to give him up, she adamantly refuses. Her family and advisers, on the other hand, see no reason for placing the menage in jeopardy for a renegade and scoundrel, who, incidentally, was at one time married to the countess's daughter. In the meantime, the Hungarian colonel has taken the daughter's present husband as a hostage until his prisoner is delivered, thus placing the countess in a further dilemma. Gettner, if released, will be shot. To the countess, however, an individual life, no matter how worthless, has sanctity. She recognizes that the good in the worst of men is as much worth saving as the good in the best of men.

Directed by Peter Brook with a strong supporting cast, which included James Donald, Hugh Griffith, Peter Bull and Margaret Johnston, the play had its world premiere at the Lyceum, Edinburgh, prior to its London opening on 30 April 1954. But Oliver had reservations about it when he attended it at its second pre-London stop, the Theatre Royal, Brighton. He wrote to 'Binkie' Beaumont criticizing various aspects of the production:

Christopher's writing is so finely orchestrated, as it were, that even the slightest notes out of tune make nonsense out of it. That is why his plays are so particularly difficult to realise with success. Darling Edith said with triumph to me, 'At last now we seem to have got it all right.' I was able to murmur praise for the scene which she does so beautifully and with sincerity in the second act, which I thought to myself only shows that she could do it all convincingly, if she were shaken out of all the insincere affectations of Lady Bountiful which make the moving speeches (of 'the troops are at the door'!!) in the first act have little meaning but vowel sounds. In forbidding Colonel Janik (John Glen) to enter the house she is so irritatingly arch, that there seems no tension at all except from Margaret Johnston.

Poor Colonel Janik appears to me so physically miscast that instead of feeling remotely in fear of this old war horse, that in the end should give pathos to the defeated giant, he cuts so insignificant a figure throughout that an important part of the story tension is lost.

Peter Bull is understandable and it is possible to hear and listen to what he has to say, but the other two are completely unbelievable components of such a community.

On reading the part of Jacob carefully again there is in my mind something not quite consistent with the conception of the part as it is realised. He seems to give the impression of being more at home behind a counter than in any form of salon.

The part of Belman has so much in describing and explaining about the story; with Hugh Griffith it is quite impossible to absorb anything but acute discomfort, because he is such a ghastly bore, with his squeaks and grunts, and it is beyond the concentration powers of anyone to pay attention to anything he is saying. Also one can't help feeling that if the countess with all her tolerance were even on visiting acquaintance with such a pest, it makes her to be despised rather than pitied. If only an actor like Alan Webb were playing that part there would be meaning to the words.

Although much of the play appears interesting and exciting it is so exacting a play that it demands more. I can't help feeling at present that it is still very difficult for the audience and the press to realize this. They may probably think it is wonderfully acted, because the words are musical, but that Christopher is so obscure that they cannot understand it. Whereas I feel that it is a really great masterpiece, but at present is not in my opinion entirely realised in a way to make it fully understandable.

I am so afraid that these things which make it difficult to get the full value from the story may make all the difference between success and disappointment.

Beaumont replied explaining that cast changes such as Oliver had suggested would be inadvisable at this late date, but thought that wig and facial make-up alterations with the aid of beards and moustaches might add to the general appearance of the three males heavily criticized by Oliver.

Christopher Fry: *The Dark Is Light Enough* was the third production on which Oliver and I shared our viewpoints of designer and author, but they weren't so interlocking as before, through no fault of Oliver's. I had been late completing the script, and had been too close to it to be able to be clear about how it should be presented. The drawing-room of an Austrian Countess in 1848 would seem naturally enough to ask for an early Victorian richness, both in decor and costume, and this Messel provided in a masterly way, while still giving the light and air which was his hallmark. But I realised too late that this winter comedy needed only suggestion, rather than imaginative actuality; all that was required was a staircase and a window looking out on to snow, the rest to be left to the words. Our two explorations were getting in each other's way — though this was not true of the set for the second act, the simplicity of the stables, where all seemed right again; and there's little doubt that if I had given Messel a clearer lead towards what I was trying to create, his genius would have supplied the answer — and how magical that would have been!

Upon its opening the play received a mixed and confused press; neither the play nor Fry's verse found critical understanding or favour. It was, however, destined for New York the following February, where Katharine Cornell and Roger Stevens presented it with Cornell in the starring role and the commercial choice of Tyrone Power as her leading man. Katharine Cornell's husband Guthrie McClintic directed, as usual, and Oliver designed new sets for the ANTA Theatre's twelve-week limited run. Although Oliver's sets were well received, the piece was compared rather unfavourably to Shaw's *Arms and the Man*, which had a roughly similar theme.

After *The Dark Is Light Enough* opened on Broadway, Oliver returned to England to organize the sets and costumes for the Edinburgh Festival productions of *Le Comte Ory*, *Ariadne auf Naxos* and *La Cenerentola*. This completed, he went back to New York again to create his designs for a new musical play with an all-black cast, *The House of Flowers*. He was accompanied by his assistant Carl Toms, and rented the house of Ruth Gordon and her husband Garson Kanin in Turtle Bay.

Carl Toms: Ruth Gordon's house was next door to Katharine Hepburn's — which Peter Brook, who directed *The House of Flowers*, had taken for a while — but it was Oliver's rented house that became the nerve centre of the production and where the designs, sets and props were created. The house was always full of *The House of Flowers* company: Truman Capote, Harold Arlen and Saint Suber, the producer. Oliver had this magic quality for attracting people to him and everybody just seemed to drift his way.

The House of Flowers was scheduled to open on Broadway shortly after Christmas 1954. The script was written by Truman Capote, based on a short story of his own, and the songs were by Harold Arlen, composer of such evergreens as 'Stormy Weather', 'Over the Rainbow' and 'That Old Black Magic'. The setting of the play was a Caribbean Island, a location close to Oliver's heart which encouraged him to create some of his most exhilarating, exotic and brilliantly colourful designs. The light-hearted story of two madams of contending bordellos (Pearl Bailey and Juanita Hall), and of the budding awareness of love in an innocent girl (Diahann Carroll), offered Oliver's imagination full play. Costumes and scenery were beyond criticism. The show itself, though much beloved in retrospect, ran into all kinds of snags and never managed to achieve more than a connoisseur's success.

Its tryout began in Philadelphia, and Marlene Dietrich, a friend of both Oliver and Harold Arlen, stripped her golden star image to become charlady, making coffee for the cast and ferrying them and the production team to and from rehearsals. She also assumed her 'private role' of helpmate, this time perched high on a stool stitching costumes. She also came to Pearl Bailey's rescue over the dilemma of her gems. Bailey began rehearsals wearing about $25,000 of her own jewellery. On stage, however, they didn't look like much. Marlene Dietrich rushed off for the costume jewellery she used in her own nightclub act — and the fakes she lent to Bailey outshone the real ones by far.

The opening night at the Alvin Theatre on 30 December 1954 glittered with the rich and famous. Gloria Vanderbilt was escorted by Frank Sinatra. Grace

Kelly, Henry Fonda, Valentina, the fashion designer, and a host of other celebrities toasted the cast as they awaited the reviews of the performance.

Walter Kerr, branded by some at that time the 'butcher of Broadway', reported: 'A pair of rival bordellos, on an island somewhere in the better-kept Indies, face each other across a dazzling stage. Oliver Messel has spilled some genie's treasure-chest of radiant pastels over the landscape, then animated it with crawling flora calculated to knock your eye out. Enormous sunflower vines smirk from the facade of Madame Fleur's.' Richard Watts Jr. wrote in the *New York Post*: 'There are a number of important contributors to the attractiveness of *House of Flowers*, and I am inclined to think that the foremost is Oliver Messel, whose taste and imagination in designing both the scene and the clothes result in what is one of the most glowing and beautiful physical productions in my recent theatre going memory. Mr Messel is an authentic artist, and he has brought to the evening a sense of colour and design that provides not only a remarkably picturesque loveliness but also a dramatic feeling for exotic appeal.'

Oliver: I loved working with Truman Capote, starting off with the picture he painted and the writing. I admired the music of Harold Arlen and I enjoyed working with Peter Brook again. I found it fascinating designing something for a Negro cast. I thought they were a fabulous cast; such tremendous vitality and wonderful talent. It gave enormous scope and enjoyment in that way. It was stimulating on one hand, but frustrating and maddening on the other because although it had such wonderful ingredients the book was never quite finished and the thing went into production before the situation was solved. It should have been worked out completely in a satisfactory way before it got launched into the terrifying business of production. Everybody's nerves got on end and people lost balance and judgment. It was so nearly wonderful but it just needed several adjustments to the story.

On his return to Britain, Oliver's order book was as full as ever. The Bath May Festival presented Grétry's opera *Zémire et Azore* on 11 May 1955, conducted by Sir Thomas Beecham and with sets and costumes designed by Oliver. Its story-line was a version of *Beauty and the Beast*, which provided the designer with ample opportunities to create those spectacular masks for which he had first become noted.

Then, in abrupt contrast from opera, a wedding. In characteristic proof of his versatile ability to leap from ballet to comedy, light opera to heavy drama, and from decorating Royal Boxes to mounting displays in shop windows, Oliver undertook the decorations for the sumptuous reception in Venice following the spectacular nuptials of the fifteen-year-old Princess Ira Fürstenberg to Prince Alfonso Hohenlohe-Langenburg, thirty-year-old car salesman and millionaire. The wedding linked two giant automobile empires; Ira of the Italian House of Fiat, and Alfonso representing the Volkswagen firm in Germany. It proved to be one of the most sensational marriages — and later, divorces — Italy had witnessed.

Contractually, Oliver had final approval of the interpretation of his designs — even about that of the stars and the directors, and to this end he supervised the making of the costumes and wigs and the construction of the sets himself, being consulted as well on lighting effects on his work throughout. Cecil Beaton also

Pearl Bailey in *House of Flowers,* 1954

had this power of veto and used it so relentlessly during the filming of *My Fair Lady* that he lost the respect of his peers.

But never once did Oliver lose the esteem of those who regarded him so highly – and they continued to commission him. Despite his sometimes quarrelsome nature and exasperating attention to minute details, those who championed him continued to admire and quickly forgive him for the many letters he sent criticizing their decisions. His steel-like determination invariably won him the day, and he became much admired for his strength of character in a profession peppered with quick-tempered practitioners who experience exhilarating 'highs' and suicidal 'lows' on an almost daily basis.

Now, again, with the bit firmly between his teeth, he reproached the Glyndebourne Festival management about alterations to furniture and costumes in the new production of *The Marriage of Figaro*, which had been made without his approval. It opened on 8 June 1955 with a cast headed by Sena Jurinac, Frances Bible, Sesto Bruscantini, Elena Ruzzieri and Ian Wallace, but Oliver had not been able to attend the first night as he had left for Copenhagen to supervise the construction of sets and the costume design for the production of *The Dark is Light Enough* at the Detny Theatre. However, he had examined the properties and costumes before his departure and wrote to the producer Carl Ebert from Copenhagen on the 19th:

I am worried about two things about my original designs for this production. The dressing table has been altered without my approval. As designed for the scene, it is

The Marriage of Figaro: the 1955 revival at Glyndebourne. Photograph by Snowdon

Messel's model for Act III of the Glyndebourne production of *The Marriage of Figaro*

the right proportion and shape for the scene. Small, oval dressing tables are a later innovation and are out of character with the rest of the design. I particularly don't want any dressing table other than the one I designed as I have avoided the dainty and think the oval ones are dainty and kitsch.

Also, the colours of the costumes were most carefully planned so that when they are in groups they compose as a picture. Cherubino should wear the page's costume, deep wine coloured velvet, in the Countess's bedroom in Act II. I believe the other costume is being worn. This may be accidental but it should not be.

We have worked happily together, dear Carl, on a number of productions. I have loved working with you and am very fond of you, and you can't feel that you have done badly over our collaboration. You must know that my experience in design is not haphazard or without knowledge. I should at least be able to rely on you to respect my work and refrain from making alterations to the design.

I shall appreciate it if these things are put right. [They were.]

By the time he had completed productions of *The Abduction from the Seraglio* and *The Magic Flute* at Glyndebourne the following season, opera had dominated his life for three years.

Oliver: I found most of the continental *prima donnas* delightful in the style and precision of Italian opera, as in the 1953 Glyndebourne production of *La*

A decoration by Messel for
Delightful Food, a recipe book
compiled by Adrianne Allen
and Marjorie Salter

Cenerentola which I adored. I remember Sari Barabas in the 1954 Glyndebourne production of *Le Comte Ory* in Edinburgh. I had left the length of the train of her dress to be shortened at the fitting. I was astonished to find that she didn't want it shortened at all. She made a beautiful gesture by which she manouevered it all so gracefully while singing the most difficult of Rossini's arias absolutely exquisitely. A designer doesn't often enjoy such good fortune.

The only artists usually hell to deal with were those from Vienna, who carried their own white cotton-wool wigs and were desperately determined to wear them. There were occasions when the battle with a *prima donna* was a performance in itself; Rosemary Wilkins and the others in the wardrobe would be watching and taking bets as to who would win. Mine was a divine act; overwhelming flattery — then devastating little pinpricks.

I attempted every device to make as much magic as possible. One major problem was over the setting for the Queen of the Night scene in *The Magic Flute* at Glyndebourne in 1956.

The scene change for this great aria was vital — placing the American singer, Mattiwilda Dobbs, effectively, yet not too remotely, for the voice to have full impact. I made the effect that of a Spanish Madonna at Seville, set under a canopy with a myriad of candles, preceded by a gauze of formal clouds made to move by front projection. The chariot of the Queen of the Night appeared dimly through the clouds and starry night, at first in the distance, and then forwards as if floating through the sky until it reached right downstage. At the end, she floated back and just dissolved into the night sky.

The Magic Flute always arouses much controversy. It was originally conceived entirely as a popular show in the oriental taste of the eighteenth century (*Chu Chin Chow* or *Kismet*), but because Mozart wrote such sublime music, it is frequently held that the whole thing should be treated with awe and solemnity. All the original stage directions as well as some illustrations of the first productions are still in existence. There seems no reason to ignore what was intended.

Interior decorating was Oliver's main occupation in 1957. His days were filled with assignments that included the Pavilion Room at the Dorchester Hotel, the Reader's Digest building in Paris, the boardroom for L. Messel & Co., and private interiors for several friends, including Billy Wallace, grandson of the distinguished architect Sir Edwin Lutyens, and one of Princess Margaret's frequent escorts in the 1950s.

His commissions during those months culminated in witty designs for *Delightful Food,* a cookbook by Marjorie Salter and Adrianne Allen with a foreword by Noël Coward, and the artwork for the Folio Society's publication of *A Midsummer Night's Dream.*

He returned to the theatre in 1958 to design *Breath of Spring,* which opened at the Cambridge Theatre in London on 26 March with Athene Seyler, Mary Merrall and Michael Shepley in the Michael Codron production, directed by Allan Davis (who was later to direct the longest running comedy in the world, *No Sex, Please, We're British!*). This fairly successful comedy by Peter Coke was set in the living room of Dame Beatrice Appleby's (Athene Seyler) flat near the Albert Memorial, a delicate cosy room designed by Oliver as if from affectionate memory, and showed how Dame Beatrice and her highly respectable guests embark on a life of crime in the manner of modern Robin Hoods. It ran for over a year before going on tour.

After *Breath of Spring* he designed a production of *Homage to the Queen* for the Brussels Fair, followed by *The School for Scandal* at the Detny Theatre, Copenhagen, which opened on 19 September 1958.

The Royal Opera House, Covent Garden, were planning a new production of *Samson*, an opera adapted from Handel's oratorio, with Jon Vickers, Elisabeth Lindermeier and, in a minor role, Joan Sutherland; Oliver was invited to suggest ideas for the visual accompaniment to the piece that had not hitherto been performed as an opera.

The 1958 production at Covent Garden of Handel's *Samson* with designs by Messel

Oliver: Working with the director Herbert Graf was one of my happiest experiences, and the day Raymond Leppard [the conductor] played through the score for me I had instant vivid impressions which formed notes I was able to decipher and make a whole series of scenes and action groupings which Herbert Graf then developed on the stage. Like *Idomeneo*, this production was designed at great speed. Other productions had taken ages before anything would materialise at all.

Oliver wrote to Professor Graf on 30 July 1958:

> I have been rather worried about the opera as my previous commitments made it impossible to really start working on it until last week. However, now everything seems to be shaping itself.
>
> At first I couldn't make the plan work out as I had in mind at Covent Garden, so I tried various other ways. Then it suddenly seemed to fall into place and the form emerged in principle exactly as the pattern that came when the music was being played through at Covent Garden, and which you liked.
>
> Leppard came here yesterday, and went through some of the music with me again, and I made some notes. I had just built up in my mind a whole imaginary picture heightening the visual effects where the existing story seems rather static, but having no knowledge of the music, before the afternoon with you, I was rather relieved yesterday to find that it all seemed to fit in with my ideas.

He later sent Graf a note on the way he felt the scenes developing:

> When Samson decides to go towards the temple, as he is led up the steps and reaches behind the archway I imagined some of the Philistines would come dancing down the steps and swirling round him, leaving him horrified and bewildered as he is led through them to the temple.
>
> Then I imagined a kind of altar or something with a flame as part of the celebration which would be placed in the middle of the archway. Then the music suggested to me that a dancing procession could whirl in from below prompt side, dancing hand in hand like a long chain, as in revelling scenes at the end of a party. Then breaking off and falling on the ground, but gradually winding up the steps, incorporating some ritual, with a centre flame piece, and then all gathering up into the temple as Manoah comes on, perhaps right down-stage O.P. side.
>
> At this point of Manoah's lament I would like to close the scene down with a gauze from behind the boxes so that when Micah sings his aria just before the collapse of the pillars a projection light from the back will make a silhouette as a vivid vision inside the great temple. Perhaps a silhouette of Samson praying for strength and pulling the columns down.
>
> I am trying to devise a means of making the silhouette of the shapes of a big temple which can be made to fall backwards, which would then appear as though it falls towards the audience. Then I feel that this could seem to burst into flames at the same time with the first crashes, the red damask material from behind the singers in the boxes should fall down and the piece of the wall behind them tear out so that the archways of the boxes would be left open showing jagged edges of ruin.

The next production Oliver designed was one of his favourites, and reunited him with Peter Glenville, who directed it. *Rashomon*, produced by David Susskind and Hardy Smith and starring Rod Steiger and Claire Bloom, was planned for an opening at the Music Box Theatre in New York on 27 January 1959 after a tryout in Philadelphia. It was the stage version by Fay and Michael Kanin of the classic Japanese film written and directed by Akira Kurosawa. The action takes place in Kyoto about a thousand years ago — at a corner of the Rashomon Gate, at a police court and in a nearby forest. Before the time of the play, Rashomon had been the largest gate in Kyoto, the ancient capital of Japan. It was 106 feet wide and 26 feet deep: its stone wall rose 75 feet and was topped by a ridge-pole. With the decline of West Kyoto, the gate had fallen into disrepair and became a decayed relic with an unsavoury reputation, a place which most people tried to bypass. In this setting, four people give different versions of a violent incident they had witnessed when a bandit attacked a nobleman in the forest.

Peter Glenville: *Rashomon* was a work of art in the way Oliver designed it. His set consisted of the most magical Japanese forest that actually moved; the trees themselves seemed to come to life. He also produced a great elevator that emerged from the pit of the theatre, supporting a witch surrounded by her cauldrons of incense.

While he was in the process of transforming this film masterpiece into stage terms, Oliver felt dissatisfied with his billing, and ever conscious of his own essential worth, wrote to Peter Glenville on 3 October 1958:

> There has been a slight complication over billing me but I don't know whether you have heard about it. Arnold [Weissberger, the American theatrical lawyer] wrote me and said that Susskind said he could not now give me the billing agreed on my contract. I replied that if I was not expected to receive the courtesy of the billing to which I am accustomed and which was in the contract, I wouldn't want to come to New York as I won't be put in a position of going anywhere if I am not appreciated.
>
> I pointed out to Arnold that you wouldn't want, or expect, my prestige to be diminished, especially as this year has been my highest peak [he had been awarded the CBE]. Even twenty years ago I received equal screen credit with separate card, etc., as George Cukor for *Romeo and Juliet*. This was unheard of in those days. It would be out of the question for me to waive a precedent of billing that no other artist usually has.
>
> Felt rather depressed when I found everything was to crumble as I was looking forward to it all with you. However, I was in contact with Arnold this evening by telephone and he tells me that everything is being rectified. I thought I would write at once to let you know what had happened in case no mention of all this had been made to you.

Needless to say, Oliver as usual had his way. His credit, 'Settings and Costumes by OLIVER MESSEL', was placed above that of both the director, Peter Glenville, and the lighting director, Jo Mielziner — himself a famous American set designer.

Although *Rashomon* was a notable artistic success, it failed at the box office. Brooks Atkinson said in his *New York Times* review, 'Renouncing realism, *Rashomon* is pure art of the theatre. Out of a legend, it conjures a mood. . . . And

Claire Bloom in Peter
Glenville's Broadway
production of *Rashomon*

Oliver Messel's settings, representing the decaying Rashomon gate and a
barbaric bamboo jungle, are like the illustrations for a macabre legend. *Rashomon*
is an incantation of things far away and long since forgotten.' Walter Kerr in the
New York Herald Tribune was equally enthusiastic:

For the best part of two acts we watch an intricate, bewildering, boldly-colored pursuit of truth
with some fascination. A bandit has raped a woman [Claire Bloom] in a lonely stretch of Japanese
forest; the woman's husband has been found with a brightly-jeweled sword through his heart. Is
the brigand a coward, or has he killed his man in a fair fight? Is the woman a flirt, a slut, or a loving
wife? As the bound husband turns stony eyes upon her immediately after she has been assaulted,
which of her secrets has he guessed? Under Oliver Messel's sky-high bamboo reeds, and against
the liquid light of Jo Mielziner's translucent green sky, the unanswered questions are tantalizing.

Peter Glenville: He devised a revolving Japanese forest, one through which the
leading female character was led on horseback by her husband through glades
and trees that glided gently by as the couple progressed towards their fateful
encounter with the bandit. Nearby was a ruined temple, later to be battered by a

tempestuous rainstorm. It was a formidable challenge for a designer, magnificently mastered.

Snowdon: The set that Oliver created for *Rashomon* was most beautiful, but he was heavily involved with the mechanics of making it work. The revolve on which Claire Bloom made her entrance on a white horse went the opposite way and it looked as though the horse was moving through the wood, yet the horse never progressed at all; it was rather like trying to go up an escalator that is moving downwards!

Oliver's settings and costumes for *Rashomon* were nominated for a 'Tony' (Antoinette Perry) Award in 1959. The other nominees for costume designer that year were Irene Sharaff for *Flower Drum Song* and Rouben Ter-Arutunian for *Redhead*, starring Gwen Verdon, and the award went to the latter. Peter Glenville, however, champions Oliver to the end:

Peter Glenville: Oliver was a magician. He was effervescent, funny, egocentric, loyal, sophisticated, wise, childish but shrewd – and a beautiful sprite. All his work had a brilliant flair and evoked both the classical world of the past and a future world over the horizon. I was lucky enough to meet him when we were both young. After my enjoyable Jesuit education he taught me to appreciate through the eye and not just through the mind. To guide me in the visual world was a priceless present.

His close friendship was another.

After the opening of *Rashomon* Oliver managed to slip away for a holiday in Barbados, in the West Indies. Surrounded by an enchanting black nation, the strong influence of his Negro art inspired by Glyn Philpot and the theme for many of the exotic exteriors he loved creating so much, he contemplated buying a house there. He could not know then that this would be the paradise island to which he would return in the early 1960s to spend the rest of his days.

7

The Marriage of Figaro, Act III;
the Metropolitan Opera
Company production, 1959

190

7 * 'Marriage' to the Met

WHILE IN NEW YORK for *Rashomon*, Oliver started working on the redesigning of the National Theatre on 41st Street, which was to be renamed the Billy Rose Theatre. With a budget of half a million dollars to complete the renovation, he worked closely with Billy Rose himself (who also owned the Ziegfeld Theatre). Its interior ablaze with gold chandeliers and rose-red, gold and white decor, its exterior an elegant oyster-grey with off-white trim and sporting a new red-and-gold marquee, it was being prepared for its reopening with Shaw's *Heartbreak House*, starring Maurice Evans.

On his return to England, Oliver started work on the film of Tennessee Williams's *Suddenly Last Summer*, directed by Joseph Mankiewicz from a screenplay by Gore Vidal. Williams's rather lurid play involved the themes of homosexuality, incest, lunacy and cannibalism. Mrs Venable (Katharine Hepburn) summons a surgeon (Montgomery Clift) with the idea of operating on her niece (Elizabeth Taylor) in order to induce amnesia, though she tries to cover up her reasons for wanting this done. The niece, who has been committed to an asylum, is the only witness to her poet-cousin's sordid escapades in North Africa which led to his death and have tormented her ever since. We, the audience, witness the scenes in flash-back as the niece unfolds the horrifying facts — her cousin being raped and murdered by beach boys — which resulted in her mental condition.

Filmed at Shepperton Studios near London, Oliver's sub-tropical, steamy Deep South set for Mrs Venable's house, with its larger-than-life exotic garden containing huge and menacing plants, was reminiscent in style of his exterior stage settings for *The Little Hut*, *Ring Round the Moon* and *The House of Flowers*.

Oliver: I couldn't find anyone to make the garden so I used this wonderful person, Hugh Skillen, who made all the head-dresses for the Margot Fonteyn productions, and he made the insect-eating plants and all sorts of exotic outsized plants. I myself made banana leaves with waxed crinkle-paper and then mixed them all in with real plants. I made all the vines from paper twisted round in coils and then covered with pale green flock.

Suddenly Last Summer was released in 1959 and resulted in Oliver's nomination for two Oscars for scenery and costume design.

His successful working relationship with Elizabeth Taylor led Twentieth Century-Fox to commission him to design her costumes and wigs for their forthcoming mammoth film production of *Cleopatra*; but this had an unhappy ending for Oliver because his designs were never used, and he was replaced on the production by Irene Sharaff who won an Oscar for her work on the film.

Stanley Hall: *Cleopatra* was an exciting project for me to make the wigs designed by Oliver. I had so admired the *Caesar and Cleopatra* film with Vivien

Cleopatra with the dying Antony: a discarded costume design by Messel for the film *Cleopatra*

192

Leigh and Claude Rains — and Oliver was such a master and genius who always extended one's potential to produce the definitive effect. Egyptian wigs *were* wigs and one had great scope in creating the fantastic. So much of my work had been to make wigs look undetectable — natural and real and growing out of the scalp, with no question of noticing a wig join or a phony effect, which would have been a catastrophe.

Cleopatra could have all the trimmings and exaggeration, and who better than Oliver to prod one along. It is said that genius involves originality, creativeness and the ability to think and work in areas not previously explored, and thus to give to the world something of a pre-eminent value it would not otherwise possess. Oliver created magic, and his wig designs for Elizabeth Taylor were sensational. Sydney Guilaroff, M.G.M.'s superb hair artist, was assigned to the production. He was a friend of Elizabeth Taylor and she had confidence in his creative ability. Miss Taylor came to London for fittings and mountains of costumes and wigs were made — when suddenly the powers that be decided that the film should be made in Rome. There were endless changes of cast and directors — Stephen Boyd was replaced by Richard Burton as Antony and Rex Harrison accepted the role of Caesar. Many British players spent months in Rome working on the slowly turning film, but Oliver was replaced.

It was known that Oliver insisted on having his contracts specify that he had the final say on the appearance of an artist on the set, and I had the feeling that Miss Taylor couldn't accept his time-consuming and demanding attention to make her into *his* idea of Cleopatra. Another point, of course, was that the film combined the young, kittenish Cleopatra (of Bernard Shaw) in her experience with Caesar, and then went on to the later, more mature Cleopatra in love with Antony. It may not have helped if Miss Taylor had seen the remarkable effect Oliver had created for Vivien Leigh in the earlier film.

Irene Sharaff, who had many successful films and Broadway shows to her credit, and who had a rapport with Elizabeth Taylor, was called in to replace Oliver. She redesigned every costume and reshaped every wig. I don't think her task was easy, but she bore it with great style and dignity.

Rudolph Bing, general manager of the Metropolitan Opera in New York, was keen for Oliver to design a new production of *The Marriage of Figaro* for an October 1959 opening, and wrote to him about this eighteen months in advance. Although Oliver accepted the invitation, the production could not proceed until certain contractual details had been ironed out — namely, Oliver's fee and his travelling expenses to America. The choice of director and the decision about who should make the costumes became additional causes of contention. When Bing suggested Carl Ebert as director, Oliver countered with Tyrone Guthrie, but Bing felt that Guthrie's style would be unsuitable for this particular opera at the Met.

Bing had explained that the union minimum for stage designers was $3,000, and this would be for operas such as *Aida* and *Macbeth* which have many set changes and hundreds of costumes. It was unfortunate that *Figaro* involved only four sets and approximately thirty costumes, but he thought that $3,600 would be a reasonable fee for Oliver. Weissberger, who handled Oliver's business affairs in New York, finally negotiated a fee of $5,000 plus $1,000 to cover the return fare to New York. On 24 April 1958 Vagn wrote to Weissberger:

Oliver is willing to do *Figaro* for this fee but cannot accept responsibility if they expect him to send his model and costume drawings over for them to copy the way they think fit. Oliver must come over with his designs himself, say in February or March, so that he can explain exactly the way he wants his work carried out. That would mean that the Met would have to pay one more fare to New York and Oliver's keep for one week, as they simply cannot expect him to pay this out of his $5,000 fee.

I am quite sure that Bing will understand this as he says in his letter: 'Once something has been designed, approved and built or painted, nothing can be changed . . .' How on earth does he expect his people at the Met to carry out Oliver's designs without having any explanation from him?

So, if they will agree to pay $5,000 plus two return visits to New York, $2,000, and one week's keep, I think we can accept.

Yours always
Vagn Riis-Hansen

This was agreed, but Bing stipulated the condition that Oliver's engagement be subject to the director's approval. Garson Kanin, who had been approached to direct the production, wanted approval of the designer before committing himself. The result of this was that either Kanin might be the director and conceivably not approve Oliver, or Kanin might not be the director and the director selected might not approve Oliver. This Oliver found unacceptable; he had gone too far in his career to consider an 'on approval' basis for negotiation.

My dear Rudi

Thank you so much for your letter. Re Carl Ebert; yes, over the last production of *The Magic Flute* at Glyndebourne he was, in confidence, rather hell to work with.

Perhaps because in initial working out of such a technically difficult production he seems unable to visualise anything until it is actually on the stage, and on principle at first fights against everything in turn. Last year, however, after battling over things I had done, everything went without a hitch. With *Figaro*, it was different, being simpler and more straightforward (no problems of Germanic or Italian conflict of conception). With his knowledge of the music he does manage to get the very best in acting out of the singers. So to me, anything for the best results.

When you first asked me, and thinking Ebert out of the question anyway because of the disagreement between you both, I suggested Tony Guthrie because his understanding of 17th and 18th century comedy is his greatest accomplishment, and at that he is probably unequalled. When you said you did not think he would be suitable for the style, I took it that you wanted someone entirely specialist in music and Mozart, like Ebert.

Now Garson and Ruth [Gordon, his wife] are two of my greatest friends in America so of course I would enjoy working with Garson. I had always looked on Garson's great *forte* to lie in his quick and brilliant treatment of modern American life and had no idea that he was an expert on Mozart. As I understood you to be reluctant about Tony Guthrie on that very account, I was astonished that you chose Garson, simply because I was unaware of his having any possible link with 18th century comedy or Mozart. If you, however, feel that he has, then by all means I would be delighted to do it with him.

All very best wishes
Oliver

But Oliver's letter crossed with one sent just one day apart by Bing:

METROPOLITAN OPERA

6 May 1958

Dear Oliver

Before going any further, I must have your answer about Garson Kanin. Obviously I cannot engage a director without knowing that he will get on with the designer, nor can I engage a designer without knowing that he can get on with the director. This, therefore, must of course go hand in hand and before I proceed with Garson in any shape or form, I would like to know whether you have merely overlooked answering that point or whether you have purposely avoided it. Needless to say, if you do not wish to collaborate with Garson you can say so quite frankly to me and I will not disclose this to him. As you know, I am not yet committed to either side and I could, therefore, easily discontinue conversations with Garson – provided I find somebody else whom we may mutually consider better. I would love to have Alfred Lunt do it (he did a delightful *Così* some years ago for us) but I am very doubtful that he would accept and commit himself as far ahead as it would be necessary for me to know. On the other hand, if you should be agreeable to doing *Figaro* with Garson Kanin, then I think no time should be lost for the two of you to communicate.

So please let me have a frank answer on this all important question.

Yours ever
Rudi

Oliver was in Paris preparing the Glyndebourne production of *Le Comte Ory* which was to open on 8 May 1958 for eight performances at the Sarah Bernhardt Theatre; and Garson Kanin, on a visit to Europe, conferred with Oliver about the pending Met production of *Figaro*. They were not in accord, and after Kanin returned to New York and reported to Bing, Oliver received the following letter, dated 19 September:

Dear Oliver

I am in trouble! Garson Kanin has, on his return from Europe only a few days ago, advised me that he is unable to commit himself now for the *Figaro* production next autumn. He gives various important reasons, mainly some serious illness in his family with which I need not bother you. The fact remains that I have no director at this moment.

I have approached Cyril Ritchard who I think would also be excellent for *Figaro* and particularly has the style and elegance for the period. But while Cyril is interested I have not yet had a final answer from him. Also, he would naturally have to get some advance knowledge of your ideas. Will you be in America in the near future? Or if not, could you have some sketches sent so that Cyril can know what you have in mind before finally committing himself? Please let me hear from you at your *earliest* convenience.

I am very sorry for this delay but as you will realise it is not of my making and I am still as anxious as before to have you do this and I hope further productions when the new house will be available in 1961.

Yours ever
Rudi

26 September 1958

My dear Rudi

Much as I would love to work with Garson, I don't think that *Figaro* would have been at all his cup of tea. Please, dear Rudi, if you really do want me to do the production do wait until I can see you before you commit yourself.

When you last spoke to me on the telephone about the possibility of Herbert Graf I was delighted with the idea as he has so much experience with music and opera, and I find him a marvellous person to work with. As with Tony Guthrie, there would be no question of seeing eye to eye.

That I should be asked to send designs to see if a producer can commit himself is something that I have never before been asked to do. I really don't wish to start sending my work on approval now, although I am very fond of Cyril Ritchard, as I am of Garson.

I have just returned from Copenhagen. The production of *The School for Scandal*, I am happy to say, is a fabulous success.

Looking forward to the pleasure of seeing you.

Oliver

The final choice of director was Cyril Ritchard; Oliver had won the hand. Few designers can ever have had such power and influence over a major production as to be in the position to select the director. By and large the director chooses the designer. Oliver, however, did not let matters lie there: now came the question of the making of the costumes. The Met had advocated the distinguished house of Brooks, with whom Oliver had worked when they made the costumes for *The House of Flowers* and *Rashomon*. He wrote to Herman Krawitz, the Business and Technical Administrator of the Metropolitan Opera on 24 March 1959:

When you first mentioned to me about *Figaro* I explained that Karinska had been asked to make the costumes. Karinska has carried out designs of mine for as long as twenty-five years, and each time she has interpreted my work it has been with knowledge and real understanding, and I have been delighted with the results.

When the Met told me that she was to make the costumes for *Figaro* I naturally agreed, as I had no reason to be anything but pleased. This does not mean that I don't appreciate the work that has been done at Brooks. I am extremely fond of Mrs Swann, Steve, Mary, Marcel, George and all those who helped me with *The House of Flowers* and *Rashomon*.

Figaro is a production that Karinska has definitely been asked to undertake by you, on the understanding that there was to be no question of competitive bidding. This was made quite clear when we met. Therefore, I know you will understand that I could not think of accepting any other arrangement other than what was agreed.

Krawitz replied assuring Oliver that Karinska *would* be making the costumes, and that there would be no competitive bidding.

Oliver had had his way again, and fortunately the production was a tremendous success with Lisa Della Casa, Cesare Siepi and Elisabeth Söderström singing the leading roles under Erich Leinsdorf's baton.

While he was planning the *Figaro* production for the Met, Oliver designed another opera for Glyndebourne to celebrate the twenty-fifth anniversary of its

opening on 28 May 1959: *Der Rosenkavalier*, by Richard Strauss, with Elisabeth Söderström as Octavian, Regine Crespin as the Marschallin and Anneliese Rothenberger as Sophie. 'Oliver Messel's settings and costumes are possibly the most beautiful he has ever designed,' Andrew Porter wrote in *The Financial Times*, and Desmond Shawe-Taylor was equally enthusiastic in *The Sunday Times*: 'Oliver Messel's designs, straight-forward in plan and often exquisite in detail and colour, were among the best he has done for Glyndebourne.'

In that same year, the Rayne shoe shop issued this publicity statement: 'London can now boast of having the loveliest shoe shop in the world. Magic afoot in Old Bond Street – and you are invited to come along to Nos. 15 & 16 and share it. Here, at the House of Rayne, Oliver Messel has created the prettiest shoe-salon in the world, a light-hearted fantasy in white, gold and iridescent silks. In this enchanted setting, the most fabulous collection of shoes is yours to choose from.' Edward Rayne had taken over the Lloyds Bank branch next door to his long-familiar Delman shop and handed over the space, both within and without, to Oliver to redesign. Outside, his task was to create a harmonious façade from two quite dissimilar exteriors. Delicate ironwork balconies disguised the different window levels, and flattened arches and fanlights set flush into dark green marble imposed a uniform character to the frontage.

Inside, Oliver created a series of vistas. Using to the full the free hand given him by Rayne, he transformed a shoe-shop into a ballroom. Damson Japanese silk paper lined one room; pale green Thailand silk another. Another room had recessed banquettes, curtained in garlanded chintz, cleverly lighted. Every detail had been designed and specially made, from the hand-painted borders to the chandeliers and show cases topped with Brighton pavilion domes.

Messel showing Edward Rayne a model of the designs and decorations he was creating for Rayne's shoe salon in Old Bond Street

Interior view of the Rayne shop after Messel's alterations

It was the first shop Oliver had designed since the Justerini & Brooks decor. When asked whether he would ever consider taking on a big store he said, 'No. It would be too commercial.'

His other commissions for 1959 were the decorations for a party John Aspinall gave at his house in Belgrave Square, and some new fabric designs for Sekers which were exhibited in the presence of Princess Margaret. In addition he undertook the design for a new theatre in Whitehaven, in the North of England, three miles from a new industrial area.

The one theatre within miles had been lost to the new community when the Royal Standard, a late-Georgian playhouse, afterwards used as a music-hall overlooking Whitehaven Bay, was demolished. Miki Sekers bought the remains of the interior for a princely £50 with the intention of rehousing them in a Georgian stable. When that scheme broke down, a more ambitious one grew out of it – to incorporate decorative pieces of the old building in a new, specifically contemporary type of theatre, designed not for plays but for intimate performances of the kind associated with festivals, recitals, chamber opera and 'celebrity concerts'.

Sekers commissioned Oliver to decorate the interior of the new Rosehill Theatre, which had an auditorium with a seating capacity of just under 200 and a foyer large enough to serve the secondary purpose of an art gallery. The budget of £35,000 was raised through private subscription. Oliver remodelled the proscenium arch on that of the Royal Standard and affixed painted panels from the old theatre to the front of the balcony of the new. The wall coverings and curtains were made of silk, green for the foyer and dark red for the auditorium, where four side-boxes concealed stage-lighting behind gilt lattices.

The Rosehill Theatre at Whitehaven, Cumbria (1959): the interior

The colour plate on page 201 should
have the following caption:
A model for the garden set of
The Abduction from the Seraglio,
Glyndebourne, 1956.

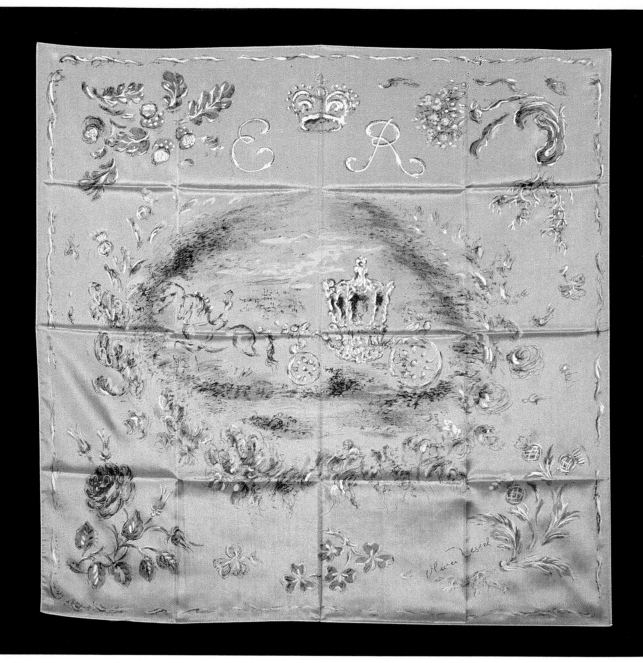

Commemorative silk scarf designed by Messel for the
Coronation (1953)

Opposite, statuette of Bacchus in the Penthouse Suite
decorated by Messel in the Dorchester Hotel

Left, Messel's Barbadian home, Maddox. Photograph by Derry Moore

Below, *Les Jolies Eaux*, Princess Margaret's house in Mustique. Photograph by Derry Moore, courtesy of *Architectural Digest*

The Gingerbread House in Barbados designed by Messel.
Photograph by Derry Moore

Three monkeys designed by Messel for Seker's silk promotions

Opposite, the Silver Rose from the Glyndebourne production of *Der Rosenkavalier*, 1959. It was designed by Messel and made by Hugh Skillen.

The opening of the Rosehill Theatre marked the start of one of the most enterprising new theatre ventures the North had seen for some time. Artists such as John Gielgud, Joyce Grenfell, Yehudi Menuhin, Emlyn Williams and Elisabeth Söderström were booked to appear for twenty-seven performances, all of which were sold out. Packed audiences admired the decor Oliver had designed in perfect eighteenth-century style. Champagne was served at the small, white taffeta-covered tables in a corner of the foyer, which was lined with sea-green silk. In the bar, the walls were covered with a white and gold brocade specially designed by Oliver and hung with gilded Chippendale looking glasses.

Later that year Oliver travelled to New York for the production of his *Marriage of Figaro* which opened at the Met in October 1959. While there during November and December he had his first exhibition of paintings and theatre designs in America, at the Sagittarius Gallery.

Oliver: It was an exciting winter but an exhausting one. I'm rather erratic about taking holidays, and in the past liked going to distant parts where people don't normally go a lot, so I went off to Barbados for five weeks after my New York work was over. I'm very fond of Barbadians — of all coloured people. I get very worked up about this race relations business. How can there possibly be two ways of regarding the colour question? People are created equal. You'd think that would be a fundamental belief by now.

Oliver had in fact fallen in love with the island and its people. He began thinking seriously of settling there. The swinging sixties were fast approaching, and with the success of such productions as John Osborne's *Look Back in Anger* at the Royal Court Theatre, the swing was to kitchen-sink drama, a style as alien to Oliver as colour prejudice itself. His thoughts were on the future and a new career in a different country — hot and remote, with a dry, warm climate that would offer both scope for his art and relief from the arthritis that was constantly troubling him.

The Met again invited Oliver to design a forthcoming production, this time the opera *Martha*, but much to his regret he had to turn it down. As his mother was seriously ill and his nephew, Antony Armstrong-Jones, had become engaged to Princess Margaret, he felt his place was at home. Though he was in financial difficulties and would have gladly undertaken the commission, he wrote to Rudolf Bing on 7 March 1960 to say that he reluctantly felt unable to accept. 'I have all the time been hoping that somehow I might be able to rearrange things and make it possible.'

I had already promised to do some work for a film, which I cannot afford to relinquish, as it may help to clear my financial position here. Also, now my mother has, in my absence, become in a very critical condition, and the whole family has to lean on my shoulders for decisions and what calming support I can give them.

The sudden news of my nephew's engagement to Princess Margaret, though a joyful relief to balance the anxiety, has created such a commotion that it necessitates the more my being available here to help.

I so very much appreciate the kindness and everything that you did to help me over the work on *Figaro*. Everyone at the Met made me feel welcome and happy, and I hate to be denied the pleasure of being able to undertake this for you.

Messel in his garden at Maddox. Photograph by Snowdon

Maud Messel, Oliver's mother

Oliver's mother, to whom he was so deeply devoted, died in March 1960. Among the flood of condolence letters were those from three of his close professional associates:

JOHN GIELGUD

9 March 1960

Dear Oliver

I know both Anne and you will be overwhelmed with messages of sympathy, and I rather hesitate to bother you with mine. So *don't answer*, please. The death of one's mother is such a very personal and strangely final business, and I know how long her friendship with my own dear parents lasted — she was so thoughtful and sweet to them always — and to me too the few times I was lucky enough to meet her. And your brilliant achievements must have given her so much pride and pleasure. I hope she took in the news about Tony before the end. It must be so exciting for you all. See you soon, I hope.

Love, as ever, and affectionate thoughts at this sad time.

John

KATHARINE HOUGHTON HEPBURN

9 March 1960

Dear Oliver

I was so sad to hear about your Mother. It is such a ghastly moment in one's life — and a moment which never seems to come to an end — when you have had such a warm relationship as you have had. I suppose when one has great joy in someone then when they disappear one has great sadness. But at least these are fine and vital emotions and the person somehow is always there. I think very few people ever seem to know each other at all — and I know how close you were to your mother, as I was to mine — and I only know how lucky we were to have had them so dear to us even though losing them one is shattered. And the thing about life is that if one gets too old the process of living becomes a burden and she has always been so very alive to you — so really she cannot disappear from you and you have the joy of knowing that she has no more of the tears, the problems. I am so sorry that you must be made unhappy. Please know that you have my warm and affectionate sympathy.

Kate

NOEL COWARD

9 March 1960

Dearest Oliver

I know how desolate and suddenly rootless I felt when my own mother died. She was an old, old lady and it was 'high time' and all that, but it didn't mitigate the sense of loss and the feeling that the most important link of all had gone.

This doesn't require an answer; it is my job to let you know that I am thinking of you and how deeply I sympathise.

All my love
Noël

Fortunately, there were several buffers to his grief. There were the preparations for the royal marriage at Westminster Abbey on 6 May with which he became involved, and the luncheon party afterwards at Pelham Place, attended by his sister and her family, their life-long companion Addy, and other friends including Mr and Mrs Emlyn Williams and Stanley Hall.

He was also involved in redesigning the party sequence of the forthcoming reproduction of *The Sleeping Beauty* ballet at Covent Garden and three more Glyndebourne reproductions of his work required his supervision: *Der Rosenkavalier*, *La Cenerentola* and *The Magic Flute*.

The Sleeping Beauty opened on 10 June 1960 in a semi-reproduction of the original designs Oliver had created for it at the Garden in 1946. He wanted to do a new version, but, as the Royal Ballet couldn't afford to pay for a new series of designs and sets, the old ones were modified. For fourteen years on both sides of the Atlantic, this ballet had proved overwhelmingly popular with the general public, and no small part of its success was attributable to Oliver's magnificent stage pictures, brilliant in colour, breathtaking in grandeur and imaginative in design.

The role of Princess Aurora was danced on the first night by Nadia Nerina, and then successively by Annette Page, Svetlana Beriosova, Anya Linden and Antoinette Sibley. The most famous of British Princess Auroras, Margot Fonteyn, was in South America, and was scheduled to dance the role when the Royal Ballet opened its sixth tour of North America at the Met in New York the following September.

In 1960 Oliver was made Honorary Associate of the Regional College of Art, Manchester, and took up his architectural career by starting work on the ambitious restoration of Flaxley Abbey in Gloucestershire, the home of Mr and Mrs Baden Watkins. He launched himself into this assignment with confidence, for although he was not a qualified architect, he was equipped with an encyclopaedic knowledge of the history of architecture which had enabled him to achieve such signal success on the stage and in films.

Although he had always been criticized by his rivals for the exorbitant fees he charged for his work, he was continually in financial difficulties; and at this time, in 1960, he explained that the fees he asked for theatrical designs were higher than anyone else's in Europe because he was 'horribly vain'. He enjoyed being offered fabulous jobs and being paid more than anyone else for doing them; it boosted his ego. A great deal of money seemed to pass through his hands, though he was not by any means extravagant; he didn't smoke, he drank only the occasional glass of wine at dinner — and gambling was not in his blood. His income was poured into his work; supplies, salaries, rent and rates. Although he loved to entertain, he was usually so snowed under with work that he had little time to go out to parties, and preferred to have people at home when the occasion arose. He generally worked at night, usually from about eight o'clock right through to twelve noon the next day. 'But I like parties all the same,' he admitted. 'Money is not important to me, except that I usually don't have it. I know my fees may sound excessive, but I put in a terrific amount of time and work to satisfy myself, and suddenly I find myself plunged into debt.'

During this period he admitted to being 'thousands and thousands in the red', but he could not think commercially nor consider taking on assignments simply because they would pay best. He preferred to work for Glyndebourne more often, but it was hardly a lucrative choice. One year, for instance, he spent eight months designing two productions for which he was paid little, as Glyndebourne could not afford his usual level of fee. 'And you can't imagine how much it takes out of me designing the sets for an opera season at Glyndebourne. It sometimes makes me quite ill. . . . Being in debt worries me dreadfully. It's my one worry.'

He had a Danish housekeeper (Mrs Poulson) and a Danish valet-butler (Leif Hansen), and a Barbadian. In addition there were his manager (Vagn), an assistant (Carl Toms, at that time) and a fluctuating pool of other helpers to support. Surrounded as he was by these devoted workers and the possessor of strings of loyal friends, naturally enough he never felt lonely. He had only to lift the telephone receiver and his intimates would be round within minutes. Yet when he wanted to live like a hermit and opt for peace and quiet, he would shut himself away in his studio where his privacy was respected.

He was always preoccupied, however, with the impermanence of his work and felt that a council house, for instance, had a longer life than one of his sets.

While working on Flaxley Abbey he became even more interested in architecture. The first house he actually designed was for Sidney Bernstein (of Granada Television) in Barbados. 'It is what I would call a modern house,' Oliver pointed out. 'But I am not inspired, as some modern architects seem to be, by airport buildings.'

Oliver: I am not against modern things: I think the road leading to Heathrow Airport has a rather pretty shape, but I would not want to live near it. On the other hand, I would have hated to live in the eighteenth century, a period I enjoy designing so much. I think the snobbishness of the period would have been quite unbearable. The segregation of the classes is something I can't bear.

Over the next two years, he continued the restoration of Flaxley Abbey, supervised revivals at Glyndebourne of *The Abduction from the Seraglio* (first designed by him in 1956 and revived a year later) and *The Barber of Seville* in 1961, followed by *The Marriage of Figaro* and Strauss's *Ariadne auf Naxos* in 1962 (produced by Carl Ebert).

He was to team up with Ebert for the last time later that year when he returned to New York to design the sets and costumes for a new Metropolitan Opera production of *Ariadne auf Naxos*. Privately sponsored by Francis Goelet and conducted by Karl Böhm, it opened on 29 December 1962 with Leonie Rysanek singing the role of Ariadne and Jess Thomas that of Bacchus. This turned out to be Oliver's final contribution to the world of opera, but he was to return to the Met fourteen years later to design a new production of *The Sleeping Beauty*.

On returning to London he supervised a BBC television film production of *The Sleeping Beauty*, and prepared fifty canvases for an exhibition at the O'Hana Gallery, his first exhibition of paintings in London since 1938.

Oliver: All the time I was designing for the theatre I was painting, and I really enjoy it more than anything else. But I don't think many people know I'm a painter at all. I've done a lot of portraits – the Maharanee of Baroda, Ulanova, the Kabaka of Uganda, Vivien Leigh and many, many more. There was nothing directly to do with the stage in the O'Hana exhibition. I very much wanted to show the West Indies and parts of Africa where I'd been. Very few people, it seemed to me, had caught the tropical feeling of these places. I enjoyed painting coloured people, and I didn't treat them like ornaments, as some painters did; I liked to register their expressions.

His next major mission was to restore the Assembly Rooms at Bath to the glory of Beau Nash's day; they had been blitzed by German bombers in 1942, and since then had served little functional purpose for the benefit of the community. It was decided that the Rooms should house a collection of theatre costumes, which was organized by Doris Langley Moore, who had mounted various costume exhibitions in museums throughout the country. However, she boycotted the unveiling of the newly restored building, for a controversy had arisen over the bar, which Oliver felt looked like a cafeteria. It was situated in the Great Octagon, and Oliver redesigned it to fit in with the correct period of the building. Unfortunately, his design was rejected by the committee and a more modern bar substituted (not designed by him). When Princess Marina attended the opening ceremony of the new rooms, and asked to see Mrs Moore, she was told that the originator of the new museum was indisposed. Mrs Moore would not attend, in fact, because she considered the modern bar to be 'shocking', and felt that her helpers and donors had been shabbily treated by the Spa Committee.

Vagn Riis-Hansen (centre) mingles with guests at an exhibition of Messel's paintings at the O'Hana Gallery, London.

Messel working on the
redecorating of Flaxley Abbey,
Gloucestershire (1962)

Equally put out at the treatment over his new design for the bar, Oliver kept the
model he had made of it as a permanent reminder of bureaucratic buffoonery. He
had, incidentally, refused a fee for his work.

Oliver: When so much effort had gone into restoring the Assembly Rooms, not
to mention the cost of over £300,000, to their best advantage, it seemed a
mistake to clutter the space up with a permanent bar over sixteen feet long [his
own design was twelve feet long].

The history of Flaxley Abbey, Oliver's next commission, is given in a pamphlet
published by the Cistercian Abbey of Flaxley. Between 1148 and 1154 Roger
Fitz-Milo, Second Earl of Hereford, raised the monastery Flaxley Abbey in the
very clearing of the forest where his father, Milo the First Earl, had been
accidently shot dead while hunting on Christmas Eve 1143. For nearly four
hundred years the Abbey of Flaxley existed peacefully. Its history was
uneventful apart from an accident in 1234 when the monks had the temerity to
shelter Hubert de Burgh, then in disgrace with Henry III; the sheriff's men, in
pursuit of de Burgh, forced a way into the Abbey by assault. From the sixteenth

century on, the Abbey changed hands several times and was added to by each new occupant, until the interior resembled a museum, each new room or wing denoting the period in which it was built.

The last time it changed hands was in 1960 when the present owner, Mr Baden Watkins, and his late wife Phyllis, bought it. It was in dire need of restoration, and it was while Mrs Watkins was on a visit to London to buy shoes at Rayne's newly decorated premises that she had an inspiration. So impressed was she by the shop that she traced Oliver and asked him down to Flaxley Abbey, where he accepted the commission to undertake the mammoth renovation and redecoration task. His mother had died shortly before, and some of the funiture from Nymans was sold to the Watkinses.

The morning-room at Flaxley Abbey. Photograph by courtesy of *Country Life*

Baden Watkins: My grandfather was chiefly in mining; iron ore in the Forest of Dean. His name was Richard and he founded the engineering company Richard Watkins and Sons in 1860. He left it to my father and his brothers and they renamed it Fred Watkins Engineering, which it has been ever since.

When my wife and I discovered that Flaxley Abbey was on the market, we came along to the auction. But in fact it was the land I was after because my son wanted to go into farming, and so we bought this colossal house (sixteen bedrooms) in order to get the land. We first of all asked Oliver to design just the drawing room and the morning room, and it went on and on after that until he left for Barbados. I daresay that if he hadn't gone, he would still be working on the house today. He had his own room and studio here and always said that he would like to retire here; but the English weather was no good for his arthritis and so he stayed in the West Indies even though he left many of his belongings here.

The morning room, on the right-hand side of the entrance hall opposite the dining room, had been rather drab. Oliver hung the walls with gold damask and made curtains and draped pelmets of the same material. The thick carpet with apple-green background, cream oval centre, and mauve borders was made in Madrid to his design. A jib-door in the right-hand bookcase leads to the bow drawing-room, which is also approached by a short passage from the foot of the main staircase. He created the room out of a series of small rooms projecting towards the garden.

Until 1960 the upper floor of the south wing had been divided into a number of pokey little rooms, and Oliver fashioned Mr and Mrs Watkins's bedrooms out of the space they occupied. Charming touches, such as a fake fireplace set into a corner, give the rooms originality. The bathrooms were redesigned to resemble film sets, each bath set into a recess framed by swagged curtains and ornamental pelmets. What appears at first to be a cupboard in one of the bathrooms becomes the doorway leading to a corridor reached by descending half a dozen steps. Much of the design is functional, but does not seem so until it is put to work.

The most ambitious part of his undertaking at Flaxley was the formal garden. When the Watkinses came to live at Flaxley nothing of William Boevey's late-seventeenth-century layout survived. Recognizing that an exact reproduction of Boevey's intricate layout between house and avenue was out of the question, Oliver sought to cover the same area with a modified version of the original layout while giving greater emphasis than before to water. He was as meticulous as ever. The love and care he lavished on the house are evident, and the Watkinses were careful never to move so much as an ashtray without Oliver's advice. The late Mrs Watkins would go as far as to telephone him in London when she wanted to change the water in the vases!

Watkins: As he was so very gifted Oliver could do anything if he put his mind to it. When he made up his mind to get a thing done, he got it done. I never saw anything like it in my life. Once he had an inspiration, he'd get a piece of paper and sketch it out. What would have taken me five years, would take him five minutes. He had one of the ceilings done, but the workers didn't get the colour exactly as he wanted. He used to have a piece of cardboard with the design and colour on it, show it to them and say, 'That's what I want.' Three times they got it wrong, and he made them redo it three times until they got it the way he wanted it. He made models of every one of the rooms with the right colours for the walls and curtains so that he could see what it would look like when it was finished. Then when the room was done, he'd say, 'I've got a pair of mirrors at Nymans that would look right there,' and I would buy them. On one occasion he came back to say that he had seen a pair of oval side-tables at Emlyn Williams's home in London which would be dead right for the dining-room. He persuaded Williams to sell them to me. He had all the glass in the windows made in Germany. When you come down the drive you'll notice the glass is diffused. When he finished the interior furnishings of a room, he would hold up a mirror and look through it over his shoulder to see that it looked right from that point of view. And he was never wrong.

When he came over, he was so pleased to find that there was nothing out of place. After all, he was the artist, and it was no good trying to tell him what the things should be like.

In 1962, while working on the Flaxley Abbey restorations, Oliver was asked to decorate the Oliver Messel Suite for the wedding of Sir Berkeley Ormerod and Mrs Beatrice Sigrist. Mrs Sigrist was the widow of Frederick Sigrist, who made his fortune in the aircraft industry during both wars, and it was their famous daughter Bobo who, as a debutante, eloped with Greg Juarez, a South American, creating sensational comment in the gossip columns at the time. The Ormerods had one daughter who married Hamish McAlpine of the McAlpine family, who built and owned the Dorchester.

Ormerod, who was in charge of the British Information Services in New York, was knighted for his work there. When he married Beatrice Sigrist they had their reception at the Dorchester. Oliver converted the outside terrace of the Suite into a conservatory and draped masses of yellow roses everywhere.

After their marriage the couple stayed in the Oliver Messel Suite every year from July to October, until Lady Ormerod's death at their home in the Bahamas in 1981; Sir Berkeley died in London while on holiday the following year.

By 1963 Oliver had completed the bulk of the work at Flaxley Abbey – his major architectural accomplishment – although there was still a great deal more to do before his assignment was ended. It had taken him over three years so far, while working simultaneously on other projects.

Aside from the decorations for the Sigrist-Ormerod wedding, he did some designs for Donegal Carpets and advised the Hon. Clive Pearson on his house in Parham Park, for which he designed the long gallery, and he supervised redecorations for the Green Street Club in London.

Over the next three years Glyndebourne presented further revivals of his productions: *Figaro* in 1963, *Idomeneo* in 1964, and *Rosenkavalier* and *Figaro* again in 1965. During this period he also accepted various commissions for portraits of Mrs Reginald 'Daisy' Fellowes, Sir Jack Campbell, the Maharanee of Baroda, and Mr Albert Baer in New York.

His thoughts, however, were far away. Barbados suited him; the climate was essential for his health; he had always admired black people and the island offered him seclusion to work without interruption. Settling in Barbados was to bring him contentment, but mixed with a certain anxiety, for it was not only his own health that was deteriorating rapidly, but Vagn's as well.

8

A model of the house Messel
designed for Lord Bernstein in
Barbados

8 * Islands in the Sun

THE HIGHEST PRAISE of the West Indian island of Barbados, where Oliver spent the last fifteen years of his life, is to be found, according to George Hunte, author of a book called *Barbados* in *Westward Ho!*, a novel of no great literary distinction but representative of British political and commercial attitudes prevalent in the decade that preceded the first settlements in the West Indies in 1869. Through his mother's eyes, Charles Kingsley was to see Barbados as 'that lovely isle, the richest gem of all tropic seas'. From recollections of the childhood she spent there as the daughter of Nathan Lucas, a rich landowner, Kingsley borrowed splendid images of Barbados at sunrise and sunset. He describes how, at dawn, 'up flushed the rose, up rushed the sun, whose level rays filtered on the smooth stems of the palm-trees, and threw rainbows across the foam upon the coral reefs and gilded lonely uplands far away', while at sunset the island became 'a long blue bar between the crimson sea and golden sky'.

Had it not been for Victor Marson, it is unlikely that Oliver would have chosen Barbados as his paradise island. Barbados's most successful hotelier, Marson had originally owned a private beach house on the fashionable west coast, which he turned into the well-appointed Miramar Hotel. After many years of success with yet another hotel, the Ocean View, on the south coast, Marson went into partnership with Donald Scott, and together with an English naval commander, Bellairs, they developed the Coral Reef Hotel; its main building, Manizilla, had formerly been the commander's private home. Marson later converted the Miramar into a small exclusive resort; while under his management it was used for the dinner sequence in the Twentieth Century-Fox film *Island in the Sun*. The beautiful flowering trees at Miramar and the avenue of cabbage palms were planted by Marson, who also became the greatest expert in the art of cookery to have lived in Barbados since Richard Ligon laid the foundation of Barbadian cuisine in the mid-seventeenth century.

Nowadays Marson, retired, lives at Highclere, a charming house set high in the hills, which looks down from a thousand feet on the rugged, unfriendly east coast.

Victor Marson: Oliver and I were very great friends and for years I had encouraged him to come and live in Barbados. He and Vagn had holidayed with me at my private house at Miramar, and as they fell in love with Barbados I felt they should stay. One day in London Oliver asked me to luncheon at Pelham Place. 'I've got something I want you to see.' And he showed me sketches he had done for improvements to a house called Maddox.

I had known Maddox quite well. A cousin of mine had lived there for years and a coloured man, Paul Clark, bought it from him. Oliver told me that he had bought it from Clark for £25,000, which was a fair price in those days. I said, 'You're mad. Do you know what it's going to cost to turn it into the sort of place

Messel and his assistant at his Barbadian home, Maddox. Photograph by Snowdon

you would have it be?' He said, 'Yes. But we'll only do bits at a time.' I laughed. I knew Oliver too well for that!

The house that Oliver had found, of simple Barbadian design, stood a little beyond Miramar on the seaside north of the fashionable Sandy Lane Hotel, opposite many other simple 'badjan' houses — a term used to describe the light timber-built huts, occupied by the locals, which are supported on brickwork so that they can be easily moved to other locations. The plan Oliver had mapped out was to convert Maddox into a place for 'indoor-outdoor' living with porches, upper verandah, lower verandah, and dining room facing outwards to the sea across thick foliage screens of tropical trees and ornamental plants. It was this idyllic spot that not only the Queen and Prince Philip, Queen Elizabeth the Queen Mother, Princess Margaret and the Earl of Snowdon visited, but every other dignitary to set foot on the island as well. The house owned by Claudette Colbert, Bellerive, is situated nearby in St Peter. Her neighbour, Verna Hull, also became a close friend of Oliver and Vagn, and Miss Hull was always generous to the two men, particularly later on when Oliver's finances caused real concern.

Claudette Colbert: The reason I went to live in Barbados was because of Oliver and I'll always be grateful to him for that. When my husband [the late Dr Joel Pressman] and I spent Christmas with Noël [Coward] in Jamaica in 1954 we loved it there and I said to him, 'We've got to have a house here; the water is great.' But Joel had to return to his practice and I stayed on for another week. And then we forgot about the idea of living in Jamaica and bought a house in Palm Springs instead.

The first time I met Oliver was at one of his parties in Pelham Place when he was designing the Oliver Messel Suite for the Dorchester Hotel in London. He had a magic way of giving parties — there were flowers everywhere and strokes of genius at every turn. He left me four of those adorable monkeys he had made for the Justerini and Brooks window in Bond Street. We met up again in New York when I was playing *Marriage-Go-Round* on Broadway with Charles Boyer in 1959. I had gone to Oliver's art exhibition at the Sagittarius Gallery where I bought one of his paintings, and we lunched together afterwards. He'd had a very busy time in New York designing the interior for the Billy Rose Theatre and the production of *Rashomon* on Broadway and was in need of a well-deserved holiday. When he told me that he had chosen Barbados, as I still had a hankering for Jamaica, I asked, 'What's the difference between Barbados and Jamaica?' and he replied, 'Night and day.' So I called my husband and said, 'When the play closes do you think we could go to Barbados and try it?' That's what we did and I fell in love with the island. Oliver knew the house that I bought — but he had nothing to do with it structurally or artistically.

When he first heard that I had bought it, he said, 'Don't do a thing to it. It's just *perfect*.' But frankly, enchanting as it was, looking across the Caribbean with a lovely garden leading down to the beach, there wasn't a *piece* of wood in it that hadn't been chewed up by termites! And it was so typical of Oliver, because he would never have touched it and the whole house would have fallen down on his head! But he loved that house and I kept it the way it was for a while because he kept saying, 'Don't do *anything* to it!' However, I finally had to do something about the woodwork, otherwise the house would have fallen down on *my* head! I

Model of Messel's set for the Anouilh play, *Traveller without Luggage* (1964)

must say, we laughed a lot about it afterwards. I didn't want Oliver to redesign any of the interior because, rather like Princess Margaret and her own house in Mustique, I wanted to do 'my own thing'. And I did, because it's the only home I have.

I was very fond of him and I saw a lot of him in Barbados – as much as I could, that is, when I wasn't on tour with a new play. We both entertained a great deal and had innumerable mutual friends – not always theatrical ones – such as Renaldo and Carolina Herrera from Venezuela. Carolina is a great fashion designer in New York and she stayed with Oliver at Maddox on many occasions, where he painted her.

But even though there were the times when I didn't see him I remained constantly grateful to him for encouraging me to settle in Barbados – where I shall continue to live until the end of my days and think of him with the deepest love.

Traveller without Luggage, which opened at the ANTA Theatre on 18 September 1964, was Oliver's penultimate contribution to Broadway, and it was followed by two other major theatrical disappointments: *Twang!!* in London and *Gigi* on Broadway. Although these were his last assignments for original theatre design on both sides of the Atlantic, where he had enjoyed such outstanding success, the outright failure of these three productions could hardly be attributed to his own involvement in them.

Adapted by Lucienne Hill from Jean Anouilh's *Voyageur sans Bagages*, *Traveller without Luggage* opened with high expectations, but managed no more than forty-four performances. Though Oliver's sets were thought to be effective, the play itself aroused little response.

He now faced the most harrowing production of his career. On his return to London after the opening of *Traveller without Luggage*, he was contacted by Lionel Bart, author of the phenomenally successful musical *Oliver!*, who had an idea for a new musical. He explained to Oliver that the Robin Hood story had been made stale by innumerable pantomimes through the years, and he intended to freshen up the plot by injecting into it some element to which pantomimes could not aspire — and this became the chief problem. He asked Oliver to design the production to be called *Twang!!* which began — and ended — in disaster for everyone who became connected with it. It was, sadly, the last production Oliver was to do in London: 'I spent months designing it, and it was absolute, complete rubbish. At first it was directed by Joan Littlewood; then Burt Shevelove, the American writer, composer and director, was brought in to try to save the production which was scheduled to open at the Shaftesbury Theatre, with Barbara Windsor as leading lady, on 20 December 1965.'

While in London Oliver and Vagn had decided to go into business in Barbados and had entered into partnership with an engineer for the venture. They planned to open a factory where sugar cane waste could be reprocessed and manufactured into construction materials such as assimilated chip-board, known as *bigas*. It was also possible to reprocess other sugar cane waste into additives for cattle feed. This idea had proved successful in South America, South Africa and Britain, and depending on the installation of the right machinery and reliable technical advice there seemed no reason why it should not succeed in Barbados as well. It was Vagn's responsibility to oversee the investment in Barbados with the technical support of their partner, while Oliver worked on *Twang!!* in London. Letters of deep concern, not only about their investment, which seemed to be faltering, but also about the behind-the-scenes dramas emanating from *Twang!!*, were sent to Vagn almost daily. The Barbadian government had provided a substantial grant for the new enterprise — and that, together with Oliver's £10,000 investment, seemed to be in jeopardy.

Slight *crise* day! My back playing me up and still no clear story to work on, and realising that I had been working over a month with no contract signed I would have no security if anything went wrong. A slight outburst of hysteria on my part claiming it impossible to proceed at least has precipitated contract arrangements. Feel better this evening; the contract and cheque have arrived!

Feel so anxious over all you have to cope with.

High sparks and big dramas!! between Joan and Lionel. Joan walked out as Lionel kept interfering and writing silly little notes, etc., etc. Now Joan has won the day for the time being, and Lionel is not allowed to the rehearsals. How the show is going, I don't know. The first act walk-through seemed a terrible muddle to me, but maybe they may comb it out. Poor Stanley Moore made the trees terribly badly, some back to front and losing the line of drawing so that they looked more like Christmas stockings.

At the same time, Vagn was having contractual difficulties over the new venture, and trouble with the installation of machinery. Oliver wrote, asking him to answer these questions:

Model of Messel's set for the ill-fated Lionel Bart musical, *Twang!!* (1965)

1. Has Jock agreed to a proper working agreement acceptable to all of us?
2. Is the full amount of money in hand now to start?
3. Is all the machinery completed and ready to go into production and the correct resins in store?
4. What date can we possibly hope to start on plain sheeting and cattle feed?
5. What was the hitch before? Was it the installations of the boiler in order to get the steam pressure, or what else was missing? I understood when we left that the production of shingles and plain sheeting and cattle feed was already starting. What has happened?

Not surprisingly, in view of the stress he was suffering Oliver contracted shingles:

How desperate is the situation? Is it bad enough for me to have to sell the Rolls? I suppose should we have to, I could get a good price for it.

If only something wonderful would turn up. Please give my love to Claudette and Verna and all at Maddox.
P.S. Joan Littlewood is back. She is always very sympathetic and pleasant to work with which is nice.

Your long letter arrived and I can picture vividly those awful meetings and the anxiety of it all.

Anne, Michael, Tony and David [Snowdon's son, Lord Linley] popped in to see me this evening before dinner. Anne and Michael are off to Italy to stay with Harold [Acton] and Princess Margaret and Tony are off to Sardinia, or wherever; it is where the Aga Khan has a doodah! David peeped in to see all the theatre models and was endearing. Miss Poulson and all the Pelham family are well and send their love.

Despite extensive publicity about radical changes and hectic activity since its Manchester opening, *Twang!!* was a dismal flop. Penelope Gilliatt reported in

225

The Observer: 'Sometimes musicals seem more capable of breeding misery than anything else in show-biz, apart perhaps from Bible epics. The tasks they set are often well-nigh barmy. In *Twang's!!* case, for instance, who on earth can ever have thought that it would work to put Joan Littlewood and Oliver Messel together? Joan Littlewood has, of course, long since left this mercilessly unfunny show and been replaced by Burt Shevelove. Oliver Messel is still involved, though not at all distinctively.' *The Times* was equally scathing, though its critic found the show visually attractive. 'Oliver Messel's decor makes the most of the contrast between gentle Arcadian settings and court glitter. The show that inhabits these elegant surroundings seems intended as a Cockney *Camelot*.'

It was sad that Oliver's swan-song on the English stage should end in such disaster. He was more concerned, however, with his new house and wrote to Vagn with instructions:

I will try and send drawings for the wooden trellis gates as soon as I can. At the moment I am utterly worn out and have started another damned bout of shingles so I have to try and take things bit by bit.

I would like Johnson [one of their staff] to get some golden shower to plant all along the staff wing so that it will just look green, then moonflowers could grow into it. On the patio entrance side I think I put some stephanotis to grow up but I don't remember if we planted it or not. It could go both sides if we have enough to spare. I also want to get some more *beaumontia*, beautiful tubular climber, and some chalice vine.

Having finally managed to sell his adjoining Pelham Place houses (to the Hon. Mrs Jessica Jane Vronwy White, who paid £30,000 for the leasehold), Oliver was prevented from travelling to his new home because of an arthritic hip. He was admitted to the King Edward VIIth Hospital for an operation. On 7 March 1966 he wrote to Vagn from the hospital:

One more uneventful day brings it that much nearer, not just one week left. Poor Pelham Place, I gather, is now stripped to the bone. George has gone down to Flaxley with another load. Brenda [Haydon, his secretary] has fled to her sanctum.

The nice day-nurse returned today and I am making splendid progress, so the stairs at Maddox will be no problem. The progress I am making appears to be unprecedented and marvelled at. The only impediment being my back which of course is achy from being in bed and I naturally get easily tired, so I am thankful to have the good special nurses.

Although Oliver had sent a good deal of his personal belongings on to Barbados, there was, of course, the question of storing the vast quantity of his designs, theatre models, costumes and masks; and as he was one for never throwing anything away, there was enough to fill a factory. Princess Margaret came to his rescue.

Snowdon: Before Oliver went to Barbados, he left all his *maquettes* in London and Princess Margaret very sweetly looked after them at Kensington Palace where they were stored in the heated and disused chapel. They had polythene covers put over them to protect them against dust and they remained there until after Oliver's death.

Although my original idea was to house them at stables which I intended to be converted into an art gallery at Nymans (and later I received an offer to put them on display in a private museum in Canada), after twelve years I gave them on permanent loan to the Victoria and Albert Museum for the benefit of the nation. And when they left Kensington Palace for the Victoria and Albert Museum, there was not one break, crack or chip in any of them, they had been so magnificently looked after.

When he emigrated to Barbados and embarked upon a new career as architect and interior designer, Oliver was almost sixty-three. He was to design innumerable houses in Barbados, and on one of its neighbouring islands, Mustique. The first of these, in Barbados, was Leamington for Mrs Drue Heinz, wife of Henry John (Jack) Heinz II of the canned food empire. It is a movie-star type house on the 'golden mile', or 'millionaires' row', on the west coast near the Sandy Lane Hotel.

Nick Paravicino, a leading estate agent in Barbados became a friend of Oliver's and subsequently handled his business affairs:

Paravicino: Leamington had come on the market, and one night when Oliver and Vagn threw a huge barbecue party at the Colony Club, Drue Heinz was there. Now Oliver and Vagn could sell anything if they wanted to, and they talked about what a wonderful place Barbados was, what they could do with Leamington if it came into their hands. They spoke so enthusiastically that Drue Heinz said, 'Look, Nick, if you can get this house for me at a reasonable price, I'll talk my husband into buying it.' I got hold of the current owners, who were in England, over the weekend; she made an offer on the Monday for, I think, £30,000, which was the popular price in those days. Oliver then redid the house for her.

Mrs Heinz came over for the first three or four winters, but then rather tired of Barbados and didn't return for a while. I used to rent it out to Katharine Graham, the owner of the *Washington Post*, who came here every winter. Then when she stopped travelling I leased it to the American government and an American Ambassador lived there for a long time. It was finally sold to Mr and Mrs Peter Caffyn-Parsons from England who spend the winter months there.

Although Oliver didn't know the island too well, he always met the right people. He had a lot of local friends on whom he could draw for advice and experience, and of course he entertained overseas visitors to the island. He became a great friend of Lyall Ward. The Ward family owned Mount Gay Distilleries, famous for their brands of rum, and a surviving Ward is our Governor-General. They are probably the most respected coloured people on the island, and terribly rich, and old Lyall Ward would do anything for Oliver.

The redesign of Crystal Springs, Mrs Stephen Catsford's enchanting house next door to Maddox, was Oliver's next commission.

He incorporated into the design an innovation he was to repeat in all the subsequent houses he undertook either to design from scratch or to convert: vistas from the front door right through the house to the Caribbean just beyond. The inside-outside feeling, reminiscent of the early Barbadian dwellings, became his hallmark.

Formal living rooms are seldom used in the West Indies, even in the large plantation houses, and Oliver's architecture evoked many features from the past: shutters and sash windows with little hoods to prevent the sun's glare, a good deal of trellis work — and stairs leading to the upper quarters built on the outside of the house rather than inside. For the floors Oliver used cement and coral stone dust, mixed, with lines drawn across them — and over-painted with a coloured sealing agent to add his desired design effect.

The original owner of Crystal Springs was Jock Cotell, a scientist from England, who sold it to Mrs Catsford. She carpeted it in white nylon and introduced air-conditioning — but when she called Oliver in to advise on the redecoration he felt there was a need of fresh air and dispensed with both the carpet and the air-conditioning plant. Eileen and Arnold Maremont bought the house from Mrs Catsford in 1971 and they lived there happily until Mr Maremont's death eight years later; Mrs Maremont has remained there. Crystal Springs started out as a beach house and, like Maddox next door, stands 20 feet above sea level. Its terraces are unique, spilling down to the private beach below with little alcoves at various levels where tables and chairs offer lazy comfort in the cool of the overhanging foliage. The house has different dining areas, and gives one the feeling of being on the deck of a ship.

The house called Alan Bay was originally built in 1960 for Alan Godsal, a member of an English family whose ancestors had settled in Barbados in the early days. It has since been bought by Peter Moores, heir to the Littlewoods football pools empire and said to be one of the richest men in Britain.

Adding iron gates and the open verandah looking onto the sea, Oliver completed the improvements in the mid-sixties.

Fustic House, on the north of the island, is owned by the author Charles Graves. Oliver did many structural alterations to this house and redesigned the interior as well. Below the gardens he carved a pool out of rock and added a decorative pagoda.

But perhaps the most controversial house that went through Oliver's hands is the one called Mango Bay. Instead of merely living in renovated houses, Oliver had longed to build something for himself, and with that objective in view he began buying up what is now the site of Mango Bay, a short distance from the popular Sandy Lane Hotel. In accordance with local inheritance patterns, the plot had been divided into tiny parcels, and he had to negotiate with more than fifty owners before he could put the property together. The result, of course, was that Oliver came to look upon Mango Bay as *his* house, even after he had sold the land to Mrs Sally Aall and her husband, and then built the house and designed the garden and the interiors for her.

Mr and Mrs Aall, who had visited Barbados periodically, wanted to buy a house there, but none that was on the market was suitable. The Aalls learnt that Oliver owned the plot of land known as Mango Bay, but Mrs Aall, who had met Oliver at parties, was determined that he should not design the house if she managed to persuade him to sell the land to her. She had her own ideas about how she wanted to decorate it and knew that she and Oliver would be in constant combat. She wasn't wrong. Oliver would not sell the property to her unless she agreed to let him both design the house and decorate the interior. It was a Catch-22 situation. She wanted the property, and realized that she could always change the house afterwards.

Mango Bay, the house in Barbados designed by Messel, which became the property of Mrs Sally Aall, and later of Averell Harriman. A watercolour by Richard Day

Sally Aall: When I got back to Barbados from America, Oliver had almost completed the house. I took one look inside and said, 'Oliver, to get from upstairs to downstairs, could I please have a barber's pole?' And he said, 'Oh, my God, I forgot the stairs!'

Well, of course, he was joking about that because he had them built on the outside in keeping with the tradition of the early estates in the West Indies. However, tradition or not, when I come down to see my guests, I might be blown to bits if there happens to be a gale — which is rare in the West Indies — or saturated in the pelting rain — which is equally rare, but I have to remember to keep an umbrella upstairs — and even that can be awkward to handle if I need to bring something else down at the same time. Although he was very emotional, underneath all that he was like steel — but he had a marvellous kind of giggle-gurgle. He was a great actor, too. For instance, when we had arguments about the house — we had plenty and he won them all! — tears would start rolling down his face and he would say, 'Sally, you don't understand me.' And that was the end of the discussion!

Building at Mango Bay started in 1968 and the house was completed the following year. A particular skill of Oliver's was to give his work an instant antique patina, and from the beginning the house looked settled, as if handed down for several generations. In this respect it was helped by fine old mahogany and tamarind in the garden, an African tulip in the front drive, and two great cordias on the lawn that stretched between the house and the sea.

The two-storied house is of solid structure, with green shutters and an open balcony that runs the length and width of the building. 'I woke up one evening at about midnight,' Sally Aall recalls, 'having heard a sound on the balcony. I put my head through the window and found one of Oliver's young workers laying the cement mix and coral stone dust slabs on my terrace with the help of a booklet called *How to Lay Terrazzo* which he was skimming through by torch-light, and then doing what it instructed, on *my* terrace in the dead of night! However, I have to admit that it was a new method devised by Oliver and one couldn't expect the locals to know how to do it from experience they had never had.'

Because of ill-health and staff problems, Sally Aall sold Mango Bay in 1984. She was fortunate, however, in finding the ideal purchaser in the Hon. Mrs Averell Harriman. At one time Harriman was Governor of New York, but he is best remembered for his Ambassadorships to the USSR and Britain. The Harrimans bought Mango Bay for a reputed $740,000 (the original asking price was reportedly $1,250,000), and it is anticipated that they will enjoy the environment that Oliver created.

Another charming house, Cockade, is owned by Mrs Pauline Haywood, who was born in South Carolina; her family have been in Barbados since the eighteenth century, having come from England to the sugar plantations. Polly Haywood spent many holidays in Barbados, and met Oliver there through Ronald Tree, a banker, former Tory MP and inheritor of a great American fortune, who went to Barbados some years after Sir Edward Cunard and Commander Carlyon Bellairs had blazed a trail by building beach houses on the deserted sand acres of the west coast. Polly and Oliver became firm friends, and their friendship deepened in the last few years of Oliver's life, as she was living in Barbados more or less permanently and was able to see him often.

When she thought of buying a house of her own, Oliver suggested the ruin of the old Haywood plantation great-house with the idea of restoring it. Unfortunately, a major road ran within ten yards of the entrance, and as Polly Haywood preferred privacy, she settled on Cockade House which at that time was called Landscape. Originally built by Wilfred Alston on the site of a seventeenth-century plantation great-house, it was virtually derelict, having stood empty for several years. Some of the original stonework remained and there were magnificent three hundred-year-old tamarinds, mahogany and frangipani.

Polly Haywood: I took Oliver to see it and he thought it was pretty ghastly. 'It looks like a post box, darling, but never mind, we'll make something wonderful out of it.' And indeed he did.

It wasn't all that easy, as a matter of fact; it took two and a half years to complete. I was living in New York at that time and spending a lot of time with my husband in the Far East. In the meantime Oliver had been commissioned to design the costumes for *Gigi* in America and therefore had to leave Cockade uncompleted. The local architect/contractor I had hired for the technical side of things had a nervous breakdown and then went bankrupt. He left the island, which meant that everyone was away, leaving twenty workmen on the site each day working without supervision.

Therefore lots of things went wrong, including the hardware for the doors and windows, custom-ordered from New York at vast expense and carefully labelled by the firm and again by me for each specific place. Since there was no supervision, they were set in the most bizarre way and could not be changed

An interior view of the house called Cockade, which Messel reconverted for Mrs Pauline Haywood

without redoing the doors and windows and re-ordering new fixtures. As a result, I have had several ladies locked in the lavatory as the locks had been put on back to front. However, none of it mattered in the final analysis, as Oliver produced the most magic effect in an enchanting garden with an overall 'Turgenev decadence' atmosphere, which has given enormous joy and pleasure to me and numerous guests for these past ten years.

I shall forever miss those teas (and afterwards drinks, which Oliver knew I preferred) when he would ring and say the newspapers had arrived from England. 'Come and share a gossip,' he would say. I shall miss sharing the love of all beautiful things with him, together with the fun and delight of just being with him.

While working on the designs and decorations for these various houses, Oliver was as industrious as ever and completed portraits for Penelope Tree, Mrs Theodora Campbell, Miss Arabella Churchill, the actress Adrianne Allen and Princess Natasha Paley, the Russian-born beauty who married Noël Coward's life-long friend, the producer Jack Wilson.

In mid-1968, Howard Koch wrote to Oliver from Paramount Pictures, to say that the director Vincente Minnelli wanted him to design the sets and costumes for the Regency scenes of the Barbra Streisand film, *On a Clear Day You Can See Forever*. Oliver declined the offer, even though he was badly in need of money, and replied on 14 May to Koch's letter:

I was so delighted when Mr Vincente Minnelli spoke to me on the telephone about the idea as I so much admire all that he does and would more than anything wish to have been able to have had this opportunity of working with him and with you.

However, when I come down to reality I realise that I have undertaken architectural projects and commitments over here on such an enormous scale which demands continual supervision that I find, alas, that it would be impossible at this time to break away. I remember the story as I was originally asked to design the theatre production

A balcony designed by Messel for Sir Roderick Brinckman's house in Barbados

for New York, and in a film it would have given more scope to be effectively realised than with the limitations of the stage.

I appreciate so much your asking me and greatly regret that at this time it isn't possible.

His order book was full. He was planning the reconstruction of Queen's Fort for Mr Frank Packard and was working on the designs for a house for his old friend Mark Gilbey (of the distillery family), to be built in Dominica. He had just completed the additions for Sir Roderick Brinckman's house, St Helena, and had been commissioned by the Hon. Colin Tennant to design all the new houses on the island of Mustique which Tennant had bought.

In 1960 Princess Margaret and Lord Snowdon had spent their honeymoon on the royal yacht *Britannia*. It was while they were on this six-weeks cruise of the Caribbean that Princess Margaret first saw the small island on which a modest house would eventually be built for her.

Mustique, in the Windward Islands, which at that time contained 1,250 undeveloped acres, eight beaches and two harbours, is three miles long and a mile wide. It has no water supply of its own; rain water from the roofs is conserved in large tanks built beneath the houses. To this day fresh drinking water is brought over by ship from the larger neighbouring island of St Vincent to the only hotel on the island, the Cotton House, which was the first building Oliver converted in Mustique.

The then Hon. Colin Tennant gave the Princess a plot of land as a wedding present, although when she first set foot on the island's white sands the precise location of the gift was undecided. The site finally chosen occupies a headland just big enough for a house and a small tropical garden. A mass of dense, thorny vegetation cloaks the steep slope down to the coves and lagoons of Gelliceaux Bay below. The architecture of the house was created by Oliver, but the Princess designed the interior decoration herself and named the house *Les Jolies Eaux*, pretty waters.

Oliver's final plans for the one-level house materialized in a U-shaped building constructed from locally quarried stone and set round three sides of a paved courtyard overlooking the swimming pool. Central to the design is the south-facing sitting-room which, when the doors are all folded back, is completely open to the air. Occupying the breadth of the house, this area is flanked by two short wings which contain the kitchen and four bedrooms. From the terrace one descends to a lower level, where there is a wooden gazebo with palm-thatched roof, which affords a panoramic view of the surrounding islands.

While working on *Rashomon* with Oliver in 1959 Carl Toms had met Lord Snowdon, who photographed the production in New York. The Kensington Palace apartment where Princess Margaret and Snowdon were to settle after their marriage had been bombed during the war, and Snowdon together with Toms had set about restoring and redecorating the premises. They worked together again on the design for Prince Charles's Investiture as Prince of Wales at Carnaervon Castle, for which Toms was awarded the O.B.E.

When I travelled to Mustique to see the houses that Oliver had designed, I visited Princess Margaret, two of whose guests were Toms, who I had known for many years, and Colin Tennant.

Tennant, a millionaire Scottish aristocrat, is tall, tanned and possesses a Douglas Fairbanks quality; flamboyantly attired in casual Caribbean wear, he dons a stetson to shelter his brow from the blistering midday sun. He became the Third Baron Glenconner on the death of his father in October 1983. At the turn of the century, his grandfather, a clever Lowland Scot from Peeblesshire, had made a large fortune out of chemical manufacturing. The First Baron was created Lord Glenconner in 1911; the Second Baron Glenconner (Colin Tennant's father) sold out the business. The chemical side was sold to ICI and Lord Glenconner became a director. The commodity trading side was sold to Consolidated Gold Fields, of which Lord Glenconner also became a director, but as he had no particular liking for business he resigned in 1967 and retired to a lovely house on the island of Corfu. His son Colin, aged 45, who had worked in the commodity business and was still working then, became chief executive of the subsidiary C. Tennant Sons Co. Ltd, where he remained until 1967. All that life could offer came his way; he had inherited wealth, married Princess Margaret's lady-in-waiting Lady Anne Coke, who bore him five children, and he was a close friend of the Royal Family.

Mustique had been owned for many years by the Hazell family of St Vincent. Their tenant farmers raised cattle, but it proved to be unprofitable and they sold it to Colin Tennant for a reputed £45,000. Tennant became Chairman of the Mustique Company Limited in 1969, but sold his major shareholding in the 'seventies for ten times the original amount, having transformed the arid island into a millionaire's paradise in which the residents enjoy the privacy of a remote existence in charming homes designed by Oliver.

Our topic of conversation was Oliver — and Princess Margaret, Carl Toms and the new Lord Glenconner exchanged their views on the subject:

Carl Toms: Oliver hated using rulers and set squares, but he would sometimes draw in freehand on the squared paper.

Princess Margaret: But the discipline he had to adopt for my house was different and with the squared paper he had to do it right for the architecture. So that's why it was an added discipline and that's why he was so good.

Glenconner: If Princess Margaret had not turned up at Mustique, life would have been quite drab. The Princess saw the need for someone of Oliver's capabilities and without his contribution to the island there would have been a loss to both Mustique and Oliver himself. Oliver appreciated scale; he got the rhythm, scale and taste right for Mustique at the end of 1969. At that time people weren't prepared to spend money here, and it was sheer luck that Princess Margaret came in at that point.

No architect would have been prepared to give up his practice to take on the Mustique commitment. Oliver was paid £1,000 to design each house — he designed fifteen in all — and the copyright of each design was assigned to the Mustique company, which is responsible for the administration of the island (under the legal patronage of the St Vincent government), for execution as part of the contractual fee. Arne Hasselquist, who is the Mustique Company's resident building contractor, saw to the construction and completion of the building of the properties.

Princess Margaret had always admired Oliver's work; as a great supporter of the arts she had, of course, seen his splendid productions at Covent Garden and had often visited his design and portrait exhibitions in London.

Princess Margaret: I told Oliver what I'd like built and so he produced a plan and we all mucked about with it up in Scotland at the Tennant house. I explained to Oliver that I wanted to get the details of the house straight from the start and that I would do the interior myself, upon which he giggled. He always giggled when he was in doubt about anything, but he was in no doubt about my wanting to do the interior. When he got down to the architecture, he drew to scale on squared paper; he was only squiggly about costume design.

During our discussion about Oliver and Princess Margaret's house in Mustique, Carl Toms enlarged on Oliver's tactics:

Carl Toms: We were working late and we were talking about something and Oliver said, 'Oh, I can cry at will.' And he did.
Princess Margaret: Do you think he was putting it on?
Carl Toms: I think a lot of it was anger and fury, and I also think he was quite capable of using it as a form of emotional blackmail. He thought, 'If they won't let me have my way over this, I'll show them.'
Princess Margaret: Fortunately, it never happened with me, because I said I was going to do the inside and he never even bartered with me. He said to me, 'You've got *carte blanche* to move anything around inside,' so I did. He did a very Oliver impractical thing by putting the kitchen on the windward side of the house and all the kitchen smells came through the house. So I got him to put it next to the dining room. But I think you will find in nearly all the houses he designed that the kitchens are in the wrong place for the dining room.
Glenconner: He certainly lost a few of my clients through that very thing. There was a Mrs Clarke who was going to build a house in Mustique, and her daughter,

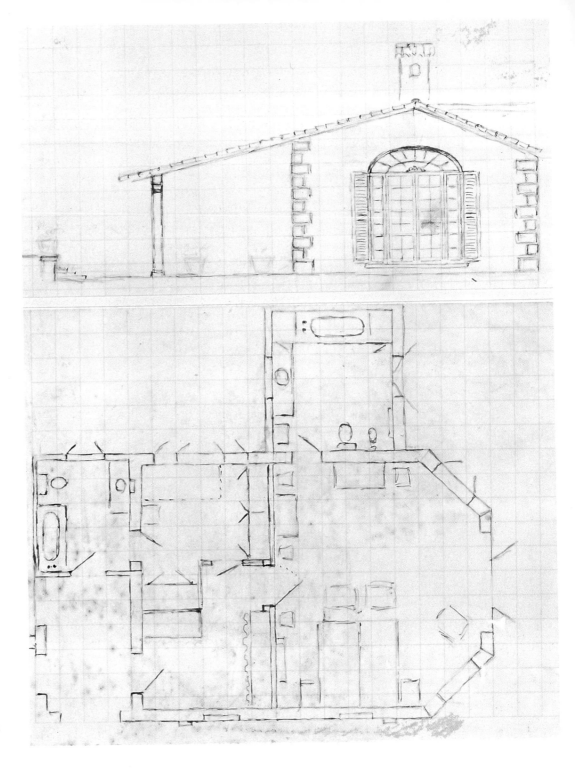

An elevation and floor plan by Messel of Barbadian projects in the 1960s

who had taken a *cordon bleu* cookery course, was set on how she wanted the kitchen. The house had a central door, as always. The kitchen was on one side of the front door, but Oliver put the pantry and larder on the other side of it. The daughter, whose passion was cooking for people, said she would like to have it otherwise, and Oliver said he wouldn't move it. Well, Mrs Clarke and her daughter left and they never came back. Strangely enough, kitchens apart, however many mistakes he made or however much one argued with him, he nearly always proved to be right.

Princess Margaret: When I came over to move in, Colin reckoned that it would take three days before I got in. The living room floor had been sealed with the wrong stuff, however, and the sun came streaming in and turned it a sickly yellow. It was the most terrible task because it took thirty men with scrapers to get it off. And there we sat in gloomsville, getting gloomier and gloomier. We used to come up every day through the kitchen door and unpack the packing cases and wash the glasses and the china but we couldn't get into the living room because the men were scraping the floor.

The best thing about Oliver was taste. He always got the shape right. He took enormous trouble in getting the proportions exact. And the worst thing about him was that if he was in a bad mood he'd write very tiresome letters!

Carl Toms: It was what I used to call his 'bee in the bonnet' time. Every time we'd be in the middle of a frantic amount of work and something attracted his attention, he would be determined to do something about it. Take the 'Kabaka of Buganda' business, for instance. We were all frightfully busy with endless work to finish and he got us to write letters to politicians and campaign to get the Kabaka back on his throne.

Princess Margaret: What is so wonderful is that this person, who of course was quite oldish when I married Tony, became a sort of beloved uncle, and he was great fun; awfully funny – but he wasn't as good a mimic as Tony!

I'm very pleased with what Oliver did for *Les Jolies Eaux*. This is *my* house, the only square inch in the world I own, and Oliver was a major contributor to it.

The celebrated American theatre and film director, Joshua Logan, recalls in his memoirs *Movie Stars, Real People and Me* (Delacorte Press) the time he gave a party in New York in honour of Princess Margaret and Lord Snowdon. Snowdon had paid several visits to New York before on assignments for American *Vogue*, but on this occasion work was not involved: 'The idea for the party started years before in London when we first became friends with Oliver,' Logan writes. 'We soon became very close to him and whenever we were in London he gave us a party, and when he was in America ours was his home. At one point we saw him daily as he painted my wife Nedda's portrait.'

When Oliver came to New York, he often brought his young nephew Tony to us for cocktails. Tony was a talented photographer who was enormously friendly and in turn as quick to laugh as his uncle.

We hadn't seen him for the several years that they had been married when Oliver wrote that Tony and Princess Margaret were going to take a trip through the United States, and asked whether we would have a luncheon for them. Of course we said yes, but soon Oliver felt it should be a little bigger, and we suggested dinner. Oliver sent us a list of the guests he felt they would like; we added the friends we thought they should meet; and it soon became a downhill sleigh ride headed for a proper bash.

We had decided to invite people we thought would interest our British visitors the most, but even that list spread into dozens, and therefore we had to eliminate some of the ones we loved to make room for those chosen by Oliver. Our apartment could, at a stretch, hold slightly over a hundred when filled, as it would be for the major part of the evening.

We decided we would have thirty-two people for dinner at four round tables in the dining-room, and ask the largest crowd to come in afterward. Impulsively, Nedda said, 'This mustn't be a stuffy party. We're theatre people – artists. Surely we should have some entertainment.' 'Oh, no!' I said. 'You can't invite people to a party and then ask them to entertain. They'd never know whether they were asked because they could entertain or because we felt that Princess Margaret and Tony would like them.'

She said, 'But we always sing around the piano or "do turns," as Oliver says. Certainly we can ask *somebody*.'

That *somebody* turned out to be the Princess Margaret, who is known for her musical accomplishment and informality at private parties.

Before embarking on the Mustique enterprise, which was rather like designing and planning a housing estate for millionaires, Oliver had work to finish in Barbados. Lord Glenconner, who is proud of Oliver's contribution to Mustique, felt that Barbados was too large for Oliver, but it was there that Oliver lived and there that he had work to finish. It was, moreover, in Barbados that he supervised a great deal of the craftswork and he was fortunate in being able to enlist the services of several of the island's experts: Heather Acquillar, a top interior designer who specialized in landscape gardening; Robert Thompson, an expert on interiors whose company supplied and made excellent furnishings; and the black craftsman Mr Massiah, who is the island's best stone carver.

Heather Acquillar: After working in England I married in Jamaica and returned to Barbados after my divorce. When I set up in real estate, I found myself working with Oliver Messel on reconstructing a house and doing the interiors. He was one of the most talented people I had ever met. But we used to have fights. One time, for instance, we fought for about a year because he was a total artist and had no idea of money; that word never entered into his vocabulary. When I had to sign cheques on behalf of a client it used to make me very nervous because I was responsible for the money which was going out. Every argument we ever had was over money!

Once, after a few months I got nervous and telephoned the owner and said, 'I think you'd better come up here because I can't stand the way I'm signing cheques.' She came up and said she never wanted to see me in such a state again. I said that so long as she did not mind my spending her money the way it was going, well and good. But I could see that the people he had working for him were building their own houses at the expense of some of these owners. He, Mr Messel, just could not tell from the bills that came in, for instance, how many bags of cement it took to make a path. He would simply initial the bill and the cement would leave the premises on the same truck when his back was turned.

He and Sally Aall, for whom he built Mango Bay, fought all the time. They weren't on speaking terms for about two years, and then she asked him to add a pool to the house, and he was delighted. Then she wanted a new garden lay-out, which he also did. But she was none too pleased when she got a bill for $35,000!

His preference for cool greens and the mixture of textures for gardens rather than colour was another thing we used to argue about. I could see his point as an artist: that is how he saw it and that is how he wanted it. I used to say, 'But Mr Messel, you and I don't live here, and if the owner wants a patch of hibiscus you've got to find a place to put it because *he's* going to be looking at it, not you.' Then he'd say, 'But that would spoil the whole effect.' 'All right', I'd reply, 'then let's just find a little corner for it somewhere.'

He liked sage green. He used it in everything he did: walls, floors, shutters, wherever he could. It became known as 'Oliver Messel green' and it was specially mixed by the gallon-load under his supervision.

The American interior decorator Robert Thompson, who has a shop in Speightstown where he has built a small villa protruding into the Caribbean, became acquainted with Oliver in this period.

Robert Thompson: I worked with Oliver on several houses. He did the architecture, or rather the design of the houses; he wasn't too knowledgeable about stress loads and that sort of thing but he knew how to make houses pretty. I have a shop here and make drapes and small pieces of furniture; and Oliver talked about going into business with me, but that took money and it was the one thing Oliver didn't have — except for good health, that is.

Oliver had impeccable colour taste but when clients preferred their own choice of colours, he always had his way in the end. Once he had a sudden passion for chartreuse and he tried to hang that on everybody, but the colour was too fierce for them and they told him so — and didn't use it.

Mr Massiah, a tall, gentle American, settled in Barbados many years before, where he established a small business moulding concrete and terracotta, and carving natural coral from the bowels of the Barbadian earth into garden pots, pillars and all other forms of garden decoration for the big houses and hotels on the island.

Mr Massiah: I worked with Oliver Messel for about thirteen years, first on the house called Leamington, then Crystal Springs and of course his own house, Maddox. He would make the original drawing on paper and then I would make the moulds from his designs. I made the adornments for Mustique and we shipped them there. Wherever he had a house I came along and did the fine work for him, artistic work of a fine nature. I liked to work with an individual who had a creative nature and to tackle things that are different. He used to enjoy working with me and I learnt a lot from him. For instance I would know the proportions of the cement and fine aggregate for a beautiful shell fountain for the pool at Mango Bay, and together we would mould it with our hands. He would make a model of the design for an ornamental garden pot out of cardboard and sponge, all with proper proportions and then it was up to me to make the mould and cast it in cement. I never got exasperated at all with him. If he didn't like the way it came out, he was really patient. He would take it over and shape it himself and show me how to perfect it. He was an admirable man and I learnt a lot from him as did everyone else who was fortunate enough to work with him.

Although Oliver worked diligently at architecture in Barbados and Mustique, with future plans for work in Venezuela, he wanted to return to his first love, painting:

Oliver: I get more pleasure out of painting and I enjoy painting more than anything else. I find with the theatre now there are so many impediments which I find maddening. When things were much easier technically you could have assistants by the dozen, which made it all marvellously efficient and wonderful. Nowadays nobody wants to be an assistant. They embark on big careers of their own when they leave art school, without serving an apprenticeship. I find that if I were to do a lot of work in the theatre in England I'd be wasting half the time doing all the assistants' work myself, and that I could not get any more money than I got some years ago. It is very uneconomic. That is why I did so many productions, but at the end have absolutely nothing financially to show for it at all. Whereas if I'd paint pictures, which I love really even more, I'd only have myself to contend with. I can go on here not having to be bothered with all the rather annoying things I have to fit in with to suit everybody else. Even the author is considered more important than the artist's desk in the theatre.

I don't like to have just a drawing and let that be that, because I like to work on every minute detail so that there's no possible misunderstanding. I work it out like a piece of sculpture, but that takes carpentry and cutting out and sticking together and if I have to do it all myself it is a life's work again. I could have painted ten pictures in the same time, which gives me more satisfaction, and I can make five times the amount of money out of it. And it's something that lasts.

Theatre is only a toy, and it's an ephemeral thing, whereas painting is not. There are so many things I want to record, so many things I feel and that I can express which aren't connected with the theatre. My life doesn't belong to the theatre any more because I don't feel the same way about it as I did before.

I see myself going on painting and doing buildings. Perhaps a ballet on occasion, but there's never enough money in it. You slog away at doing something and then there's nothing left at the end but expenses. Each time, for instance, that I worked in New York, I charged exorbitant fees and got enormous expenses, but at the end of it there is nothing left except the sort of glamour of the theatre. The last play I did in New York, for instance, *Traveller Without Luggage*, was the sort of thing I loved doing. It was appallingly acted and as the director didn't understand it very well, it didn't work at all. It needed Peter Brook or Peter Glenville or somebody that understood what it was meant to be.

But returning to architecture, I would love to do something in a totally new way, but there's nothing new in life; there's nothing that hasn't been explored in some shape, and architects kid themselves if they think it's a perfectly modern way. There's nothing modern. It's merely that they copy one another. If an architect has got any individuality, it comes out anyway, whether he's basing it on something else or not.

And Oliver certainly had individuality in abundance, as proved in Mustique where he designed the majority of the houses. Two of them are featured on a couple of the Mustique postage stamps as a fitting tribute to their finest artist.

When Colin Tennant contracted Oliver to design the houses, he also asked him to locate the sites for them. The houses all look out to sea and have a stamp of elegant French *provençal* about them. Oliver had a penchant for making big houses appear to be small from the outside, which is exactly right for the diminutive island. They have a squared symmetrical look, with the front door in the centre, flanked by shuttered windows. The rooms are spacious, light and uncluttered. Small guest houses in the grounds provide privacy for host and guest alike, and the owners themselves often occupy the guest houses, retaining the main house for entertaining. Sea Star, the house Oliver designed for the ballerina Nadia Nerina and her husband Charles Gordon, is a typical example of this, with its reconstituted coral stone façades and undisturbed views of the neighbouring islands.

Oliver often faced considerable difficulty with the construction of houses in Barbados, but in Mustique he had the professional support of Arne Hasselquist.

Arne and his wife Anita decided to leave Sweden because of crippling taxes, and travelled round the world on the proceeds from the sale of all their worldly possessions. It was a calculated risk, but they decided to find life anew elsewhere. They were both twenty-five years old; he was an architect and she an interior decorator. They knew they would always find work in these fields, and never looked back. Travelling through the West Indies they fell in love with St Vincent and the Grenadines, where they lived a Robinson Crusoe life on a little island called Palm Island. Arne built a hut, then a house, for them to live in, and got a job helping to develop an island called Petit St Vincent which had been bought by an American. He had a free hand to build twenty-two little cottages and to construct roads and a jetty, and to organize water and electricity supplies.

It was at this point, in 1969, that Colin Tennant bought Mustique, and commissioned Arne to do a similar job for him.

Arne Hasselquist: Colin invited me over to see Mustique. There were ten black families living here from the old slave days on the sugar plantations. When I arrived, they worked half the day on the plantation and the cotton fields, and the other half tending their patches of land, on which they grew sweet potatoes. The island had no telephone, no road, and certainly neither electricity nor water, but it did have millions of mosquitos, hence its name.

I started the Mustique Construction Company, which was responsible for the building of all the properties on the island. It was quite difficult in the beginning because we had to row the first sacks of cement ashore and build accommodation for nine workmen, then another ten — and that is how we started expanding. I began work on the Cotton House which had been a warehouse. It was to be converted into a hotel and that was when Oliver Messel came into the picture. He was chosen as the architect.

When I went to see him in Barbados I was pleased to meet Vagn because he was Danish; as I am Swedish we could speak the same languages. After Oliver had done the first sketches of the Cotton House Hotel and the cottages in the grounds for guests, I did some of the structural drawings. We worked together for about three months and then we had the most tremendous row. Oliver thought my columns in the Cotton House were too thick. They were six inches; he said they should be four and a half. I said, 'Look Oliver, I can't take them all down. If they were four and a half inches they might very well not be able to hold up the roof, and snap! Besides, with the hurricanes we have here, they have to be strong enough to stand for ever.'

Afterwards, of course, I realized that when Oliver was doing mainly stage settings the pillars could be very small and flimsy, because the set was only going to stay there for a few months; but when you build a solid house it is going to stay there for a long time. Oliver started shouting and screaming, but I held my ground. And then he resorted to tears, but I wouldn't give in. Then he had a terrible row with Colin Tennant and said, 'This bloody Swede makes everything too clumsy.'

Vagn and Oliver photographed at Maddox by Cecil Beaton

Luckily, we worked out a precise pattern of how things would progress. We were able to give fixed prices for the houses and their construction to customers, so they knew where they were. They were beautifully designed by Oliver, and were costed and constructed by us. The clients liked Oliver very much and his relationship with them was helped by the fact that all finance went through the Mustique Company. When he wanted to change anything he told the clients how much it would cost and that they were to liaise with me over money.

Oliver's plans for the houses in Mustique did not require volumes of mechanical draughting, but the imagination, vision and knowledge to create an indigenous style suited to the conditions of the West Indies. He designed each building differently, at the same time composing an overall harmony and adapting each establishment to the requirements of the individual.

The Cotton House and Lady Honor Svedjar's two houses, Phibblestown and Continots, were designed like French farmhouses. Lady Honor, whose first husband was 'Chips' Channon, was Oliver's first private client in Mustique. He designed her houses with concrete roofs, but these proved unsuccessful because the wood supporting them underneath was apt to move.

Many prototype samples of West Indies features, such as special louvres, windows and hoods, were designed by Oliver, and he also found it easier to educate and train the local craftsmen in the interpretation of his $\frac{1}{2}''$ scale plans drawn on squared paper than to expose them to more complicated mechanical drawings which were bound to confuse them.

Having studied the ground carefully, Oliver took advantage of its own best views, then its relation to the surrounding buildings. It usually took about five weeks of solid work in order to produce the initial basic design. Together with Arne Hasselquist, he supervised the construction to completion and personally advised on the interiors, ordering furniture, fabrics and adornments from England and the United States.

Aside from working hard in Mustique and Barbados, Oliver and Vagn contributed substantially to the old and needy in Barbados. They founded a 'Meals-on-Wheels' organization, for which the cooking was done in the kitchen at Maddox.

But they were concerned about Vagn's health. He had been a heavy smoker, and in 1972 he developed cancer. He had to be rushed to London for medical treatment. Oliver suffered a minor heart attack at the same time and, through the generosity of Sidney Bernstein, was flown over to London where he and Vagn were able to share the same ward.

They returned to Barbados after their respective operations, and Vagn died later that year on 2 December.

Oliver: Vagn had the great capacity for giving out warmth and hospitality to all his friends. He had an extraordinary talent for the art of living. He wrote a series of articles on rare and special recipes for *Harpers Bazaar* and *Vogue*. He had a unique gift and imagination for the organization of festive occasions to delight those around him, and through his infinite capacity for taking pains over every detail he set a standard of civilized perfection which left a lasting impression on those who knew him.

As he had been a close friend and co-host of Princess Margaret and Lord

Snowdon on their numerous visits to Maddox, it was their wish to give support the needy of our parish, Saint James, by appearing at a charity ball in aid of the Red Cross Meals on Wheels and the Challenor School for the Mentally Retarded (9 February 1971). This greatly helped to establish sufficient funds to inaugurate the kitchens next to Saint James Church. Apart from seeing to the preparation of all food and special diets, Vagn set out each day to visit the homes of those in need, even long after his illness became an increasing tax on his strength.

It was the special quality of the sincerity of his concern that often helped to speed up assistance over urgent problems of housing and medical aid, as well as food.

Oliver had sent their London doctor a pair of cuff-links left by Vagn, and at the same time apologized for a small outstanding debt of £100. The doctor replied:

> Would you please not worry about the £100. I shall wait until you can spare it. I know how difficult things are and how doubly difficult it must be for you to manage now without Vagn. I am only glad that you have occupation and are not too depressed, although I am, frankly, a little worried about the loneliness. In a way I am very glad that your back makes you rest such a lot because that will protect your heart and in an odd way is the best thing that can happen to you. Do have a check-up. It is silly to save the money on health, and when you have done it, please send me the cardiogram and all the results of the blood tests for my opinion.

Oliver had been asked by the Prime Minister of Barbados to assist in the redesign of Queen's Park, a public building which had fallen into decay. It contained various leisure facilities, including a small theatre which vandals had wrecked, and a cricket pitch; but roving bands of sheep had wreaked havoc with the decorative plants and the aviary, and the fountain lay dormant.

Oliver: It was at the Prime Minister's request that I accepted to give my services to undertake the overall planning and design for a cultural centre and garden setting at Queen's Park. A special Queen's Park Committee was founded on which I served. But crisis after crisis arose, starting with the construction crew demanding more money and their having to be laid off as a consequence. After working on the project for three and a half years, the committee decided to dispense with my services, and a new designer was commissioned to do the work.

The Queen's Park Theatre which Oliver had also been asked to design was finally built, but the recreation centre's development was removed from his control. Naturally distressed by this, and determined to fight to the bitter end, a characteristic that came naturally to him, Oliver wrote repeatedly to all concerned — but they were as determined to proceed without him as he was set upon vindicating himself.

As a trusted friend of Oliver's and a highly respected inhabitant of the island, Sidney Bernstein was drawn into the controversy. On 1 August 1973 he wrote to Frank de Buono, another friend of Oliver's, who had worked for the late Ranee of Sarawak (another neighbour), and who had taken over Oliver's business affairs and the running of his household after Vagn's death:

Messel's costumes for the American production of the musical *Gigi*, by Alan Jay Lerner and Frederick Loewe: the actors are Alfred Drake, Agnes Moorehead, Terese Stevens, Maria Karnilova and Daniel Massey

I appreciate the difficulty in getting Oliver's affairs sorted out. In a letter to me the other day he said that without your help he would have been suicidal and could not have survived.

Try and get Oliver to stop thinking about Queen's Park. It's over as far as he is concerned and I'm writing him to that effect. It's no good him developing a mental cancer about the Parks and Beaches Commission. He has other things to do and must learn to accept unchangeable situations. I know it's easy to say this, but he must start thinking about new opportunities available to him.

Although Oliver took Bernstein's advice, he remained unrepentant. Fortunately there were other contracts to consider and he accepted a commission to design the costumes for the prospective Broadway production of Lerner and Loewe's musical *Gigi*, which had been a film with Leslie Caron, Maurice Chevalier and Hermione Gingold.

Produced by Edwin Lester for the Los Angeles Civic Light Opera Association, the musical was to be directed by Joseph Hardy with settings by Oliver Smith.

In keeping with the tradition he had established, Oliver demanded an inordinately high fee, as well as generous expenses and a limousine throughout his American stay to supervise the making of the costumes; but he made ever greater demands and then reprimanded his lawyer, Arnold Weissberger, for negotiating unfavourable terms. Weissberger wrote to him on 5 November 1973:

I may say that I have negotiated contracts for some of the world's most famous designers, and I have never gotten a better contract for any of them than I got for you. Never has any designer gotten the provisions for expenses that you got. You asked for a limousine, which is without any precedent whatsoever, and which Lester refused to put in the contract; I spent hours with him on the 'phone after the contract was signed, persuading him that you should have a limousine, which he finally provided for you. No designer today gets what you wanted and no designer today gets as good a contract as I got for you.

I do not ordinarily allow my anger at a client to manifest itself — especially when the client is an old friend as you are — but when I negotiate the kind of top-notch contract that I got for you and then the client castigates me so unfairly, I think I may be permitted the luxury of flaring up.

Having allowed his temper to cool, Oliver was finally persuaded to take a smaller initial fee, $5,000 — and a larger box-office percentage. But this proved unwise as *Gigi*, featuring Alfred Drake, Agnes Moorehead and Daniel Massey, with newcomer Terese Stevens from Britain making her American debut in the title role, was another failure — the third in succession for Oliver after the *Twang!!* and *Traveller without Luggage* disappointments. *Gigi* opened in San Francisco on 15 May 1973, and after an extended tour came into New York, where the title role was taken over by Karin Wolfe. Although the familiar numbers, like 'Thank Heaven for Little Girls', went down well, evoking memories of Maurice Chevalier's endearing performance in the film, the new songs were found to be pallid. There had been incessant rewriting at rehearsals and several changes of costume design, but it was generally considered that the show simply wasn't yet ready for a New York audience. Oliver's costumes were very much in the turn-of-the-century idiom, bringing to the stage the colourful atmosphere of the Belle Epoque; though he and Oliver Smith enjoyed a favourable press the rest of the show did not, and it was withdrawn after 103 performances.

9

Messel's workroom at Maddox

246

9 *Maddox

Oliver: From the fragments of a small derelict old plantation house under the shade of some magnificent mahogany trees, I transformed Maddox into one of the most unusual and romantic houses in Barbados. Retaining all the character and charm of the buildings of the West Indies, I redesigned the house to suit the ideal way of living in the tropics today. With balconies, loggias and terraces overlooking the sea, all the main living areas are open and part of the garden.

The whole setting already appears to have the maturity of some hundreds of years, yet the rebuilding of the house and the creation of the luxurious tropical garden have in fact taken only three years to accomplish. The initial structural work was carried out by a local builder, Clyde Smith. I collected a special group of craftsmen for the embellishment, who worked under my direction and that of my new assistant Carl Chandler. It gives me special delight to feel that the place has been made by friends. The garden has materialised in such lush profusion through the dedicated work of Johnson, who had worked with me from the start, when there was nothing but a slope of mud and rubble.

The house is situated on coral rocks overlooking the Caribbean but set back a little from the sea. The different levels have given special scope to the landscape planning of terraces, paths, pools, and steps leading down to the beach below. It is from that private beach that Princess Margaret set off for her water-skiing pleasures when she and my nephew stayed with me on so many occasions.

I planned the garden like a painting, focussing the main attention on the composition of the pattern and colours of tropical plants and leaves for their beauty rather than for their rarity. It is the only garden in Barbados where banana trees, daturas and the most exotic of the hybrid hibiscus thrive in profusion right down to the shore.

In the house, although some special furniture was brought from England, many of the most interesting pieces have been made to my design by skilled craftsmen on the island.

The overall effect of the garden is rather like a Rousseau jungle; but a controlled jungle which is inhabited by little monkeys who swing down to my terrace when I breakfast and perch on the table, begging for handouts, which I give them with pleasure.

Arlen Brooms, a Barbadian subcontractor, worked for Oliver for over ten years. He was employed by him on a permanent basis and spent several months working on the structure at Maddox, fifteen months on alterations of Charles Graves's home, and another ten years on the controversial fantasy, Mango Bay. Brooms's general impression of Oliver's work, much in accord with others who had collaborated with him, was that although Oliver was not a qualified architect he knew more about the history of architecture than many eminent practitioners, through the many years he had spent in the theatre and films, and in Italy.

Head of a Negro, painted by Messel in 1963 and exhibited the next year at the Sandy Lane Hotel in Barbados

Brooms: Mr Messel was more of a designer in his approach to architecture than an actually qualified architect. He tended to work from imagination – and the next day he would change both his mind and the work he had told me to do. I was a fairly fast worker and he would often say that I was travelling too fast for him! He came to the site twice a day, and each time he changed his mind; then the following morning he changed it again. He would often say, 'Lord, this isn't exactly what I want,' and we would have to pull it down, no matter how far we had got with it, and start again. However, I soon got used to him changing his mind.

I had thirty men working for me and we would work from his drawings on square-lined draft paper and it was not easy to decipher the designs into practical, workable terms and reorganise the daily duties of the workforce at the same time while he kept changing his mind.

He was very quiet and peaceful, but if he did not get his way he would lose his temper very quickly and then retire to bed for a couple of days until he had calmed down!

His workmen were employed on a full-time basis and operated from the back of the garage at Maddox. From there they would be sent off to any of the houses he was working on either in Barbados or Mustique. For instance, we made the oval windows and doors for Princess Margaret's house at Maddox and they were shipped over to Mustique by schooner together with all the other fittings for her house.

I remember one afternoon at four o'clock Mr Messel saying, 'I want this new terrazzo floor laid tonight.' I said, 'That's impossible,' and he insisted, 'I want it done tonight!' So he sent for more workmen, brought them some rum and corned beef, and we finally finished the job by morning. When an idea came into his head, he wanted it carried out there and then without question.

There was a domestic staff at Maddox, between seven to ten in the days when Oliver and Vagn were still entertaining. Ruby was the upstairs maid, Johnson the trusted gardener and general *factotum*, absolutely indispensable to Oliver. Naomi was another maid, Carl Chandler was Oliver's assistant, and Evelyn the cook helped wait on table when either the Queen and Prince Philip, Prince Charles or Princess Margaret visited.

Evelyn: When he entertained, there was normally lobster for dinner or lunch, otherwise veal, fish or ham. But Mr Messel ate very little when he was on his own. He could live on barracuda, which he loved.

I prepared a dish of chicken Kiev for the Queen and Prince Philip, which they said they enjoyed very much, and when Princess Margaret and Lord Snowdon stayed for periods of three weeks at a time, they would normally lunch or dine very informally on the terrace. Princess Margaret loved water-skiing and was very good.

The Princess would often go down to Oliver's private bay where the boat and skis awaited her — but considerations of security curtailed her impromptu sporting activities to some degree. Her private detective was always close at hand and lived in the guest house in the grounds of Maddox throughout her visits.

After Vagn's death, Nick Paravicino paid the staff, settled the monthly household accounts and attended to Oliver's business matters.

Paravicino: Oliver was the most humble and friendly person in the world but he was hopeless with money. This, somehow, didn't matter to people. They accepted the fact that he was creative, and that, together with his charm, was enough for them. He treated his Barbadian black staff like his family and always insisted that they eat with him when he was not entertaining. When he was working alone in his studio upstairs, one of them would invariably be working at his side. He had no colour prejudice and lost his temper when he found anyone who did. He was Church of England, but never went to church particularly. But he did so much good he didn't have to go to church. He did, however, go to St James's Parish Church with Princess Margaret when she stayed at Maddox.

Messel's bedroom at Maddox

He loved dancing and when the Festival came along he would dance and dance. He spent a week at the Mustique Festival where he won first prize for the fancy-dress costume which he made himself, and when he returned he said he hadn't slept for four days.

On Christmas mornings he would have a present for all the folk at the top of the road above his drive. He would wrap each gift himself and write their individual names on the tags, and then go along to deliver them himself.

Evelyn: His bedroom always looked a frightful mess because he worked from there. It was impossible to find anything. His sister Lady Rosse was staying here when the Queen visited and she tidied up his room before the Queen came. Mr Messel was furious. He said, 'Where are all my things? Bring them back. Bring them back. You can't move this — it's precious. And that's precious too. Put it back. Put it back!'

But Mr Vagn was very tidy. He kept his bedroom beautifully neat and spotless. He was a very particular man. When Mr Messel went into his room, he would say, 'No, no. Back to your own room, please. You're not going to make a mess of mine!'

In 1975 Oliver's health was fast deteriorating. While working on the designs for Colin Tennant's new house on Mustique, he was admitted to the Queen Elizabeth Hospital in Barbados. From there, he wrote to Carl Chandler on 14 June:

I have been here for just over a week in the intensive care unit under observation, and I hope to be allowed back to Maddox today after the doctor has seen me. He is youngish, clever and dedicated.

Of course, the thought of being cut open like a partridge fills me with horror and I would much sooner simply pop off without any fuss. If there is any possible means of surviving for a bit longer without the ordeal I would naturally wish to cling to it. [The heart operation was found to be unnecessary.]

It is a terrible scramble for me to survive financially, although I am in the middle of Colin's Turkish fantasy which is interesting and exciting. Although we now get along very happily it is difficult for him to realise that I need solid remuneration to be able to live. Barbados is very empty at the moment. Dear Verna Hull is in New York and Polly Haywood in London. A very charming new friend, Madame Machado, from Venezuela flew over to see me. I have designed a Gingerbread House for her on Mustique; she has been to the hospital each day and will stay at Maddox over the weekend. How lucky I am to have such wonderful friends. My one dread is to become a burden to them.

Without Vagn to chase his clients for payment of their fees, Oliver faced the task of having to write to them himself. However, a large commission came his way when, at the beginning of 1976, the American Ballet Theatre decided to mount a new production of *The Sleeping Beauty* to open at the Metropolitan Opera House in New York for a season starting on 15 June, prior to performances in other major cities. The stars of the piece were to be the two great dancers who had recently defected from the USSR, Natalia Makarova and Mikhail Baryshnikov; and the directors of the Ballet Theatre, Oliver Smith (with whom Oliver had worked happily in the past) and Lucia Chase, asked him to recreate his original designs of 1946 for the Sadler's Wells Ballet.

As a measure of the esteem in which the Americans held him, Oliver was able to negotiate the best contract he had ever agreed to sign. It offered him a fee of $12,000 for the re-working of the scenery and costume designs and the overseeing of their execution in New York. He was provided with first-class air travel to New York and was paid a further $100 a day towards his living expenses. He was to have a costume assistant as well as a scenery assistant, who were to fly over to Barbados to work with him on the re-creation of the designs; and he was to enjoy top billing, above that of Petipa and Tchaikovsky, with the words '*Entire production designed by:* Oliver Messel'. No changes would be made to his designs of floor plans without his prior written consent and he retained the copyright in his designs, which could not be copied or reproduced without his written approval. The British designer Richard Berkeley Sutcliffe was to obtain the original designs and models from Kensington Palace where they were lodged, to have them insured and sent by air to Barbados.

Princess Margaret: Unfortunately, someone has lost the originals. When they wanted them, I telephoned Tony and asked whether it was all right to send them as Oliver had asked for them and he said, 'Well, you'd better.' And I did. But it was an error, a disaster to send them, and we've never got those designs back. Every time I go to New York I ask, 'Where are Oliver's designs?' 'We haven't the faintest idea,' they say.

But my spies are still at work there!

Lord Glenconner's 'Turkish Pavilion' on the island of Mustique; this was Messel's last architectural commission. Photograph by Charles Castle

I can put Princess Margaret's mind at rest about at least fifteen of the original designs, for I discovered them when wading through Oliver's files and trunks sent over from Barbados after his death for safekeeping to the home of his nephew Thomas Messel in Gloucestershire. At the suggestion of Lord Snowdon I delivered them into the custody of the Victoria and Albert Museum where the rest of Oliver's art material is on permanent loan. Other original designs hang in the Oliver Messel Suite at the Dorchester Hotel, where they have been for the past thirty years.

On the opening night of *Sleeping Beauty* Oliver Smith sent Oliver a note:

It is impossible for me to fully express my gratitude to you for your extraordinary efforts in the realization of *The Sleeping Beauty*. Your designs for the settings and costumes are exquisite, right, evocative and truly among the most beautiful designs in the history of the theatre. That you would undertake such a stupendous job is an act of extreme generosity and love, and Ballet Theatre, all of the performing artists, and the world audience are in your debt.

I do feel you have also supervised the production superbly, and I agree with you that it looks even more ravishing than the original very beautiful creation.

I thank you with my whole heart. I can never thank you enough.

253

One person, however, had reservations about the costumes. Robert Helpmann had performed in the original 1946 production; and some time later was called upon to stage a production of it in Paris.

Sir Robert Helpmann: When Nureyev defected from Russia, the first ballet he did was *The Sleeping Beauty*, in Paris, with Rosella Hightower dancing Aurora. It was being staged by Bronislava Nijinska [Nijinsky's sister] for the Marquis de Cuevas company, but she only got as far as the Prologue after six weeks of rehearsal. She simply couldn't remember the Marius Petipa and Nicholas Sergueyev choreography, so de Cuevas sent for me and I staged it for him.

I was lying on the beach in Honolulu on holiday in 1976 when I received a cable from the Met. They had started restaging *The Sleeping Beauty* and couldn't finish it either, so I was asked to complete the production.

When I got there I found none of the scenery had been made, and the costumes were terrible. Every colour was different from the original even though Oliver had based them on his original designs. The costumes were coarse and dreadful. In fact I opened it in Washington. I played Carabosse, the Wicked Fairy, in all the performances there and the first night in New York.

The costumes just didn't have Oliver's touch even though he came over to supervise the making of the scenery and the costumes. He wasn't well at the time and when he returned to Barbados I rang him up and said, 'Oliver, it's not like you,' and he said, 'Oh yes, that's what it was in the original.' And I said, 'No, Oliver. It isn't what it was. It is *not* like what it was.'

When he returned to Maddox in July, Oliver wrote to his secretary, Brenda Haydon, in London:

Here I am back home but still living in a dream world of all the unbelievable fantasy and drama of the last weeks of New York. After these last years of grief and continual worries, I could never have imagined that God had stored up all this wonderful adventure that I should be showered with such glamour and hitherto unheard of accolades.

I was coddled, pampered and surrounded with love and appreciation. Each one of the some 300 costumes, made at a cost of two hundred dollars, emerged as if it was a museum piece, one more lovely than the other; the craftsmanship superb and the materials of nothing but the purest silk. The radiance of the colours alone was something out of this world, far more beautifully made than for the original production, when, of course, we were slightly handicapped by the shortage of materials. Even now, as all stocks of materials are synthetic or drip-dry, the real silks are hard to find and needed weeks of searching.

Colin has just been here in very good mood and is anxious for me to get on with my designs for his new house on Mustique. He had already approved the original designs but he has now changed the site with different conditions, so have to start again. Never mind.

What Oliver left out of his letter was any account of his collapse on the stage of the Met.

Oliver: On the Saturday before the show opened I collapsed (not from the excesses of New York!) but from the strain of work. I felt a heart pain which ran through the chest and back and down one of my arms. I was said to have turned a very strange colour, and I was carried off to hospital. In my delirium I asked someone to telephone a friend of mine, Father Walley (a tall black American whom Oliver had known for some time), who was on holiday in New York.

As I arrived at the hospital, emergency cases were kept waiting and treated like cattle. Suddenly he appeared, and being a priest he was able to bully them into action. They laid me out on a slab; it was all rather like a Hogarthian prison or morgue, with rough attendants stripping off one's clothes. He soon put a stop to their rough treatment.

There was something faulty in my cardiogram. Heart damage, I presume, from the previous episode and irregular heart beat I had suffered in Barbados. So I was dragged into the intensive care ward and strung up with all those horrible tubes stuck into every vein, just as before. I was told to remain absolutely flat on my back for two or three weeks and if I so much as went outside I would fall down dead on the spot.

They couldn't tell exactly whether I'd had a real heart attack or just a warning of angina. Father Walley managed to force his way back in later that evening. He laid his hands on me and gave me his blessing. I don't know if it was my imagination or if it was some kind of miracle, but I suddenly felt much better, with no pain at all. According to the recording machines my heart beat was much stronger, and I realized that they couldn't keep me there against my will.

I explained to the doctor that during the war, life was in the balance from day to day and that as such vast sums had been poured out by the Ballet Theatre and risked in order to perpetuate my work — and for my glory — I felt it my duty to be there for the important technical rehearsal the next day, Sunday, and for the dress rehearsal on Monday. If it was God's will that I should die, this was the way that I would have chosen to go, by not shirking my responsibilities. Everything hung on my being there for the placing of the lighting which no one else knew about and which rested on my judgment. It was a risk I intended to take.

Father Walley arrived with my clothes on Sunday midday, and promised to be with me throughout with emergency pills. The rehearsal went well but I was much needed over many decisions and preparations for the next day's dress-rehearsal.

Then came Tuesday and the glorious excitement of the opening night with all of New York agog. What a night! Had I been lying in hospital and missed it all I should have died of sheer frustration.

All the thrilling first nights of my experience were nothing compared to this. Verna [Hull] and I sat in the stalls so that we could observe the finer details more clearly and make notes of any tiny thing that still had to be completed before my return to Barbados.

During the intervals I was mobbed by kind-hearted enthusiasts pouring out their congratulations. At the end of the performance, Makarova brought me onstage in the centre of the entire company to receive curtain calls. When the curtains dropped she led me through them to face this magnificent auditorium at the Met overcrowded with an ecstatic audience. The house shouted and called again and again as though I were some great prima donna like Callas! Tears welled into my eyes. I could barely see. I had never received nor expected such a moving accolade throughout my fifty years as a theatre designer. Later, it took nearly an hour to get through the stage door after signing autographs.

Instead of feeling the worse for all this experience — naturally, I rested as much as possible afterwards — I am told that I look years younger. I have certainly never felt better for a long time, so perhaps a miracle has happened.

Unfortunately, it had not. His health continued to deteriorate, and his financial situation didn't improve either. His loving friends rallied: Sidney Bernstein, Claudette Colbert, Verna Hull — and Polly Haywood, who provided the oxygen cylinder that was installed in his bedroom at Maddox.

There was, however, still hope — and interest in him from abroad. A few months after his return from New York, he received a letter from Peter Stafford, the Managing Director of The Dorchester [between 1976 and 1979], inviting him to fly over for the Jubilee celebrations and to stay in the Oliver Messel Suite as a guest of the hotel. In a long reply to Stafford explaining why extended travel would be impossible, Oliver wrote on 26 March 1977:

When following the hip operation for arthritis I was told I might always remain an invalid I had to decide to move my home to where the sun is warm. In fact apart from the spine naturally remaining a slight problem, I otherwise recovered perfectly from the hip operation, and have been able to get up around the hills of Mustique like a mountain goat. It was probably a good idea to start life anew, and in place of the theatre I carved a whole new career in architecture, in the last 10 years having probably designed more buildings than most architects achieve in a lifetime: the whole initial development of the island of Mustique (about 30 buildings or more); some houses for other Caribbean islands, and quite a number here.

At the moment I have just finished the designs for the Hon. Colin Tennant's own house for Mustique — an exotic kind of Folly! A Turkish Pavilion with domes which is to be set in a beautiful Palm Grove by the sea with a wonderful view over other islands. The domes are not high ones like the Pavilion at Brighton which was based more on Indian sources, but are the lower domes as in the Persian and the Turkish kiosks or pleasure pavilions. There are at the moment some changes and developments in the Management of the Island of Mustique, which may be more enterprising and mean more work as the Venezuelan group have taken to the Island, which is good! As, alas, we poor English have little money to build with. The immediate future seems so committed to seeing through these various projects as well as fulfilling some portrait commissions that alas I see no hope of being able to fly over for the Jubilee Celebrations or for a little while.

If ever anything comes up that designs for any new specialities might be required for any new developments at the Dorchester please remember that nothing could give me more pleasure.

He completed the designs and elevations for the Turkish Pavilion and, although building had begun on the site, he was not to see the completion of his finest building.

On Thursday, 13 July 1978, he was seated on the balcony outside his bedroom door at Maddox. The last to see him alive were his trusted staff and friends: Evelyn his cook, Ruby the maid, Johnson his faithful helper, his assistant Carl, and Robert Thompson who was returning home from an errand and called in to see him.

Ruby: I worked for Mr Messel for the last eleven years of his life. He treated me like one of the family; he actually treated all his servants like his family because he had no family here. He always suffered with his heart and arthritis but that didn't prevent him from working. Sometimes when he came downstairs he'd feel ill and would go back up to his studio for a rest. But when I went to check on him he wouldn't be resting, he'd be working. In the mornings when I came in I would go up to check on him before I got his breakfast. When I came in on that last day it was just after nine in the morning. He told me that he had already had breakfast so I went downstairs.

Robert Thompson: I stopped by to say hello to Oliver just before noon on that day. He was sitting outside his bedroom on the balcony taking in the sun. Poor man, he looked so small and fragile, as though his shirt was too big for him. Ruby appeared with a glass of Ovaltine, but he declined it saying it was always filthy stuff. Ruby said, 'But sir, you haven't eaten anything for ever so long.' I said, 'Since she's gone to the trouble to make it, Oliver, wouldn't you just try a tiny sip?' He patted my hand and said, 'Oh, I suppose I'll just have to eat something or I'll die, won't I? It's just that I have no appetite.' He took the glass and drained it with great difficult gulps. We chatted on for a little while and had a few laughs and then Johnson came. Oliver said he'd like to go inside. As he rose, we embraced and I left as Ruby and Johnson helped him into the bedroom.

Ruby: I went downstairs after his assistant, Carl, had arrived, but the internal telephone rang and Carl asked me to see to Mr Messel who was calling for me. I went up and applied the oxygen. He responded to it and told me to take it off, which I did. He told me that although the doctor said he was getting better he wasn't feeling better at all. He seemed short of breath. I said, 'Sir, why don't you let me put you in the garden so you can get some fresh air.' 'That would be a good idea,' he said. I went to the chest of drawers to get his clothes, and when I got back to the bed, he was lying with his eyes shut. He opened his eyes and said rather weakly, 'Oh, dear darling Ruby don't leave me. God bless you, dear. Don't leave me.'

Then he lay back and shut his eyes. He gave one breath – huh! – just like that. Then I telephoned Mr Thompson who told me to call the doctor. Dr Gilmore used to visit him at Maddox for the past two years. He was working in the intensive care unit at the hospital where Mr Messel had been. Dr Gilmore arrived – and pronounced him dead. They knew it was the heart because of the long history of heart failure.

Robert Thompson: His two nephews, Tony [Snowdon] and Thomas [Messel], flew in from London and arranged a very beautiful and touching service in St Peter's Church. There were many floral offerings and just as many candles. Oliver's coffin was covered by a marvellous needlepoint rug Vagn had made.

Father Broome, in his eulogy, apologized to the choir for lack of light to help them read the lyrics, but explained that this candlelight-and-flower service was Oliver's express wish.

After the funeral in Barbados, his body was flown back to England where another funeral service took place at Staplefield in Sussex, near Nymans. After the cremation, his ashes were buried in the magnolia garden at Nymans beneath the Greek urn which was placed there as a dedication by his sister Anne.

Lord Glenconner: It was tragic that Oliver died just when he did, in 1978, because it was shortly after that that property values escalated in Mustique, and he would have appreciated the international interest shown in the island that he helped to create.

Princess Margaret: However much one argued with Oliver, he nearly always proved to be right. It was just sheer luck for the island that he was there at the right time. He was one of the greatest contributors to it and his houses on it stand as a kind of wonderful memorial to him.

Lord Snowdon: Oliver was probably the greatest stage designer in the inventive way he used perspective. There will always be a historical interest in his work which can only grow and grow through exposure.

It is evident that Oliver's life had been endowed with culture, an inordinate appreciation of the arts and the inventive and practical talent to create with his hands.

Although he came from a background of artistic and financially secure ancestors, and he inherited all the taste that flowed through the lineage, there were fortunately no inherent senses of guilt or insecurities in his forbears' make-up, and therefore he developed happily without having to look over his shoulder at any dark clouds in his family's past. From an early age he had enjoyed a monthly allowance from his family, thus enabling him to be independent and to travel extensively in pursuit of history and the arts; and as further proof of his strength of character and independence, when he found himself in financial straits – and there were many – he relied mainly on his own industry, talent and creativity as a means of survival. He never once took his family's generosity for granted and continued to show his gratitude to them in many different ways until the end.

Throughout his theatrical career, he had the good fortune to have his work interpreted by some of the finest craftsmen available from all sections of the theatre, whom he trained in his own methods and without whom he would not so easily have reached the heights he achieved in all his productions.

His easy charm, his quick wit and style in all things aesthetic, coupled with his extravagance and flair as a party-giver, attracted friends to him from all spheres: the theatre, politics, aristocracy and royalty. He gave of himself and his pleasure in giving brought love and admiration; he never lost the friendships of the many people who drifted into his orbit and he retained their loyalty and affection throughout his lifetime.

He found great companionship with Vagn in the last thirty years of his life, and the homes they shared in London and Barbados were filled with friends, assistants and domestic staff; his almost childlike happiness in mixing them all together created an atmosphere of the true family life that had escaped him through the pressures of his profession from early on.

Although he was never physically strong, in the later years of his life he resented the process of aging and the illnesses that became recurrent. Arthritis caused constant pain and two mild heart attacks set him back considerably. Loath to complain, he suffered without inflicting his anxieties on those who loved him so dearly.

Lord Snowdon

A late portrait of Messel by his nephew Snowdon

As an artist he was temperamental and had occasional bad moods; he could fly into a fit of anger about what he considered to be an injustice, and his insistence on writing tiresome letters could not be easily curtailed. Many of these were misguided in their intent, and some were vehement in their content. Even these letters, though, seldom engendered animosity in their recipients, for they knew his artistic temperament well enough to understand that such correspondence was invariably written when he was under stress coupled with his search for perfection in all things.

He didn't smoke or drink (he might have an occasional aperitif or a little wine), and although he worked into the early hours he rarely burnt the candle at both ends. He was the first to leave a successful party – generally his own – when work on his bench upstairs called for completion. He had no excesses – except,

259

perhaps, for hard work and in striving for perfection – and in the last fifteen years found a way of life in Barbados that would have been the envy of many, surrounded by a caring staff and a constant stream of devoted friends. However, at the time when he began his architectural work in the West Indies, he lacked the support of brilliant craftsmen and technicians. Although he was an inspired designer, equipped with the infinite knowledge of the actual history of art and architecture, he lacked the distinction of being a qualified architect and draughtsman. He yearned for technicians of the calibre he had found in London, Hollywood and New York. Hence these were often frustrating times for him, and when he lost his health, and finally Vagn, he felt desolate in a foreign country, even though the few faithful friends rallied round him.

The administration of his complicated financial affairs by Frank de Buono, who died shortly after joining his staff, and Nick Paravicino who understood the running of his household, the responsibility of the staff and liaison with Oliver's New York lawyer Arnold Weissberger over contractual matters, hardly replaced Vagn's long standing involvement. Always at his right hand ready to advise and protect him, Vagn, to whom Oliver was so deeply devoted, left a huge void in Oliver's life when he died.

After Oliver's own death, Maddox, which was left to Lord Snowdon, was sold to cover some of the outstanding debts and mortgage repayments. However, it will always be a glorious reminder, like many of the other houses he designed, of his rare talent.

Sir Robert Helpmann: In my opinion Oliver is yet to be replaced. I don't see anyone anywhere in the world who comes anywhere near him. I'm constantly looking for designers like Oliver, but they simply don't exist. The quality of the music and the subject – he just happened to be able to put all that into his designs.

Sources and Acknowledgments

Without the permission of The Earl of Snowdon, who allowed me access to Oliver Messel's archives, letters and press-books – and, moreover to Oliver's invaluable artwork, I would not have been able to produce this book. To him I offer my deepest thanks. Gratitude too, in abundance, I owe to Oliver's sister Anne, Countess of Rosse, for her support and recollections, together with those of Thomas Messel and his wife Pepe, whose help and patience were unstinting. Spencer Herapath was instrumental in authenticating the family tree.

To HRH The Princess Margaret, Countess of Snowdon, I proffer gratitude for permitting me time with her to discuss her admiration for Oliver's work and to see her house in Mustique, designed by Oliver, on the occasion of one of her visits there, together with Lord Glenconner, founder of the island as we see it today. I am grateful, too, to the Princess for her permission to reproduce her speech at the Theatre Museum and to reproduce the photograph of her house in Mustique taken by Derry Moore for *Architectural Digest*.

Aside from the many devotees of Oliver's listed in the index who gave freely of their time for interviews and permissions to reproduce from their copyright works, I single out particularly Sir John Gielgud who wrote the Foreword; Carl Toms, whose many years working with Oliver enabled me to lean on his knowledge; and Stanley Hall, who knew Oliver not only through working with him but also as a close personal friend.

On the visual side of the book, grateful thanks are extended to the Victoria and Albert Theatre Museum, notably to Alexander Schouvaloff, who authorized Roger Pinkham and Leela Meinertas to provide me with any help required to satisfy the needs for the quality of a book such as this and for their permission to reproduce extracts from their Oliver Messel catalogue.

The contributors and lenders are numerous; I particularly thank Sir Harold Acton, Lord Bernstein, Peter Brook, Richard Buckle, Claudette Colbert, Mary Ellis, Christopher Fry, Peter Glenville, Derek Granger, Beryl Grey, Leif Hansen, Sir Robert Helpmann, Derek Hill, Howard Hook, Evelyn Laye, Dame Anna Neagle, Lea Seidl, Baden Watkins, Dorothy Ward and Polly Ward.

While researching in Barbados I received unfailing help and information from Mrs Sally Aall, Heather Acquillar, Mrs Pauline Haywood, Mrs Eileen Maremont, Nick Paravicino, Robert Thompson and Oliver's former helpers, Brooms, Carl, Emily and Ruby. My hostess Janet Meyer was charming and helpful, and her co-guest Janet Brown a daily delight. In Mustique I valued particular support from The Earl and Countess Alexander of Tunis and Mr and Mrs Arne Hasselquist. I thank them all.

I extend gratitude as well to the many photographers, newspapers, press agencies and copyright owners of work reproduced herein, including John Adams, Lord Snowdon, the Cecil Beaton estate, *Country Life*, Noël Coward's estate, J. W. Debenham, Dorothy Dickson for permission to reproduce the C. B. Cochran letters, Dulwich Museum, Glyndebourne Festival Opera, Graphic Photo Union, Guy Gravett, W. H. Grove & Son, Milton Goldman (Arnold Weissberger's letters), Katharine Hepburn, Peter Hope Lumley, Justerini & Brooks, Keystone Press, John Kobal, George Konig, Marjorie Lee (for the Dorchester Hotel), Alex & Reid Lefevre Ltd, Lenare, Angus McBean, Metropolitan Opera House Association Archivists (Rudolf Bing's letters), Metropolitan Opera Guild, Derry Moore, Neame, Bertram Park, John Perry (Hugh Beaumont's letters), Mrs Eva Reichman (Max Beerbohm's letter), Archivists of the Royal Opera House, Covent Garden, Saska, Frank Sharman estate, Edwin Smith, Paul Tanquery, Van Damm Studio, *Vanity Fair*, The Victorian Society, *Vogue* – and the many others who do not have credits printed on their work.

Needless to say, Thames and Hudson who published this book deserve my gratitude for the contributions of their editors and designers.

CHARLES CASTLE

Chronologies

The following Chronologies are adapted with permission of the authors of the catalogue prepared for the Oliver Messel exhibition which opened at the Theatre Museum, Victoria and Albert Museum, on 22 June 1983.

Stage Productions

1925 12 Nov. Coliseum, *Zéphyre et Flore* (ballet); masks

1926 23 Apr. London Pavilion, *Cochran's 1926 Revue*; 'The Masks', costumes, masks

1927 19 June Strand, *The Great God Brown* (play); masks

1928 22 Mar. London Pavilion, *This Year of Grace*; 'Lorelei', costumes, settings. 'Dance Little Lady', costumes, masks. 7 Nov., Selwyn, N.Y., costumes, masks

1928 24 June Arts Theatre Club, *Riverside Nights* (play); 'Nigger Heaven', costumes, masks

1929 27 Mar. London Pavilion, *Wake Up and Dream*; 'The Wrong Room in the Wrong House', 'Wake Up and Dream', 'The Dream', 'A Girl in a Shawl', costumes and settings. 'What is This Thing Called Love', settings

1930 27 Mar. London Pavilion, *Cochran's 1930 Revue*; 'Piccadilly 1830', 'Heaven', costumes, settings

1931 19 Mar. London Pavilion, *Cochran's 1931 Revue*; 'Stealing Through', 'Scaramouche', costumes, settings

1932 30 Jan. Adelphi, *Helen!* (play); costumes, settings

1932 9 Apr. Lyceum, *The Miracle* (play); costumes

1933 27 Jan. Gaiety, *Mother of Pearl* (play); settings

1935 2 May Drury Lane, *Glamorous Night* (play); settings

1936 6 Oct. Old Vic, *The Country Wife* (play); 1 Dec., Henry Miller's, N.Y., costumes, settings

1937 15 July Royal Opera House, Ballets Russes de Colonel de Basil, *Francesca da Rimini* (ballet); 24 Oct., Metropolitan Opera House, N.Y., costumes, settings

1937 27 Dec. Old Vic, *A Midsummer Night's Dream* (play); costumes, settings

1940 29 May Old Vic, *The Tempest* (play); costumes, settings

1940 5 Sept. Arts Theatre Club, *The Infernal Machine* (play); costumes, masks, settings

1942 14 Jan. New, Sadler's Wells Ballet, *Comus* (ballet); costumes, settings

1942 8 May His Majesty's, *The Big Top* (revue); costumes

1945 25 Sept. Criterion, *The Rivals* (play); costumes, settings

1946 20 Feb. Royal Opera House, Sadler's Wells Ballet, *The Sleeping Beauty* (ballet); 9 Oct., Metropolitan Opera House, N.Y., costumes, settings. Revivals: 14 Sept. 1950, Metropolitan Opera House, N.Y.; Los Angeles; 1955, N.B.C. T.V.; 1952, 1956, 1958, Royal Opera House; 1958 B.B.C. T.V., Act III; *see also* 1960, 1976 below

1947 20 Mar. Royal Opera House, *The Magic Flute* (opera); costumes, settings

1949 11 May Globe, *The Lady's Not for Burning* (play); 8 Nov. 1950, Royale, N.Y., costumes, settings

1949 15 July Adelphi, *Tough At The Top* (play); costumes, settings

1950 26 Jan. Globe, *Ring Round the Moon* (play); 23 Nov., Martin Beck, N.Y., 1951, Folkes, Copenhagen, costumes, settings

1950 20 Aug. King's, Edinburgh (Glyndebourne Opera at the Edinburgh Festival), *Ariadne auf Naxos* (opera); costumes, settings

1950 23 Aug. Lyric, Shaftesbury Avenue, *The Little Hut* (play); 7 Oct., 1953, Coronet, N.Y., settings

1950 21 Dec. Royal Opera House, *The Queen of Spades* (opera); costumes, settings

1951 10 Mar. Broadhurst, N.Y., *Romeo and Juliet* (play); costumes, settings

1951 15 June Glyndebourne, *Idomeneo* (opera); costumes, settings. Revivals: 1952; 1953, Edinburgh Festival; 1956; 1959; 1964

1952 14 Apr. Streatham Hill, *Under the Sycamore Tree* (play); 23 Apr., Aldwych, costumes, settings

NOTE: At this point Carl Toms joined Messel as assistant until 1958.

1952 18 June Glyndebourne, *La Cenerentola* (opera); costumes, settings. Revivals: 1952, Edinburgh Festival; 1954, Berlin; 1956, Liverpool; 1959; 1960

1952 10 Oct. Aldwych, *Letter From Paris* (play); costumes, settings

1953 2 June Royal Opera House, Sadler's Wells Ballet, *Homage To The Queen* (ballet); costumes, settings. 18 Sept., Metropolitan Opera House, N.Y.; Detroit; San Francisco; 1958, Brussels

1953 24 June Glyndebourne, *Ariadne auf Naxos*, second version (opera); costumes, settings. Revivals: 1954 (also Edinburgh Festival); 1957; 1958; *see also* 1962, below

1954 30 Apr. Aldwych, *The Dark Is Light Enough* (play); 23 Feb. 1955, ANTA, N.Y., costumes, settings

1954 10 June Glyndebourne, *Il Barbiere di Siviglia* (opera); costumes, settings. Revivals: 1955, Edinburgh Festival; 1961

1954 22 Aug. King's, Edinburgh (Glyndebourne Festival Opera), *Le Comte Ory* (opera); costumes, settings. Revivals: 1955; 1957; 1958 (and Paris)

1954 30 Dec. Alvin, N.Y., *House of Flowers* (play); costumes, masks, settings

1955 11 May Theatre Royal, Bath, *Zémire et Azore* (opera); costumes, settings

1955 8 June Glyndebourne, *Le Nozze di Figaro* (opera); costumes, settings. Revivals: 1956, 1958, 1962, 1963, 1965

1956 15 June Glyndebourne, *Die Entführung aus dem Serail* (opera); costumes, settings. Revivals: 1957, 1961

1956 19 July Glyndebourne, *Die Zauberflöte* (opera); costumes, settings. Revivals: 1957, 1960

1958 26 Mar. Cambridge, then Duke of York's, *Breath of Spring* (play); costumes, settings

1958 19 Sept. Det Ny, Copenhagen, *The School for Scandal* (play); costumes

1958 15 Nov. Royal Opera House, *Samson* (oratorio); costumes, settings

1959 27 Jan. Music Box, N.Y., *Rashomon* (play); costumes, settings

1959 28 May Glyndebourne, *Der Rosenkavalier* (opera); costumes, settings. Revivals: 1960, 1965

1959 Oct. Metropolitan Opera House, N.Y., *The Marriage of Figaro* (opera); costumes, settings. Reworked from Glyndebourne production of 1955

1960 10 June Royal Opera House, The Royal Ballet, *The Sleeping Beauty* (ballet); part-redesigned costumes and settings from 1946 production

1962 19 July Glyndebourne, *Ariadne auf Naxos*, first version (opera); costumes, settings

1962 29 Dec. Metropolitan Opera House, N.Y., *Ariadne auf Naxos*, (opera); costumes, settings

1964 18 Sept. ANTA, N.Y., *Traveller Without Luggage* (play); costumes, settings

1965 20 Dec. Shaftesbury, *Twang!!* (play); costumes, settings

1973 15 May San Francisco, *Gigi* (play); costumes. Then St Louis, Detroit, Toronto; 13 Nov., Uris, N.Y.

1976 15 June Metropolitan Opera House, American Ballet Theatre, *The Sleeping Beauty* (ballet); costumes, settings, reworked from Royal Opera House production of 1946

Films

1934 *The Private Life of Don Juan*, London (United Artists), directed by A. Korda; costumes

1935 *The Scarlet Pimpernel*, London (United Artists), directed by A. Korda; costumes

1936 *Romeo and Juliet*, U.S.A (Metro-Goldwyn-Mayer), directed by G. Cukor; costumes (with Adrian), settings (with Gibbon)

1940 *The Thief of Baghdad*, London, directed by M. Powell; costumes (with Armstrong and Vertès). This won two Academy Awards, for Technicolor and special effects.

1946 *Carnival*, London (Two Cities), directed by S. Haynes; costumes (for Sally Gray)

1946 *Caesar and Cleopatra*, London (I. P. Pascal), directed by G. Pascal; costumes, interiors

1948 *The Winslow Boy*, London (B.L.P.A.), directed by A. Asquith; costumes

1949 *The Queen of Spades*, London (World Screenplays), directed by T. Dickinson; costumes, settings

1955 *Arms and the Man*, London (Korda), directed by P. Glenville; costumes, settings. Partly designed, then film dropped

1960 *Suddenly Last Summer* (Horizon), directed by J. L. Mankiewicz; costumes, settings

1963 *Cleopatra* (?). It seems there may have been some involvement by Messel on this film but it is difficult to establish what.

Index

Index